A PLUME BOOK

THE NEW YORK REGIONAL MORMON SINGLES HALLOWEEN DANCE

ELNA BAKER is a Mormon stand-up comedian, writer, and solo performer who specializes in comedic storytelling. She lives in New York City.

Praise for *The New York Regional Mormon Singles Halloween Dance*

"A wicked-funny debut. Baker is both self-absorbed and generous, whip-smart and naive; she apologizes for none of it." —*People*

"With unrelenting cuteness . . . Baker spins a witty girly-girl story, a romantic caper for ladies about trying to find a job, a boyfriend, and, ultimately, herself. A sexy, lubricious outing by a formerly zaftig comic." —*Kirkus Reviews*

"Elna Baker leads with her heart . . . and hilarity. . . . One dash *Sex and the City* and one dash *Eat, Pray, Love*, her memoir is an unflinching, kinetic revelation, opening a secret door on the pull between faith and carnality, expectation and desire, family and self."
—Mike Paterniti, author of *Driving Mr. Albert: A Trip Across America with Einstein's Brain*

"Is there a stronger subject than the struggle for love, or a better way to face it than to laugh? Baker has got the curse to live ⁓⁓rdly, the gift to tell it honestly, and the nerve to break our hear⁓ ⁓ her talent." —Andrew Se⁓⁓ ⁓f *The Story of a Marriage* and *The Cor⁓*

"Elna Baker's memoirs of Mormon chastity a⁓ ⁓⁓ted with such passion and wit and unbridled ⁓ ⁓ehow her life comes out as pure erotic advent⁓ ⁓unshine hedonism. She's a dazzlement, a li⁓ ⁓ox and an absolute original." —⁓ ⁓een, author of *Ravens* and *The Juro⁓* ⁓tor of The Moth

The New York Regional
MORMON SINGLES
HALLOWEEN DANCE

Elna Baker

A PLUME BOOK

PLUME
Published by the Penguin Group
Penguin Group (USA) Inc., 375 Hudson Street, New York, New York 10014, U.S.A. • Penguin Group (Canada), 90 Eglinton Avenue East, Suite 700, Toronto, Ontario, Canada M4P 2Y3 (a division of Pearson Penguin Canada Inc.) • Penguin Books Ltd., 80 Strand, London WC2R 0RL, England • Penguin Ireland, 25 St. Stephen's Green, Dublin 2, Ireland (a division of Penguin Books Ltd.) • Penguin Group (Australia), 250 Camberwell Road, Camberwell, Victoria 3124, Australia (a division of Pearson Australia Group Pty. Ltd.) • Penguin Books India Pvt. Ltd., 11 Community Centre, Panchsheel Park, New Delhi – 110 017, India • Penguin Group (NZ), 67 Apollo Drive, Rosedale, North Shore 0632, New Zealand (a division of Pearson New Zealand Ltd.) • Penguin Books (South Africa) (Pty.) Ltd., 24 Sturdee Avenue, Rosebank, Johannesburg 2196, South Africa

Penguin Books Ltd., Registered Offices: 80 Strand, London WC2R 0RL, England

Published by Plume, a member of Penguin Group (USA) Inc.
Previously published in a Dutton edition.

First Plume Printing, October 2010
1   3   5   7   9   10   8   6   4   2

℗ REGISTERED TRADEMARK—MARCA REGISTRADA

The Library of Congress has catalogued the Dutton edition as follows:

Baker, Elna.
The New York regional Mormon singles Halloween dance / Elna Baker.
p.   cm.
ISBN 978-0-525-95135-3 (hc.)
ISBN 978-0-452-29649-7 (pbk.)
1. Baker, Elna.   2. Mormons—United States—Biography.   I. Title.
BX8695.B28A3 2009
289.3092—dc22   2009029447
[B]

Printed in the United States of America
Set in Minion Pro with GothicBlond Husky
Original hardcover design by Daniel Lagin

Penguin is committed to publishing works of quality and integrity.
In that spirit, we are proud to offer this book to our readers;
however, the story, the experiences, and the words
are the author's alone.

Author's Note

Aside from my immediate family, the names and other identifying characteristics of the persons included in this memoir have been changed. And while all of these events are true, certain characters and events have been composited for the sake of clarity and brevity.

Mom and Dad,

I could never have done this without your faith, support, and constant encouragement. Thank you for teaching me to believe in myself, in God, and in my dreams.

This book . . . aside from the nine F-words, thirteen Sh-words, four A-holes, page 257, and the entire Warren Beatty chapter . . . is dedicated to you.

You might want to avoid chapters twenty-one, twenty-two, twenty-three, anything I quote Mom saying, and most of the end as well.

Sorry. Am I still as cute as a button?

Love,

Elna

Contents

A Mormon in New York

I am at the New York Regional Mormon Singles Halloween Dance. That's right—it's a Halloween dance not *just* for all the single Mormons between the ages of eighteen and thirty who live in Manhattan, it's for all the single Mormons in the tristate area. That's a lot of virgins in one room. And I'm one of them.

Tonight I'm dressed like a Queen Bee. The best part of my costume is my stinger. I bought a black funnel from the hardware store and stuck it on my butt. When I walk, it wiggles back and forth. Genius. I was certain that some Mormon guy was going to see me and fall head over heels in love. I joked to my friends that the Queen Bee was going to find a drone. Instead, I'm by myself at the punch bowl stocking up on generic-brand Oreo cookies. When I'm wrong, I'm wrong and strong.

The worst part is, I should've known better. This is my fourth New York Regional Mormon Singles Halloween Dance in a row. Every year, I come hoping to meet "The One." And every year, I leave by myself, vowing never to come again. But by the time 365 days have passed, I've completely forgotten this commitment. In the end, I am here for one reason and one reason only: I want very much to fall in love, and it would be nice if I could fall for another Mormon.

Cue: this place. And by *this place* I mean a lame dance held in a church gym. Although, to her credit, the church activities' committee director has made a halfhearted attempt to disguise the gym. Black and orange streamers are taped to the basketball hoop and silly monster feet cover the lines on the linoleum floor. Since we're all over the age of five, no one is fooled; clearly this is still the gym.

Let's not forget tonight's DJ, Brother Mo, who's wearing a polyester suit and tie with no trace of irony. He occupies the stage at the far end of the gym. To his left there's a long plastic table for refreshments: lemonade and cookies, as if we're a little league soccer team.

Then there are the dance rules. The most important one, announced over the pulpit on Sunday, is that there is to be no cross-dressing or wearing of masks. I understand the logic behind no cross-dressing, though I doubt that if a man were to dress like a woman at this function he would suddenly realize his true identity. But masks? I personally have never put on a mask and suddenly felt the urge to hold up a convenience store or reenact the orgy scene from *Eyes Wide Shut*. But that's just me.

The other rules are unspoken. There is to be no inappropriate dancing or lascivious behavior at the church dance. No grinding. No Levi-loving. And the only "humpty" allowed is a costume of an egg. That's why there are too many lights overhead and only "safe" songs like "Cotton-eyed Joe" on the sound system. When slow songs do play, people joke that you should be able to fit "the standard works" between you and your partner. *The standard works* is a Mormon term referring to all of the religious books we study. So when you're slow dancing, the *Old Testament, New Testament, The Book of Mormon, Doctrine and Covenants*, and *Pearl of Great Price* should be able to fit in the space between you and your dance partner—or you're dancing too close.

If it weren't already painfully obvious, these events are organized to facilitate marriage. How else would we Manhattan Mormons meet, marry, then make more Mormons? (Take *that*, Sally and your seashells on the seashore.) No one acknowledges this, though; that's another unspoken rule of the Mormon dance. We're all just here to "have fun." The effect is pretty horrifying. It's like watching a bunch of assembly-line workers at a factory pretending they're there because they love screwing nuts on bolts. I want to shout, "Can't we just acknowledge that we are here to eventually screw a nut on a bolt?" But no one would get the joke, and the ones who do would be terribly offended.

Contrary to popular belief, there are Mormons who live in New York City. I don't know how many of us there are all together, but there are probably eight hundred single Mormons and at least twenty thousand former Mormons. I've been in the city for four years now. I moved to New York to go to NYU for acting, I graduated in May, and I started work as a toy demonstrator at FAO Schwarz.

While I am Mormon, I'm not from Utah. I was born in Seattle, but I grew up in Madrid and London because my father's job moved my family overseas. My dad works for Boeing; it's not that exciting. But it meant we moved around a lot. When I was nine we moved to Madrid. When I was thirteen we moved to London; when I was fifteen we moved to Seattle; and when I was seventeen we moved back to London.

When I finished high school at the American School in London, my parents wanted me to go to BYU, Brigham Young University, in Provo, Utah. It's where they went to school, and it's where my older sister went. They were worried that if I didn't go to BYU I'd stop being Mormon, and I wouldn't meet anyone to marry—well, they were right about the second part.

I remember when I got my acceptance letter from BYU via the British Royal Mail. I opened the thick envelope, looked at the emblem of the busy honeybees all working together, and then read the word *Congratulations*. It felt good. Any letter of acceptance makes you feel good. But when I got my letter of acceptance to NYU, something was different. I opened the package on my way up to my room, read the word *Congratulations*, and started to sob, right there on the stairs. I sat down and I cried. I didn't realize how much getting into NYU meant to me until I had those huge tears pouring down my cheeks. And that's when I knew I had to go to New York City.

My mother was terrified. She's the more conservative of my parents, and when she's not busy being a mom, she spends her time forwarding cheesy e-mails about Christian miracles, or signing petitions against Abercrombie & Fitch's pornographic ads. To her, New York was the city from the movies made in the seventies, where you heard gunshots out your window and pimps screaming at hos. Not that there were many scenes like that in the PG-rated movies my mother was inclined to watch. But still, New York was a scary, dangerous place. A month before I went off to college, she sat me down for a mother-daughter talk.

"Elna," she said nervously. "The first thing that will happen when you move to New York is, you might start to swear."

I wanted to say, "Oh *shit*, really?" But I knew that only my dad would think that was funny. Instead I nodded my head and said, "Mmm hmm."

"And Elna," she continued, "swearing will lead to drinking."

I had somehow missed the connection.

"And drinking will lead to doing drugs."

The conversation was starting to get more amusing than even I had anticipated. "And Elna," she said, pursing her lips and looking directly into my eyes, "what would you do if a lesbian tried to make out with you?"

I didn't think double takes existed outside of *Three's Company* until that moment. I was used to her saying words like *church calling*, *relief society*, and *bishopric meeting*. Not the word *lesbian*, let alone *lesbian* and *make out* in the same sentence. It was awesome. But I was also slightly offended. If you followed my mother's logic, each step was a progression toward becoming more of a sinner. First

I'd swear, then I'd drink, then I'd do drugs. By that point I was getting used to the narrative, so I assumed sex with men would be next. But no—my mother skipped that altogether and jumped to my becoming a lesbian. Did my mother honestly think that I had a better chance of getting action from a woman than a man?

These are all questions I didn't ask her directly. But at this point I'd almost forgotten she'd asked me anything: What would I do if a lesbian tried to make out with me?

She was sitting there, arms folded, waiting for an answer.

"I'd say, 'No, thank you . . . lesbian.'"

My mother rolled her eyes. "There's one more thing," she said, resuming our heart-to-heart.

Sex with men, sex with men, sex with men.

"There are these clubs in New York where men pay larger women to dance with very little clothing on; *don't do that.*"

Our mother-daughter talk ended with that golden nugget of wisdom. I left thinking, *Great, my mom thinks I'm moving to the big city to become a lesbian stripper. Apparently, when she told me I was "special," this is what she meant.*

My father sat me down a few days later for another leaving-the-nest talk. His advice was a little different.

"Elna," he began, "never forget these three things." He paused for dramatic effect. "Number One: Never wear a dead man's socks. Number Two: Never let 'em see you sweat. And Number Three: Never touch a fat man's stomach."

I waited for him to clarify, to add a line that would somehow make all the other words he'd said make sense. But he just patted me on the shoulder and left me in the living room to contemplate his wisdom.

That was all the advice I was given before moving to New York City.

I wanted more, or at the very least a tender good-bye. Only this was interrupted when the check-in clerk announced that my bag was too heavy. My father opened it in the middle of the terminal. I watched as he pulled out items of sentimental value, told me I didn't need them, and threw them away.

That's when my mother saw it, among my tightly folded clothes: a rainbow scarf. I wasn't keeping it from her. I'd owned it for several years, and had purchased it because it reminded me of Punky Brewster in a retro eighties sort of way. She snatched it out of my suitcase.

"You can't wear this in New York!" she exclaimed.

"Why not?" I asked.

"Everyone will think that you're gay."

My mother thought gay people had a monopoly on rainbows. In my opinion rainbows were for everyone, just like unicorns.

"Mom, I'm not gay," I responded.

"I know, but you should avoid the appearance."

"That's why I bleach my mustache."

I tried to get my scarf back. I told her how much I liked it. I explained how cold I would be without it. I even tried to usher her into this century by explaining that wearing rainbows didn't automatically mean a person was gay. The Lucky Charms leprechaun was not necessarily a homosexual. The Care Bear with the rainbow on his tummy did not have a life partner. He didn't even have genitals.

Eventually my mom gave me money to buy a new scarf. But she was not, under any circumstances, going to let me take the rainbow scarf to New York City.

Both of my parents walked me to the security gate. I hugged them good-bye, swung my backpack over my shoulder, and joined the line. Just as I was about to go through the metal detector, I turned around. *Good-bye,* I waved.

"Remember who you are," my mother shouted. *Remember who you are, Remember who you are* echoed through the hall of Heathrow. I still laugh when I think about it. Not because of the message, but because my mother was quoting the slogan of an old church campaign. I even have one of the *Remember Who You Are* key chains. They gave them to all the Mormon youth. I've never used mine though; I was always worried someone would see it and think I had Alzheimer's.

I arrived in New York in August 2000. I took a cab from JFK to the address listed on my housing contract, Tenth Street and Broadway. As we crossed the Williamsburg Bridge, I stuck my head out the window so I could see the city. Everything was new. I'd never had that experience before. My cab driver, Hassan, was a new person. The city sparkling on the horizon was new, and I was about to go to my home and it was all going to be completely new to me. I love the feeling of possibility. For another twenty minutes in Hassan's cab, anything was possible: my dorm room and my roommate could be anyone and anything I imagined. But twenty minutes later they'd be whatever they were. I wanted to invent a word that described that place, the state between unlimited possibility and reality. But I couldn't think of one, and the Germans probably already invented one anyway, *Weltinnerschnitzelrealititz*.

When I walked into my dorm room, the first thing I noticed was a big rainbow flag hanging on the wall. The only way it could have possibly gotten better would have been if my roommate walked in smoking a cigarette and offered to give me a lap dance.

I'd never actually met a lesbian until I met Lisa. It turned out Lisa had never met a Mormon until she met me. And despite all the things we were supposed to be, we hit it off right from the start. We complained about the size of our bathroom, and we played Ani DiFranco at full volume while we hung clothes in our tiny closet.

Over the course of the year, I never once felt uncomfortable. Well, that isn't true. The only time I ever felt uncomfortable was when Lisa brought home a prosthetic male "piece." It was a rather large strap-on and a disgusting salmon color. (I'd obviously never seen one before.) She wore it under her clothing—I guess to feel more in touch with her inner man. That didn't bother me. But it was disturbing trying to do my homework when "The Thing," as I referred to it, was lying on her dresser or, better yet, the kitchen counter. I'd glance up from reading my theater history textbook, and "The Thing" would somehow find its way into my view. It was always perched up, eager, watching me—one eye and all. I didn't share this information in my phone calls home. If my mother couldn't handle rainbows, she wasn't going to like prosthetic schlongs.

I guess this probably isn't the kind of stuff most Mormons would even acknowledge. But how can you ignore what's going on around you? Whether you participate in it or not, your roommate is bound to wear a strap-on. But then again, I've always been different from most Mormons.

When I came to NYU, I was kind of on the fence about whether I wanted to be Mormon anymore. I obviously didn't tell my parents this. It was just such a big thing to be, a Mormon. And it's not the sort of religion you can just do because you don't want to disappoint your mom and dad. It requires major commitments: It asks for your life. And while I understood that I was influenced by my Mormon upbringing, I knew that I was many other things. In addition to being Mormon, I was Elna.

I like that I think saying my name will describe exactly who I am; it's so self-involved. But I like being named Elna. As far as I know, I'm the only one. I used to hate it, though. I thought it sounded like a Spanish man clearing snot from his nose *"El—Naaaaah."* Then I learned what it meant: Elna comes from the Greek word *Helene*, which means "light." When I found that out, I looked up the word *light* in the dictionary to see if there was anything in there that described me in particular. Here's what I wrote down: "Light: The guiding spirit or divine presence in each person" and "Light: Illumination derived from a source."

I liked the second definition best. I identified with it because I always felt like I wasn't just light; I was illumination derived from a source. To me that source was God.

Still, having a strong connection with God did not stop me from questioning my faith every ten seconds. Mormonism can sound pretty far-fetched: Joseph Smith digs up golden plates and translates them into a book, *The Book of Mormon*. This book ends up being a history of the ancestors of the Native Americans, who originated in Jerusalem and believed in Jesus.

When you write it all out like that you can't help but reconsider. Once I tried explaining it to a friend who had made the mistake of thinking the founder of the Mormon faith was John Smith. I told him that it was actually Joseph Smith, and then I went into all the things that I believed. I thought I was doing a good job explaining everything until he said, "So basically John Smith and Joseph Smith were two different people but, according to you, Pocahontas was actually a Jew?"

I guess the miracles one is expected to believe in the Mormon faith are no different from the miracles you are supposed to believe in any faith. My problem is I was always a skeptic.

When I was four and my mom first told me the story of Moses parting the Red Sea with his hands, I looked at her and said, "Yeah right, Mom." My mother tried to convince me that Moses had indeed parted a sea just by lifting his arms. I rolled my eyes and patted her on the knee like she was a crazy person.

By the age of six, I was already asking my mother, "When do we graduate from church?" At this point I had entered school and understood that while school was "not fun," it was necessary. But there was a light at the end of the tunnel. Some day, many years away, I would be done with school, and the word for that was *graduate*. To my dismay I was told that the word to describe being done with church was *death*.

And I wasn't exactly enthusiastic about getting baptized. Mormons are baptized at eight years old. When I turned eight, every kid I knew was getting baptized. They didn't seem to put much thought into it. It was just how things went. I, on the other hand, had a lot of theories. According to my parents and teachers, when you were baptized you were washed clean. So why get baptized at eight? None of us had done anything. Why not wait until we were seventy? That way you could lead a fun life, do whatever you wanted to, and have a Get Out of Jail Free card at the end. I don't know how I knew at such a young age that Mormonism would interfere with me having a "fun" life—but I did.

I ended up deciding to be baptized a month after I turned eight. I can't pass the buck on this one; it was my decision and mine alone. My father even assured me, "Just because everyone your age is getting baptized, it doesn't mean that you have to. Your mother and I want you to choose this on your own." He said I should pay attention to my feelings. "Baptism is a leap of faith," he said. "You can never know for sure if something is right, but if you listen to your heart and it tells you to go forward, then take a leap of faith."

I didn't like this. When I was forced to do things, it gave me something to fight against. Now that the ball was in my court, I felt an enormous sense of pressure. How was I supposed to decide what I was going to be for the rest of my life when I didn't know what the rest of my life was going to be like? And so I prayed about it. After my prayer, I tried to be as still as possible so that I could hear my heart. I listened, my heart felt warm, and I felt good inside. *Good*—a word I usually used to describe water fights and pancakes in the shape of Mickey Mouse. So I decided to take the leap and get baptized. But unlike with most events in my life in which I demanded ridiculous amounts of attention, I insisted that my baptism be low-key. I didn't invite many friends, and I didn't want a big party—I was embarrassed to do something I was *supposed* to do, so I made sure that my baptism was a private affair.

After I was baptized, everyone my age at church wanted to know if I knew the church was true. That is to say, if I believed Joseph Smith had a vision, if I believed he had in fact translated golden plates, and if I believed in *The Book of Mormon*. There was only one way to find out if the church was true: I was supposed to pray and get a confirmation from God. It was a weird Christian fad, like WWJD bracelets. Kids in Sunday school said that they had prayed and asked God if the church was true and they got an answer. You weren't cool unless you tried. It reminded me of the time Kelsey Mann, a girl in my first grade class, said "Bloody Mary" three times in the mirror of the school bathroom. She said a woman appeared in the glass, reached out, and scratched her forehead. After that, every girl had to try Bloody Mary and every girl reported a more outrageous encounter. Finally the principal announced over the loudspeaker that there would be "No more Bloody Mary," and the popularity contest came to an end.

Praying to find out whether our church was true was a similar popularity contest. If you prayed, your answer had to be spectacular. Because whoever had the best revelation was the best Mormon. I prayed. I knelt next to my bed, and I said, "God, is the church true?" I listened. I wanted an angel to appear to me; I wanted something to happen that would make a great story. Instead, I felt nothing.

To my mind, it wasn't fair. Billy Goodman had felt something, and he wasn't even that good a Mormon—he had tried a sip of beer once. I was a saint compared to Billy Goodman, and I got nothing? For the next two years I tried over and over again. Eventually it became so routine that I forgot what I was even asking for. In my nightly prayers I'd say, "Thank you for the beautiful weather, bless so and so, oh, and by the way, is the church true?" Each time I'd wait, hoping God would feel like giving me an answer. But it was always the same: I felt nothing. I was about to give up, when one Sunday, while I was sitting in church, a speaker at the podium said: "I can feel just by the spirit in this room how true this church is."

That caught my attention. I tried to identify the feeling in the room. It felt very peaceful. Every time I had asked God if the church was true, I hadn't felt lightning, but I had felt peace. Perhaps I had been getting an answer all along. It was not a dramatic moment—no angels appeared to me—but I decided then that my church was true. Of course, someone could easily argue that when the speaker said, "I can feel just by the spirit in this room how true this church is," I listened and felt nothing, the same nothing I had felt every time I had prayed, and somehow the two nothings combined added up to something. I try not to go there.

Crap, I'm apologizing for my Mormonism again. Sorry. I should stand up for my beliefs. Instead I find that I downplay my faith in mixed company because I know most New Yorkers think of religious people as whack jobs. But I should tell the truth: Spiritual feelings have a way of confounding me. Even though I'm the one experiencing them, they feel like they're coming from an outside source. And in addition to my questioning, I've had several spiritual experiences that caused me to have faith. There was the time I went on a church hiking trip. We were all told to go off into the woods and pray. I found a quiet spot and prayed, and I asked to know if God was there. I looked up at the moon and felt the presence of something bigger than me. I felt someone wrap their arms around me, as if they were hugging me, and I started to cry. As I cried, my body rocked back and forth and I knew it wasn't me who was doing it. Ever since then, when I look at the moon, I can't help it: "Hi, God," I'll say.

I've also studied the teachings of my religion. When I was nineteen I read *The Book of Mormon* cover-to-cover for the first time.

And while I was reading it I felt like I was leading a better life, and making better choices. I don't know how to explain experiences like this to people, because I cannot explain them to myself. So instead I usually hide them and voice only my doubt—which doesn't make me look like the most faithful of God's servants. But I'm being honest. I think most religious people experience just as much doubt as they do faith; they just don't admit it. And I don't think doubting makes you bad. I think it makes you smart.

My main problem with my faith is that any inconsistency makes me question everything. For example, a few Sundays ago, some idiot stood up in church and started talking about how we were having such a mild autumn. He went on and on about how pleasant the weather was and then jumped to, "So really if you think about it, it's a sign that Jesus Christ will be coming soon." And so began my usual downward spiral: *The weather is warm because of climate change— not because Jesus is on his way. How can I belong to a church where people believe such crazy things? I mean, nowhere in* The Book of Mormon *does it say mild autumn equals Jesus, but technically I'm supposed to believe in the second coming. Do I? I don't know. How can I possibly sign my name to something I don't entirely agree with?*

My dad says I think too much and that if I'm not careful my thoughts will undermine my faith. When he was nineteen, he was driving across the desert in Arizona on his way to serve a two-year Mormon mission, when it occurred to him: What if none of this is true? The thought paralyzed him. He pulled over and sat on the hood of his car for several hours, just staring at the horizon. And then, all of a sudden, he got an overwhelming feeling that God knew who he was and that God was proud of his choices. My dad says that he has doubts all the time, but he doesn't allow them to make him question that moment when he was nineteen. I guess I'm still waiting for my big moment—the point of no return.

* * *

Oh, hold on. A guy, Dave, totally hot, just made eye contact with me. He's dressed as Paul Bunyan, which would be cool if two other guys hadn't also thought of it. Wait, I think he's walking in my direction. Oh, my gosh, he is. What do I do? Okay. Just play it cool. Show him your stinger.

Well, that was miserable. I'll repeat the scenario so you understand just how good I am at creating awkwardness. Dave walked up to me and said, "Amanda, right?"

"No, I'm Elna."

"Elena?"

"Elna," I repeated.

"Elma."

"No, Elna with an *n*."

"Oh, okay, Elma." I nodded my head, as if he'd gotten it right.

"How's it going?" Dave asked.

"Fine," I said.

"Cool," he nodded. I waited for him to continue; when he didn't I volunteered, "Where's Babe?"

"Who?"

"The blue cow."

"What blue cow?"

"Sorry. Ox, the blue ox."

Dave looked incredibly confused.

"Paul Bunyan traveled with a blue ox," I explained.

"I'm not Paul Bunyan," he said, annoyed. "I'm Brigham Young."

I almost choked on a cookie. "Sorry," I said, "the fake beard threw me off."

I should've stopped there, but instead I added, "So the women who've been congregating around you all night, they weren't your multiple wives?" I thought this was pretty funny. Dave didn't even laugh. Mormons don't know how to laugh at themselves.

"Is your sister here?" he said. There it was, the real reason he'd come over to talk to me.

"She's around somewhere," I answered, trying my best not to sound disappointed. Dave waited for more information. When I didn't give him any, he said, "Oh, okay. Well if you see her, tell her I'm looking for her."

"Will do," I answered. Then I turned to the side so my stinger was visible and open for admiration. But Dave was too busy walking back to his multiple wives to even notice. Lame. I should've known he was just going to ask about Tina. *Tina, Tina, Tina.*

My older sister, Tina, also lives in New York. She moved here to go to law school right after I graduated from NYU in May 2003, and now we live together. It's hard being Tina's sister. She's like the patron saint of Mormonism. For her, going to church is actually enjoyable. Tina is obsessed with being good. She's never done anything wrong. For example, my curfew growing up was 1 A.M. Tina's was 11 P.M. One time she asked my parents why I got to stay out so much later than her. They answered, "We never set your curfew for eleven. You just kept coming home at that hour, so we decided not to stop you." That's Tina. Guys at church love Tina; she goes on dates all the time. It's not fair. Whatever.

It's not like I want to get married like most Mormon girls do. Most Mormon women get married between eighteen and twenty-one. I just think it would be nice to have a boyfriend. I'm twenty-one years old, and I've never had a boyfriend. That's not normal. And it's not for lack of desire—I've been on a quest to fall in love since I was six years old. It's just, well, I don't normally get attention from men.

I failed to mention this earlier: I'm big. I am a larger girl. I wear size 18/20. I didn't want to bring it up because I didn't want that to define me, just like I don't want Mormonism to define me. People think your weight should define you; they think all fat people go crazy for the smell of bacon. I don't even like bacon.

When I'm in a bad mood and I want to make myself feel worse, I blame my weight for my lack of a love life. But it can't be the only reason. I like to give the world the benefit of the doubt. I think that no matter how you look, if you're a good person, people will see that. And it's not that men hate me or ignore me. I have a lot of guy friends, but I'd like to have a boyfriend. I'd like to learn how to kiss and how to flirt. But because I haven't ever had any romantic experiences, I haven't figured out how to seduce men or how to excite them, though that's probably for the best, since I'm Mormon. But I feel like there's this whole other side of life—romance—that I'm missing out on.

It's not just romance. I'm clueless when it comes to sex. I took Sex Ed when I was living in Spain, only it was in Spanish and I couldn't understand the teacher's accent. I spent most of the class staring at the diagrams and making up stuff. My understanding hasn't improved much since then. Aside from my lesbian roommate's strapon, I don't even know what a penis looks like. I tried drawing one once. I showed it to my best friend, Kevin; he thought it was a tugboat.

I did, however, almost have a giant penis encounter once. In high school I was cast as a chorus girl in a musical on London's West End. There was a one-man show playing opposite us called *The Man with the Absurdly Large Penis*—the true story of a man with a three-and-a-half-foot penis. The show's title was so amusing that I considered sneaking in, but exercised self-control and took a handful of *The Man with the Absurdly Large Penis* postcards instead. Naturally my mother found them in my room, accused me of being a pervert, and added parental controls to my computer.

I've always had bad luck with this type of thing. Anytime I think about doing anything even remotely immoral, I get caught. Because of this bad rap, I could tell that my parents were secretly worried I'd stop being Mormon when I got to college. I think that's why they badly wanted me to go to BYU, and why they were terrified by the prospect of their daughter living in "Babylon." (My mom called New York "Babylon" once, and I've never let her live it down.) But New York had the opposite effect on me. Instead of making me want to let loose, it made me want to be true to myself. NYU was a school of lost children, full of kids who were "different" in high school. Then the different kids decided to come to the same place, and all of a sudden being different wasn't all that special. It was a fad. Kids were struggling to think of new ways to wear ties. It was a *belt*. It was an *armband*—as long as it wasn't just a tie, it was a declaration of identity. The more different you were on the outside, the more different you were saying you were on the inside. But because everyone was doing it, everyone was exactly the same. Being Mormon made me different for real.

But it wasn't just that. My first Sunday in the city, I went to church. There was such a peaceful openness to the space, and everyone was so inviting and familiar, that it became a refuge for me. At school I was constantly defending my choices. At church I could just be Mormon. It was like going to a big family reunion. Sure, I didn't know any of my relatives, and none of them looked cool, but at least I felt at home.

So I decided to stick with it, and after four years of being a Mormon in New York, I've become a reluctant spokesperson for my faith. I'm constantly answering questions or explaining my religion. After having at least a hundred conversations, one thing has become very clear: People just don't get Mormons. They think I'm Mormon because I haven't read enough books yet.

I wait to tell people about my faith after I've known them for at least a month, because, once they know, that's it for me. I'm ruined by preconceived notions. It's like the moment I want to invent a word for the state of being between unlimited possibility and reality. If I'm at a bar and the person I'm talking to asks me, "Why aren't you drinking?" I enter that place. I know that when I answer them, "It's because I'm a Mormon," I will go from being anything they can imagine to being defined. Immediately we stop talking about books or films. Instead, every question is about whether I'm a polygamist, whether I've had sex, whether I wear magic underwear, and whether I believe in dinosaurs.

For the record: I'm not a polygamist, I have not had sex, I don't wear magic underwear, and I do believe in dinosaurs. I don't mind explaining my faith, because at least I can dispel any Mormon myths, but it's hard to be classified as a "Mormon girl" when I don't even totally relate to other Mormons. And there are Mormon stereotypes: Mormons have big families; they're from Utah; they wear modest clothes; they're friendly, naïve people; they have white teeth; and they're Republican. But that list only scratches the surface. Aside from these basics, there's a general perception of Mormons that does not apply to me: Mormons are known for saying no. No sex, no drugs, no alcohol, and no caffeine. NO.

And this whole "saying no" philosophy makes me seem like a very boring person. But I'm not boring because, while I say no to *certain* things (sex, drugs, alcohol), I try to say yes to everything else. I honestly believe there's a certain power behind the word *YES*. It wasn't until my sophomore year at NYU that I realized exactly how effective saying yes could be.

It happened on career day. You see, every fall, NYU sponsors a career fair where companies set up booths and recruit graduating students. I was a drama major, so they didn't even bother with us— they sort of saw what was coming long before we did: a life of unemployment punctuated by odd jobs. But if you were a Stern business student, there were all these booths set up with tons of recruiters and the most amazing free trinkets.

One day I was passing through the career fair on my way to class when a man behind one of the tables caught my eye and asked me, "Are you a Stern business student?"

I paused and thought the answer over. If I said no, the conversation would end. If I said yes, any number of things would happen.

"Yes," I answered hesitantly.

"Are you interested in a job at Morgan Stanley Dean Witter?" he continued.

"Yes," I said with more confidence.

For the next five minutes I answered yes to every question he asked, and before I knew it, I got a free triangle highlighter with a different color on each end. *Amazing.* I had inadvertently discovered the secret to life: When in doubt, just say yes. I proceeded to stop by every single booth and answer yes to all questions. By the end, I had a bag full of free stuff.

Technically this could be perceived as lying, and Mormons aren't supposed to lie. But I don't look at it that way. I love the adventure of seeing what I can get away with. And as long as no one gets hurt, I think it's okay.

I didn't intend to become a serial convention crasher. But a few months later, I was walking by the Javits Center (a convention center in New York where they hold expositions and car shows) when a security guard stopped me and asked, "Are you looking for the paper convention?"

I sensed opportunity. "Yes," I answered.

He escorted me through a set of double doors, and there it was, laid out before me in all its glory: the paper convention. There were hundreds of booths, and hundreds of paper demonstrations. But the best part was that on each table there was at least one free thing. I went from table to table saying yes, and by the time I left I had a year's supply of stationery.

A few months later, I was at the Marriott Marquis in Times

Square meeting some friends for breakfast. Halfway through our meal I glanced under my chair and noticed a laminated piece of paper with a safety pin glued to the back of it. When I turned it around I saw it said, "Bob Barnett—7-Eleven Convention." Immediately I thought: *YES!*

I pinned the badge to my male friend's shirt and we left breakfast in search of the 7-Eleven convention. A sign in the lobby directed us to the banquet hall and a huge banner reading 75 YEARS OF 7-ELEVEN.

We walked into the banquet hall. Inside, we met Suzie and her husband from Rhode Island. We met Phil from Connecticut. And while my friends collected as many trinkets as they could, I met Carol, the woman who had organized the whole event. We got to talking, and Carol, who had obviously worked very hard, asked me for my feedback on that week's events. "I go to conventions all the time," I answered, "and this is the best convention I've ever been to."

Carol's face lit up. "Did you need tickets for today's events?" she asked.

"Yes," I answered, careful not to sound too eager.

Carol reached inside a manila envelope, fished through a few papers, and pulled out four tickets to Radio City Music Hall, four tickets for a bus tour of Manhattan, and four tickets to Madame Tussauds. She handed them to me and then asked, "Will I be seeing you on tonight's cruise?"

"YES," I said, louder than I'd expected to.

And then I waited, eyes wide, for Carol to offer me tickets. When she didn't, I added, "You know, Carol, I sent all my paperwork in for the cruise, and I never got anything back."

"What?!" Carol answered, visibly shocked. Then she held her hand to her chest and said, apologetically, "Just wait here one moment."

I watched as she scurried across the room. Left alone, I started to have second thoughts. I looked down at the embroidered carpet. There were so many things that could go wrong. Carol could ask me for my name, or she could ask who my boss was. What if the real Bob Barnett turned the corner, demanding his badge?

When I looked back up Carol was walking briskly toward me.

"I am so sorry about that!" She stuck her hand out, and handed me four tickets. I read the ticket stub: *The* Spirit of New York *Harbor Cruise and Dinner.* I looked at the price; each ticket was worth $150. "YES!" I said.

That night my three friends and I got all dressed up, took a cab to Pier 26, and walked across a long wooden platform to the *Spirit of New York* ship. I handed someone our tickets and we were escorted into a room filled with chatter. There were at least five hundred 7-Eleven employees, my friends, and me. We started mingling. I didn't make up a pseudonym or job. When people asked me what I did for 7-Eleven, I'd casually answer, "Come on, man, leave work at work. We're here to have fun!"

After about an hour of mingling, a man in a tuxedo rang a bell, and everyone sat down at three long tables. Waiters entered with silver trays. My waiter asked me in a polite voice if I wanted fish or steak. I felt like I was a dignitary, and this amused me. I wanted to whisper to him, "I'm just an actor, same as you."

Dish by dish the waiters served us a four-course meal. At the end of the dinner, one of my friends turned to me and said, "Elna, I dare you to make a toast."

I couldn't help it. "YES," I said, nodding my head with approval. I held on to the stem of my wineglass and lifted it into the air. But I don't drink and I'd never made a toast before so I had no idea how to go about it. With my glass in one hand, and my knife in the other, I made the sound *tink, tink, tink.*

Everyone shut up. I was surprised. Who knew the glass and knife combo had such power? I looked out at the crowd. I hadn't exactly thought through my toast, but I was driven by a force far greater than my hesitation—the desire to pull off the impossible.

"I'd like to make a toast," I began. "To 7-Eleven, for redefining convenience."

I raised my glass in the air. For a moment there was silence. I looked at the sea of faces, the bosses, the secretaries, the CEO. They looked right back at me and all at once they burst into applause. "YES!!!!" they replied, raising their glasses high into the air. It was one of the greatest moments of my life.

And it's why I love saying yes. When you say yes you can start and end the day in two totally different places. Yes takes that space between unlimited possibilities and reality, and stretches it out so that anything can happen.

My life is a constant balance between saying no to substances, sex, porn, and Starbucks, and saying yes to adventure. I am a Mormon in New York.

A Mormon in New York seeking another Mormon in New York.

Which brings me back to the beginning: The New York Regional Mormon Singles Halloween Dance. Me, in the corner by myself, with too many cookies and a notebook. To make matters worse, I just witnessed a thirty-five-year-old man—definitely a virgin—dressed in a duck costume doing the electric slide.

God, there has to be another way.

AGE 18

What I believe:	What I used to believe:
- The church of Jesus Christ of Latter-Day Saints is true.	- If you vacuum over the vacuum cord the vacuum cleaner will explode.
- The Book of Mormon is true.	- I discovered a constellation
- God and Jesus live!	Monica Elna Jackie which I named after my friends and me.
- Joseph Smith was a modern day prophet.	
- Someday I will get married in the temple, die, go to the celestial kingdom and then become a God and create a world.	- "A hand-job" and "a hand-massage" mean the same thing.
- God has a body like me.	- I will grow up and become pretty some day.
- The purpose of life is to get a body + make choices with it.	- Lesbians use rubber gloves for safe sex.
- No drugs, alcohol or caffeine for me.	
- I am here to be tested.	
- Masturbation is EVIL.	
- In being honest, true, chaste and benevolent.	

- Sex before marriage is the second worst sin next to murder.

- I should strive to live a life free of sin.

- If a man really loves me he'll "wait."

- I am supposed to be a missionary for my church.

- There are no atheists in a fox-hole.

- No matter what you look like, it's what's on the inside that counts.

- If you do what's right, God will bless you.

- There is a man out there specifically for me. I hope I can find him.

- When I look at the moon, I see God.

Kissing, Take One: School Bus

We were waiting for the bus to leave the school parking lot, when a boy in my fourth grade class shouted, "Look! They're tongue kissing!" I pressed my face against the window along with the rest of the kids. Two eighth graders were standing in between the school buses, frenching. I'd never seen anything like it before. His hand was in her hair and both their faces were moving from side to side, slowly. Someone on the bus started counting out loud, "One, one thousand, two, one thousand, three, one thousand," calculating how long it took before the couple came up for air. *They made it all the way to ten, one thousand.*

When I got home I ran directly upstairs and into my older sister's room. I knew she'd be home in an hour, so I had to work fast. I pulled her yearbook off the shelf. My sister's yearbook was my holy grail. I loved looking at it. Not only did it give an inside account of the lives of the upperclassmen, but popular boys would write things to Tina, things that I memorized word for word, replacing her name with mine.

But today was about a different game. I scanned the faces of the upperclassmen until at last, I found them—the French-kissers—

Gabriella and Michael. Michael was cute, but it was Gabriella who I wanted to be. She had tan skin, long brown hair, and a pouty face. I circled her with a highlighter, like she was something I needed to study and decided some day I'd be just like her, some day I'd be the *pretty girl*, French-kissing.

I'm Not from Utah

During one particularly boring church young women's class I made a list of predictions for all the girls in the room and myself.

Young Women's Class Predictions:

- Nana got married at nineteen to a returned missionary named Dave. They have five kids and live in Utah.
- When Kelsey turned eighteen she married Bryan Hunsaker (ewww). They now have six kids and they live in Washington.
- Elna was married at twenty. She is an actress in California and has four kids with her handsome husband, Josh.
- Julie married a BYU football quarterback when she was nineteen. They have three kids and live in Provo.

I wrote this on loose-leaf notebook paper, added hearts and a drawing of a Mormon temple, and sealed it in an envelope. *To be opened in the year 2000,* I wrote on the outside. It was the quintessential date, 2000: the future.

Several years behind schedule, in the year 2008, I flew home to attend a family renunion and came across this letter while I was hiding in the attic from my relatives. I read it over and considered what

I knew about each person. The funny thing is, I was right about everyone, except me.

I was born in Tacoma, Washington, and I lived in Bonney Lake and then Sumner, two fairly rural suburbs of Seattle, for my first nine years. My grandparents, cousins, and church friends all lived close by. I knew every dog on my block, one neighbor had horses, another had llamas—that was as big as my world got.

In case you haven't heard, Mormons are big on families. It's supposed to be God's unit on earth. Home is considered mini-heaven, which is probably why all Mormon commercials are shot in an ethereal soft-focus. We spent a lot of time together as a family. We'd say morning and evening prayers together and have daily family scripture study.

But not all of it was religious. My parents were young, twenty-two and twenty-one, when they met. They dated for three and a half weeks before they got engaged, and they were married after three months. It takes me four months to decide on a new haircut, so I can't imagine being engaged after three and half weeks. Although I've always wanted to go on a first date and say: "If I were my mom, and you were my dad, we could be married by the time I have my next cycle." Only that might be weird. Um, it is. But my parents are happy and still very much in love, so I guess it worked for them.

After they got married, they immediately started having kids: first Tina and, eighteen months later, me. By the time my parents had Julia, Britain, and Jill, they sort of knew what they were doing. But with Tina and me, parenting was an experiment. My dad's favorite story to tell us about our childhood is the story of the Dilly Bars.

My dad loved Dairy Queen. In particular he loved Dilly Bars, chocolate-covered circular ice cream bars on a popsicle stick. One day he came downstairs when Tina and I were playing with our toys and interrupted us. In a scary voice he said, "The Dilly Bars are coming." Then he screamed and ran out the front door.

My sister and I were five and three, and we had no idea what my dad was talking about. We ran to the window and watched as he drove away. When he didn't immediately return, we got scared. We positioned ourselves on top of the couch, rested our feet on the ledge, and leaned against the front window, waiting. My mother came over to see what we were doing. We asked her where our father was.

"He went to get Dilly Bars," she answered, unaware of the effect of this information. Tina and I froze, remembering my father's final words: "The Dilly Bars are coming." We were terrified. Who were these Dilly Bars and what had they done with our father?

When my dad returned twenty minutes later, he saw us at the window with our faces pressed against the glass and decided to play a joke on us. He parked his car behind the house and crawled across the lawn on his stomach until he was situated directly under the window. He unwrapped two Dilly Bars, held on to their sticks, and slowly lifted them above his head.

When you're a kid, the world is just starting to make sense and yet you still have this expectation that anything can happen at any time. When the two dark brown circles appeared outside the window and bobbed back and forth, Tina and I thought it was an event on par with an alien invasion. We screamed at the top of our lungs. Tina started crying, "The Dilly Bars! Not the Dilly Bars!" I peed my pants.

My dad rolled back and forth on the grass, laughing and slapping his leg. We, on the other hand, had nightmares involving ice cream bars for weeks.

While my father was busy playing pranks, my mother raised us. She used to play the piano for us kids to dance to. It was one of our favorite things to do. We'd spin in circles to "The Entertainer" until we were sick, and then lie on the floor and giggle. My mother was always pregnant. I remember nuzzling my head into her round belly, listening to my new sibling's heartbeat. I knew Julia, Britain, and Jill before they were born; I knew them as heartbeats in my mom's tummy. It makes me feel like I somehow own them. That's how Tina must feel about me.

Then there's my father. My dad did not want four girls. He wanted boys. Instead, he raised my sisters and me to be strong women. I hated him for it. I hated it when he'd throw me off the high diving board, or force me to ask strangers for directions when I wanted to be shy. I especially hated when he would scoop me up and stand me on top of the fridge. He'd tell me to face the wall, and without looking back or bending my knees, I was supposed to fall backward and trust that he would catch me.

My father had a way of making our home a party. On one occasion, he came home from a boring day at the office and yelled, "Line up, tallest to shortest." He'd seen this in *The Sound of Music* and had been using it ever since.

All five of us kids lined up against the wall.

"Do you guys know what cereal killers are?" he asked.

We shook our heads no.

"You guys are the cereal killers!" he said emphatically.

He piled us into the van and drove us to Fred Meyer. While he bought us masks, gloves, and squirt guns, we each got to pick out any cereal that we wanted.

From there we headed to several of his friends' houses, assembling in a clump on their doorsteps while Tina, my oldest sister, rang the bell.

As the door opened we cocked our squirt guns with one hand, and held up our cereal boxes with the other: "Hands up," we yelled. "We're the cereal killers!" Then, at my father's instruction, we went into his friends' houses and forced them to eat cereal.

It's only when I tell stories like these to friends that I realize exactly how bizarre my childhood was—bizarre yet simple. But something happened in the spring of 1991 that changed the course of this simplicity. My father got a job offer to work for Boeing in Madrid, Spain. We'd never been out of the country. He brought home a map of the world and pointed to a potato chip–sized country on the other side of the ocean. Spain.

I didn't understand countries, leaving, or the other side of the world. And it was hard for me to wrap my head around the idea that if I left Sumner, it would still exist. As a result, in the weeks preceding our move, I became a bit of a hoarder. Especially food. I had to try every single candy bar at the grocery store for fear that I would never see them or get the opportunity again.

The day before our departure, we went to Fred Meyer to get a few things. We were standing in the checkout line when I spotted a large gum-ball machine. *There probably isn't gum in Spain,* I thought. *Oh, how I will miss it!* I tugged on my mother's sleeve. "Can I have quarter?" I asked. "I *need* a piece of gum."

"Absolutely not," she answered. "You've had too many sweets today."

My mother didn't understand the gravity of the situation. So what if I'd already had M&M's? M&M's aren't gum. I needed to say good-bye to *gum.* I waited for her to get distracted, reached my hand into her coat pocket, and pulled out a quarter. That's the joy of having four brothers and sisters; you can get away with this sort of thing. I crept over to the gum-ball machine, put the quarter in the slot, and twisted the knob. A blue gum ball spun around and around until— *whack*—it hit the small metal door. *Blue.* I held it up in amazement. *I wanted you!*

Were it not for the fact that I chew like a cow, I would've gotten away with it. But unfortunately, as we turned onto our street, my mother heard me chomping on my piece of gum. *Why had I disobeyed her, where had I gotten the money, didn't I understand how busy and stressed she was?*

My punishment: I had to walk the rest of the way home. It was actually a good thing for me to do; it gave me the chance to say good-bye. As I turned up our gravel road, Zeb, our sheltie, ran down to meet me. Leaving him with my grandparents was more sad than anything. *I won't forget you.* I scratched him behind his ears. *I promise.* Reaching my hand into my coat pocket I took out the rest of my M&M's. I fed Zeb the entire bag, one by one. There's no other way to say this: I was a fat kid and this was the most selfless thing I could think to do; give up my chocolate.

I looked up at our house. The sun was going down and light was shining through all of the windows. "Good-bye," I said. There's a particular feeling I get when I say good-bye. It's not nostalgia; it's more like I miss something even while it's still there. In my adult life this happens when I'm incredibly happy. I'll look around and my eyes will fill with tears because I know it can't last forever. But this was my first experience with it—the first time I recognized *just because you like something doesn't mean it won't go away.*

My dad's getting the job in Spain was a huge leap for my parents. They were still living like poor newlyweds, only with five kids. And so, when Boeing offered to either ship ten thousand pounds of their belongings or give them ten thousand dollars to buy new things, they took the money and paid off their debts. We went to Spain with only the luggage on our backs. Prior to leaving, my mother checked to see how many bags we were allowed. Two checked bags, two small carry-ons. Multiply that by seven people, you get twenty-eight bags. Back then there wasn't a weight limit to luggage; the only limitations were on size. According to the airline, the largest bag a person could check was eight feet by three feet. They don't sell bags this size. And so my mother sewed her own. She made ten giant eight-by-three-foot duffel bags and filled each one to the brim. In addition to those body bags we had four rolling suitcases, and fourteen small carry-ons.

Two adults, five children, and twenty-eight bags left the Seattle airport in route to Madrid. It wasn't a direct flight either. We stopped in San Francisco and my parents collected all twenty-eight bags and re-checked them. From there we flew to New York City where they did it all over again. It was chaos, the airport was overcrowded, and the other passengers were giving my parents dirty looks. I was only nine, but I knew enough to understand that their thriftiness was humiliating. In the midst of piling up the body bags, my mother looked up. She'd lost Britain. He was three at the time and he'd wandered off somewhere in baggage claim. We split up and searched the airport. He was missing for a total of five minutes. My mother nearly had a meltdown; in an attempt to save money and still bring as many things as possible, she'd sacrificed a child.

Once our bags were checked and my brother was found, we went into the bathroom to change into our nicest clothes. Officials from CASA, the Spanish equivalent of Boeing, were greeting us at the airport in Madrid and my mother wanted us to look our best. She'd bought an outfit for the occasion, a silk mustard pantsuit, high fashion for the early nineties.

It was a nine-hour flight to Madrid. The airplane was a newer model and each seat had its own TV. Tina and I thought this was incredible. We could watch TV and our parents couldn't control what we watched or how long we watched it. Instead of sleeping, we made the most of this opportunity and watched movies for nine hours straight. Meanwhile, the little kids slept on my mother. Julia had her head on one leg, Britain was sleeping on the other, and Jill was resting in my mom's arms, her head on a thick mustard shoulder pad.

Halfway through the flight my mom got a terrible migraine. She handed the baby to my dad, moved the sleeping little kids, and walked to the bathroom. It was only in the light that she noticed them: three giant drool spots, one on each knee and another running down her shoulder. She looked in the mirror. Her silk mustard suit was ruined, her eyes were bloodshot, and she was exhausted. She opened the toilet lid and started vomiting.

We arrived in Madrid the following afternoon. Tina and I had gone a total of twenty-four hours without sleep. To top things off, the CASA officials were three hours late. By the time they got there, Britain's outfit (he was wearing a white suit and playing on the floor with his toy train) had turned dark gray. It wasn't the first impression my parents had imagined: twenty-eight bags and five zombie children in stained clothes.

We drove to our hotel and dropped off our belongings. My biggest concern with moving to Spain was that I would never see American food again. Ironically, the first thing we did was head to a McDonald's. I was too tired to appreciate it. Both my older sister and I fell asleep on the plastic table. When we woke up an hour later, still in McDonald's, my father said it was the next day, and for some reason we believed him.

I remember looking around at Ronald and the Hamburglar and being genuinely perplexed. *How did an entire day go by? Where did I sleep? What did I do? Why was I at McDonald's again?* I couldn't remember a thing. *Even time is different when you live in Spain.* I cried.

We adjusted to the life of vagabond children rather well. My mother was worried that the Boeing execs would change their minds and make us go home at any moment, so she insisted we see everything that we possibly could. We spent the weekends driving from city to city. "Not another castle" became a family catchphrase. One summer we drove through twenty-five countries. My parents never made plans, either. We'd just pull into the center of town and ask the first person we saw what to see and where to stay.

I was ten years old and got to experience history before I'd read or heard about it. I learned about the Battle of Normandy while I was looking at a huge field of white crosses. I learned about concentration camps while visiting Auschwitz. And I learned about the slave trade on a slave ship off the coast of Portugal. At the time I already knew I wanted to be a writer, so I wrote about these events through the eyes of a young girl who was experiencing them. I thought my stories were great, too. It's only now that I realize what they really were: *World War Two, The Holocaust,* and *Slavery,* written by and starring Elna Baker.

But each experience helped expand my knowledge of the world—which is what my parents were aiming for. During a family trip to Morocco, they dropped off us kids at a carpet factory and paid the foreman to make us do manual labor. Tina, Julia, and I sat on a bench next to three other little girls. They tried to teach us how to weave a carpet by smiling, quickly pulling the strings, then crossing them. It reminded me of a popular playground game, Cat's Cradle: one girl wraps a piece of string around her hands, another takes the string, creating a new pattern. Only in this circumstance there were hundreds of strings and the pattern we were making was an actual carpet. I tried to help, but I kept getting in the way. At one point I pulled on Tina's sleeve. *This is a really bad day,* I was about to complain, when a different tan girl turned around. I'd mistaken one of the Morrocans for my sister. It totally startled me, like when you gulp down water and get Sprite. *She could be my sister and my sister could be her.* It made me realize that I couldn't take my life for granted. Other kids didn't get to have my life. And this upset me. Because no matter how I looked at it, I couldn't figure out why it was fair.

- Elna was married at twenty. She is an actress in California and has four kids with her handsome husband, Josh.

* * *

I always considered my upbringing to be a positive thing. Only back at the family reunion, rereading a prediction for a future I hadn't experienced, I started to rethink things. It wasn't just the letter. It was something my sister Tina had said to me earlier in the day.

We're old maids. Not to most people, but within the context of the Mormon culture, single and over twenty-one means we're way past our prime. We are "career-driven women," and so we are abnormal, especially because we were trained to want marriage. I grew up singing songs in church with lyrics like: "I have a family here on earth / They are so good to me / I want to marry in God's temple for all eternity."

For the most part my failure to live up to my personal destiny is only apparent when I call home and talk to my mother.

"I'm writing a story about—"

"That's neat," she'll cut me off. "Did you meet any new guys at church last Sunday?"

My mother desperately wants all of her children to be wed, but because Tina and I are the oldest, we get the brunt of it. At the dinner table she'll pray out loud, "Bless Tina and Elna that they will be able to find their eternal companions."

Eternal is the key word. Mormons don't believe in hell. We believe there are three different levels to heaven, like how they divide A-list, B-list, and C-list celebrities. In the highest level of heaven you can become a God and create your own world. But here's the catch: In order to do this, you need to be married for time and all *eternity* to another Mormon in a Mormon temple. As if aging, social pressure, potential weight gain, dried-up ovaries, and a mother's constant prodding isn't enough to motivate marriage, I have to find a partner *for eternity*, and I can't even sleep with him first. A choice that could result in bad sex for eternity.

There's another catch: If I choose not to get married in a Mormon temple, I forfeit the ability to be with my family in the afterlife. I'm convinced that this is why my mother puts so much pressure on marriage: She's afraid of losing me after I'm dead.

And yet, in spite of all her meddling, my mom was the only member of her extended family with five unmarried kids at her family reunion. *What's wrong with the Baker children?* our relatives whispered. *I mean, they're attractive.*

One of my great-aunts actually pulled me aside and said, "When are you going to give up your big dreams and settle down?"

I pointed out that the words *give up* and *settle* weren't exactly inspiring to me. Then I found Tina and related the story to her. At the ripe old age of twenty-eight, she finds it even worse. Apparently someone had just tried setting her up with a twenty-one-year-old returned missionary who we may or may not be related to, and I quote, "But if you are, it's distant."

"Why do our lives only matter if we're married?" Tina complained.

"Because we're women," I answered. Only this didn't help cheer her up, so I tried another route. "Has dad ever pressured you to get married?"

"No."

"You see? We're fine. Once he starts interfering, then we know we're in trouble. Until then, we're in the clear—"

"He did say something once that really bothered me," she interrupted.

"What?"

"He said, 'Did we do you kids a disservice by showing you the world?'"

"Why would he think that?" I said defensively.

"Because he said that now, when mom and him want us to make simple choices, choices they know will make us happy, we can't seem to do it."

Kissing, Take Two: Wade

B y the time I was sixteen, everyone I knew had been kissed except for me. In hopes that the day would come, I tried to prepare myself mentally for my first kiss. I memorized an article in *Cosmo* entitled "The Art of Kissing." "Gently press your lips to his, flick your tongue lightly." I practiced in the air, on my hand, and on a pillow. But the suggestions were too advanced for me. They were based on the premise that the reader had already been kissed. What I wanted to know more than anything was: What does another person's tongue feel like when it's in your mouth? Is it like a slug, or something more romantic—a rose petal maybe?

Then it happened, in the most uneventful way possible. I was jumping on the trampoline when my twelve-year-old neighbor Wade decided to join me. Wade was small for his age, and he was known for being super horny. "I've had like eight blow jobs!" he once told me, a fact that I seriously doubted because I'd just barely learned what a blow job was and I was sixteen.

Anyway, Wade and I were jumping on the trampoline when Wade made an unexpected move: He put his foot underneath mine and tripped me. I flopped backward onto the trampoline and, before I could catch my breath, he jumped on top of me, and stuck his tongue down my throat.

I screamed and tried to push him off, but at the same time, I was curious. There was a tongue (the very thing I'd been reading and wondering about), and it was in my mouth. So I stopped screaming and pressed my tongue against Wade's. It felt weirder than I thought it would—fat and slimy.

In the midst of this kiss, it dawned on me that anyone could turn the corner and see us lying there. I screamed and pushed Wade away for a second time. But just as I did this, I got curious and pulled him back. Pressing his little body into mine, I kissed him hard, not because it felt good, but because it didn't. Everything I'd read described kissing as pleasurable. This wasn't pleasurable; it was disgusting. My worst fears were confirmed: *I'm a terrible kisser!*

It was clear that the kiss was going nowhere. I pushed Wade off me, deflated. We lay there on the trampoline, side-by-side. I can only imagine what we must've looked like from above, me an extra-large, him an extra-small, like a mother bear and her cub.

Wade broke the silence. "Can you at least give me a blow job?"

Kissing, Take Three: Paul

I n high school I was the queen of crushes. I think *crush* is the perfect word to describe it, too, because it simultaneously means "to have a brief infatuation with someone unattainable" and "to be violently squashed." That's usually how my crushes would end.

Case in point, my biggest crush of all time, Paul Stowe. Paul and I met when I was in high school in Seattle. He was a senior while I was a sophomore, which made him automatically cooler than me. Plus he was the drama club president, which meant he did funny skits in the high school assembly. Everyone in the whole school knew him by name, and I aspired to be one of the lucky few whose name Paul Stowe knew.

Our friendship began because I was Mormon. Paul had never met a Mormon and he was curious about my beliefs. One day after drama club he asked me some questions. I answered them as open-mindedly as possible. And so began our routine: Every Tuesday after school we would sit in his car and have long conversations about religious dogma. Paul was a nondenominational Christian, and he loved to ask things like, "Why are we here on earth, Elna?"

I'd launch into an explanation, his eyes would light up, and I'd watch him shift back and forth in his seat with excitement. When he got this way he looked like he was trying not to wet himself; I guess

God had that effect on him. We spent hours in Paul's car. While I talked, Paul would listen intently; but when Paul talked, my eyes would glaze over and, instead of listening, I'd think about kissing. I still don't know exactly what nondenominational Christians believe, because the whole time Paul was explaining his faith, I was making up scenarios in my head that ended with our making out.

This went on for several months. We would go to drama club meetings and find ourselves in Paul's car talking about existence. The best part was that we really believed we were only one or two questions away from figuring it all out.

One day in the midst of one of these discussions, Paul started talking about snow, and how looking at fresh snow really helped him "get it." He described the perfect whiteness of snow. He described how the little crystals sparkled, and then he explained that one could not look at snow and not believe there was a God.

The words came out before I could stop them. "I've never seen snow," I said. Paul was shocked. I was shocked, too—it wasn't true. I'd seen snow dozens of times. I'd been skiing; I'd been to the Alps. But it was too late. I'd just lied for no reason at all and the only way to take back the lie was to admit to it. And I wasn't about to do that.

"How is that even possible?" Paul asked.

I made up a story about how in Spain there was no snow, and how every time I'd been to Seattle it was summer. I went back and forth, giving far too many examples. In the winters of '91 through '94 I was in Madrid, in the winter of '98 we were living in Seattle, and while it did snow there we'd taken a family trip to the Bahamas. And so on.

To Paul this wasn't just a list of poorly planned vacations—it was a real tragedy. He explained that snow had guided him, that snow had helped him understand his inner light. That's when it occurred to him: "Elna, the mountains are only three hours away. We should just drive to the mountains and see snow right now!"

I made a mental pro/con list. On the one hand, I really liked Paul, and if we spent six hours in the car together the mathematical odds of our making out would increase dramatically. On the other hand, I would have to act like I was seeing snow for the first time. And how do you do that? How do you have an experience you've already had, for the first time? I looked at Paul. He had his usual *I am so excited I'm going to pee my pants* look. Then I thought about all the times we'd just sat in the school parking lot. The keys would be in the ignition, the tank would be full of gas, but Paul and I never went anywhere.

"Okay," I said. "Let's do it! Let's go see snow!"

Three hours later, at the base of Mount Rainier, clumps of partially melted snow started to appear alongside the road. I pressed my face against the window and tried to react genuinely. "Is that what I think it is?" I began. Paul grabbed a sweater from the backseat of his car and threw it over my head.

"Not yet," he said. "No peeking till we get to the top."

For the next twenty minutes, I sat in my seat with his sweater over my head. I inhaled the cologne in its fibers, and tried as hard as I could to memorize his scent. I started to feel a little bit bad. Paul was so proud of himself for being the first person to ever show me snow. But it was all a lie. I realize that at any moment I could have compensated for this guilt by telling the truth, but that would have been too obvious. Instead, I decided to go deeper. I decided that when Paul took that sweater off my head, I was going to give him the performance of a lifetime.

I felt the car slow down and veer off to the side of the road.

"Stay right there," Paul said and opened his door. I was like a musician running through her set. I thought of all the possible reactions I could have: surprise, joy, gratitude, confusion. I practiced saying the word *snow* in my head. I could say it lightly like a damsel in distress, I could shout it like the word *surprise* at a surprise party.

Or I could say it softly, reverently, like an *amen* at the end of a prayer.

Paul opened my door. I felt his soft hand on my hand. I grabbed hold of him and he helped me out of the car. My feet made a crunching sound below me as I stood up. I could feel the cold air on my bare arms.

"Ready?" Paul asked.

"Ready," I said. He pulled his sweater off my head. We stood facing a large clearing covered in snow surrounded by a semicircle of tall pines. Everything sparkled. I thought about what Paul had said about God. I didn't need to act surprised; I was surprised. Three hours previously I had been in the school parking lot, and now I was in the middle of the forest. It was as if we'd gone through one of those *Star Trek* transport machines. (I don't watch *Star Trek*. It's just an analogy.)

Paul searched my face for a reaction. I took a deep breath—it was time for me to deliver. I went with possible reaction number seventeen: I threw my hands up to my face like Macaulay Culkin in *Home Alone*. "Snow!" I hollered, the word echoing from the mountains above. "Snow, snow, snow, snow." I twirled in a full circle, and then I bent down and picked up a handful of the new white powder. I gazed at it. "It's so beautiful," I said. "Yikes," I added, shaking the snow from my hands and to the ground. "It's freezing!" As if I'd never touched frozen water before. It was a terrible performance, overdone, reeking of melodrama—but Paul loved every minute of it.

"Race you to the trees," he said. I took off running. I'm really slow, so any head start helps. Paul didn't run after me. Instead, he bent down, scooped up a pile of snow, packed it between his hands, aimed, and threw it across the clearing. It hit me in the middle of my back. "Rude," I yelled. I could feel the wet spot through my T-shirt, but I ignored it and ran faster.

When I made it to the trees, I glanced back at Paul. I could hardly process it. I was living out a daydream. I, Elna Baker, the chubby uncool girl, was in the woods with Paul Stowe, the guy who ran the school assemblies, and he was holding a snowball and he was chasing me! I threw back my head and felt the cold air on my cheeks as I ran. I imagined Paul catching up to me. I imagined him grabbing my right arm and spinning me into him. I imagined him dipping me, and I imagined him kissing me. It would be perfect. He would kiss me like I always thought lovers would kiss, softly, confidently, like a declaration.

I was so engrossed in my fantasy that I didn't see the log. My right foot caught it at a perfect angle. Despite my weight and size I was catapulted into the air. I floated for a total of three seconds. As I flew toward the ground I thought about staying up there, but years of being a klutz have proven that landing is inevitable. I hit the ground with a *thud*, my body rolled over itself three times, and my head smacked into a rock.

I sat up, embarrassed and hurt. My hands immediately went to my throbbing head. But before I could assess the damage, Paul was there, bending over me and holding back a laugh.

"Are you okay?" he asked, kneeling down beside me. "Are you hurt?"

I was about to say no when Paul leaned in and pulled a twig from my hair. We had never been this close. He was eight inches from my face. I could smell his cologne. I looked into his green eyes, his lips, his braces (okay, so he had braces, but he was still hot). After all my daydreams the moment had finally presented itself. I was going to kiss Paul Stowe. That's when I felt it in my hand—liquid. I knew without having to look that it was blood. *No*, I thought. I had to stop it. If I wanted to get kissed I had to will the blood back.

Paul was still looking at me, looking directly into my eyes. *Kiss me, kiss me, kiss me*, I tried to telepathically communicate. Then, a warm bead of liquid slid down the side of my face. I watched Paul's expression change from admiration to sheer horror.

"You're bleeding!"

I took my hand off my forehead. It was covered in blood. I wasn't just bleeding—my head was gushing.

"Don't move," Paul said. He stood up and looked around, as if he'd find a first aid kit hanging from one of the trees. "Oh, shit," he said, followed by, "It's okay" and "We gotta put pressure on it."

Paul frantically searched through his pockets in an attempt to find something that he could hold to my forehead and use to stop the bleeding. I, on the other hand, was too disappointed to do anything. I had spent six months engaged in deep religious conversations just so I could get kissed—and now that the moment had arrived, my forehead had spit blood.

I took a handful of snow and pressed it up against the wound. It didn't help. The blood mixed into the snow, and the snow melted down my arm. *Alas*, I thought, *my newfound friend does not serve this purpose.*

Paul was not handling the situation as calmly as I was. "We have to get back to the car," he said.

I stood up, but my right foot—the one that had caused all the drama—buckled underneath me. Each step I took hurt more than the one before.

"Here," Paul offered, "let me carry you."

"That's okay," I insisted. When you're fat, you never let people try to carry you. They think they can, but they can't.

"Elna, we have to get back to the car and put something on your head as soon as possible."

"You go," I offered. "I'll wait here."

"I'm not leaving you." Paul was suddenly very serious. "You could pass out. Come on—let me carry you."

Paul reached one arm under my butt and tried to lift me. "Wait!" I practically shouted. To this day I regret the words that followed.

"I have my period," I said, "and I have a pad in my pocket." It wasn't a new thought. When Paul had searched his pockets, I had searched mine, felt the pad, and then decided against it. But desperate times call for desperate measures—Paul could not try to carry me.

I pulled out the Maxi pad, carefully unwrapped it, undid the wings, and stuck it to my forehead. At the time I was only thinking about how to stop my head from bleeding, and how to stop Paul from picking me up. But when I caught a glimpse of Paul's face, frozen in amusement and disgust, I wanted to rewind. I wanted to put the Maxi pad back and I wanted to bleed to death slowly.

But you don't get second chances. I thought about this on the long car ride home. Paul sat in the driver's seat staring straight ahead, both hands on the wheel, and I sat beside him leaning against the window, a bloody Maxi pad still pressed against my forehead. *After all of our profound discussions in the high school parking lot, this may very well be the meaning of my pathetic life.*

Shortly after our road trip, Paul started dating another senior and we stopped hanging out after school. Sometimes we'd see each other in the hall and he would call me "Paddy." When he used this nickname in front of other people I'd lie and say my middle name was Patricia.

A few months later, I moved back to London, Paul went off to college, and that was the end of Paul and me. Or at least I thought it was. Then, the summer before I went to NYU I returned to Seattle to visit my grandparents and get a summer job. I was working at the local movie theater when Paul came in with a few friends. I gave him free popcorn and a drink.

"We should hang out sometime," Paul said casually.

"Great," I answered, a lot faster than I should have. We ended up going out at least twice a week for the entire month of July. One summer evening, we were at a Mexican restaurant having cinnamon tortillas when I started babbling.

"You know, I feel like I've really matured this year," I said. "I keep thinking that I'm going to meet someone, but I've never actually been ready. Now I feel like I'm aware enough of my individuality to have a boyfriend." It was all nonsense.

"I'll be your boyfriend," Paul said. I choked on the water in my glass. Had I heard him right? Had he really just said that?

"You want to be my boyfriend?" I asked, looking hard into his eyes.

"Yes," he said. "Elna, do you want to go out with me?"

It was like hearing the unimaginable. He had spoken the words that were supposed to break the spell. I felt a change come over me. Right there in front of Paul a circle of light surrounded me and swirled around like a tornado. I transformed. Not from a moth into a beautiful butterfly, which is always what I thought would happen if I could just get a boyfriend. But from an intelligent articulate person into a semiretarded schoolgirl.

"You want to be my boyfriend! So cool, good, so good boyfriend!" I blabbered.

"What?" Paul asked.

I glanced down at my chest, where huge red blotches were starting to form as they do when I'm embarrassed.

"Boyfriend," I said pointing to him and giggling. The giggling would not stop.

When he said, "Elna, why are you acting this way?" I just laughed and laughed. When he said, "Stop that," I repeated, "Stop that," and then I laughed and laughed. I knew exactly how fatal this behavior was. I wanted to grab myself by the shoulders and scream, "Snap out of it." Instead, I blew bubbles in my glass of milk.

Paul broke up with me three hours later. "I feel like you've changed," he explained.

I tried to explain that I hadn't changed, I tried to convince him to give me another chance, but all I could do was giggle and ask for high fives.

While we never went out again, technically my adolescent daily affirmation came true: Paul Stowe was my boyfriend, once, for 180 minutes. I should've been more specific.

My Grandmother's Dress

I always wanted to be beautiful. I'm not talking inner beauty either. I wanted to be hot. As a kid I would daydream about it. I had this picture of my mother's mother that I would stare at; she was twenty-five at the time, tall, thin, her hair pinned back in a 1940s-style and she was wearing what I called the "Sacred Dress." I knew this dress was sacred because I could try on all her dresses except for this one.

My grandfather had served in the Korean War and while he was stationed in Japan he bought my grandmother this silk brocade fabric. She looked through all the magazines and carefully selected a dress in *Vogue* that was worthy of the material. She saved up for the pattern and, at night, when her babies were asleep, she would work on her dress. It took her two years to finish. The result is a dress that fits tight around the ribs, has cap sleeves and a V-neck, and flows out in a full skirt.

I would stare at the picture of my grandmother in this dress and daydream the same dream each time: I was all grown up, I was beautiful, I was wearing the dress, and I was on a date with Brian Egbert, the most popular boy in first grade.

I had daydreamed this so often that one day I couldn't take it anymore. I snuck the dress out of my grandma's closet. I stood in front of the mirror, delicately pulled the dress over my head, and then tried to zip it. *It didn't fit.* I was seven years old and I was too fat to fit into my grandmother's dress.

I was always chubby. Okay, not just chubby, I was clinically obese, but can we skip the semantics? I used to make up friends with birthdays so that I would have an excuse to bring cupcakes to school and then eat them for lunch. I was that kind of chubby, the lying-for-baked-goods kind.

And it didn't help that Tina was gorgeous. On our family trip to Morocco when I was twelve years old, a man saw my sister on the street and stopped my parents to say: "Your daughter is the most beautiful creature on this earth. I will give you a thousand camels for her." My parents said: "No, thank you" (and scooted Tina behind them). So the man turned to me, looked me up and down, and said: "I'll give you a hundred camels for her."

Nine hundred camels, I thought. *There is a nine-hundred-camel difference between my sister and me?*

The rest of my life can be described as a pursuit to be worth more camels.

Even at a young age I understood: Because of the way I look, I am worth less. I tried to have a sense of humor about it. I remember lying in the bathtub and squeezing my stomach fat for fun. I rolled the white chubbiness into a circle and decided I had a tangerine of excess fat. Through elementary school I continued to measure my fat in increments of fruit. When I was nine I had an orange of extra fat and then at eleven a grapefruit of extra fat, and then a melon, and then . . . I decided not to measure myself anymore because it was no longer a fun game, and I didn't want to use the word *watermelon.*

Things only got worse from there. I was going through the back of Tina's yearbook, my favorite activity, when I recognized two signatures. They belonged to the two most popular boys in my fourth grade class: "How come you're so pretty and Elna isn't?" and "I wish your sister looked like you." I was devastated. Not because I thought they were being unfair, but because I agreed with them. My mother consoled me: "Don't get mad, just get even" (a truly Christian philosophy). The next day I signed their yearbooks: "You will regret your comment in my sister's yearbook next year when you beg to go out with me. Of course, I will refuse." But that never happened; no one ever begged to go out with me.

God, please make me beautiful, I want to look like Tina, turn me into someone special. I would've traded everything to be beautiful. This went against everything I was raised to believe. In fact, if you ask any Mormon the question "Why are we here on earth?" they will give the standard answer they've been taught since childhood: "To get a body."

I remember my primary teacher holding up a paper doll and reading a quote from a Mormon apostle, "You have been given a body so you can exalt yourself to a nobler condition. . . . The intelligence that is in man . . . give it a physical body and you have enlarged its powers immeasurably."

In other words, the primary purpose of life on earth was for me to get a body, any body; to appreciate it, make choices with it, and use it for good works; and then, when I am done with it, "to shuffle off this mortal coil" and return to God. By the age of five I had learned the meaning of life. There was only one problem: I got the wrong body—and I'd been hating it ever since.

Only, something happened my sophomore year of college to change my perspective. I went to a writing retreat and on the retreat I was given an assignment to write a story that began with the line: "My body finally speaks." The last thing I wanted to do was to let my body speak. At the time I weighed two hundred fifty pounds; once it got started it might never shut up.

I sat in front of a blank piece of paper and thought, *Okay, fine, body, you want to speak? Now's your chance.* I didn't anticipate the effect this offer would have. Without any effort on my part, words started flowing onto the page.

I am made up of skin, and muscles and fat, my body began. *I have a heart that pumps blood and a foundation of bones that are as vulnerable as paper because they too can become ash. But I move, and I can jump, and I feel, and I can do all of these incredible things . . . but you don't love me. When are you going to realize—this is your only chance.*

Reading these words over, it felt like someone had knocked the wind out of me. *Wow. Body certainly doesn't hold back when body speaks.* It was a wake-up call. I left the retreat with a new mission: I was going to stop wishing that I was beautiful and I was going to learn how to love myself just as I was. And so, to start this off, I created a mantra: *I am what I am.* And I would repeat it every day: *I am what I am, I am what I am, I am what I am.* It was like my sound track. A little repetitive and not necessarily iTunes worthy, but it was my sound track nonetheless.

After doing this for a few months, I stopped hiding food and I started accepting my bad habits. Until one day, I was waiting on the subway platform during rush hour when a man passed me. He looked me up and down. I genuinely thought he was checking me out until he said in his loudest voice: "Damn girl, you better lose some weight!" It was like being back in fourth grade and opening my yearbook. But this time I had a defense. *I am what I am, I am what I am, I am what I am*, I repeated silently while the other people on the platform avoided making eye contact with me.

On the ride home I thought deeply about what I was trying to do. My entire life, I had defined myself by how others perceived me. I needed more than a mantra to change this habit. So I decided to pray about it. I didn't pray to be skinny (I'd tried that one a million times before); instead I prayed to be able to see myself through God's eyes so that I could realize my potential. I did this every day for a year, and I can't tell you how or why it worked, but eventually something just clicked and I felt like someone greater than me, some force from on high, loved me tremendously. And this feeling encouraged me to let go. I stopped using my weight as the trigger for a downward spiral of self-loathing. What was the point if it only made me feel bad? Instead, I accepted the way I looked. Not completely, because that's impossible, but I considered myself in a way I never had before, as an actual child of God, someone worth being created.

While I'd never fit into my grandmother's dress, I decided that I'd get one of my own. And so I went to a plus-size store in Harlem and picked out the loudest, sexiest dress I could find. It was hot pink Lycra, and the label said *Stop Staring*.

Kissing, Take Four: Jeff

I originally moved to New York to make it as an actress, but it'd been five months since my graduation from NYU and I was still unemployed. I wanted to persevere, but if I went to one more audition and heard, "You're great, but . . ." I was going to go insane.

The *buts* always ended different ways. For the sake of my ego, I stopped listening. Usually it had something to do with the way I looked: "We're looking for someone of a different build"; "You just don't match the male lead"; or, my personal favorite, "This character eats less than you."

It was embarrassing. After my parents had spent forty thousand dollars a year on my education, I was calling home and asking them for more money. I felt like the family gamble. I was the child who went to an expensive school and the child who promised she'd succeed. I was finished now and the gamble wasn't paying off. I had to get an acting job, and I had to get one soon.

At the end of my rope, I read an ad in *Backstage*: "Actors wanted, FAO Schwarz." I didn't care what they wanted us for; I ran to the audition. When I got there, I had to read a monologue by Princess Pretty, and then test-demonstrate an unknown toy. I looked down at a blob of magnets, called it "the amazing whirly-bob," and connected the pieces, mugging enthusiastically. I got the job.

Working as a toy demonstrator was actually more complicated

than you'd expect; there was a ranking system for the actors and certain toys were considered better than others. For the first few weeks I had to rotate from toy to toy so that Chad, the FAO toy demo manager, could analyze my acting strengths before placing me on a specific product. I demonstrated anything from robo transformers to plush puppets. My least favorite, the preschool veterinarian kit, came with a stuffed puppy and doctor tools. For six hours I was supposed to fake diagnose an inanimate object and get other people excited about it. I would interrupt families as they strolled through the store, saying, "Spot is sick. Will you help me figure out what's wrong with Spot?" And then I would hand the child a stethoscope while the parents waited impatiently. I might as well have said, "You and your family want to be left alone, but I'm an actor and I need attention."

After two weeks of rotating, I was assigned to the Lee Middleton Doll Collection. It was a coveted position. Lee Middleton Dolls were supposed to be special, they were made to look exactly like real babies, and they were weighted in the head and in the bottom so that they actually flopped like real babies. Every day I dressed in a nurses' uniform, and I worked with two other nurses-slash-actresses in the "adoption center," a small cottage on the second floor of FAO Schwarz.

A typical day of work would go as follows: Parents and their children would go from incubator to incubator admiring all the babies. If they wanted to hold a particular doll, we would ask them to point it out to us. Then we would carefully lift the baby, playing up the fact that it was "real," and hand it to them through the cottage window.

If they decided that they were serious about "adoption," we would open the gate to the white picket fence that surrounded the cottage and invite them in. Then we would sit across from the prospective parent (usually a seven-year-old girl) in one of two rocking chairs and begin an adoption interview. "Do you promise to love and care for the baby?" "Will you read to the baby?" "Will you change the baby's diaper?"

"Yes," the little girls would answer with such sincerity.

And then the final question: "What would you like to name the baby?"

The girls always chose frilly names like "Princess Tiffany of Fairy Flowerland."

We would write "Princess Tiffany" on the doll's hospital bracelet, along with the D.O.B., which usually happened to be the previous day, and then we would fill out a birth certificate. We would hand the birth certificate to the little girl's parents and say, "Now all you have to do is pay the adoption fee (*wink, wink*)."

Chad instructed us never to use words like *cost*, *purchase*, or *buy*, that would "break the illusion of the world." All transactions were considered adoptions and the adoption fee was $120. And I should mention here—while the Lee Middleton Dolls were "special" they were a far cry from being worth $120. So we were encouraged not to mention the price until the end of the interview because at that point the child's hopes would be too high for the parents to back out.

When the parents returned from the register we'd have the baby wrapped in a blanket—blue for boys, pink for girls. And then we'd check their receipt, hand the doll to their child, and say, "I'm sure baby Tiffany will have a wonderful home."

One annoying aspect of the job was that when it was slow, I wasn't allowed to socialize with the other nurses "on duty." Again, according to Chad, that would also break the illusion of the world. If we weren't working with a customer, we had to hold, rock, or bounce the display baby doll.

The display baby doll was on display for a reason. It could not be sold. Something terrible happened in the factory on the day of its birth because the doll's fingers were not like the other babies. They had been molded together—making it look like it had flippers instead of hands. As if that weren't bad enough, it had curly red Chuckie hair and scary green eyes, and its head weighed at least five pounds more than all the other babies' heads. As a result, when you lifted the baby, its head would automatically flop back, and its little flippers would flip up—making him look like a tabloid monster baby.

Which is how the doll earned its nickname: Nubbins. And because Nubbins was for display purposes only, he didn't have an incubator like the other babies. Instead, he was kept in a cupboard. This was especially disturbing because Nubbins had a knack for looking dead. So when you opened the cupboard you'd find him slumped over onto his enormous head with his arms flopped behind him, like he died in Downward-Facing Dog.

September and October are traditionally slow months at FAO Schwarz, and with no customers to attend to, we spent a lot of time holding, rocking, and bouncing Baby Nubbins. So much time that we actually started to resent him.

To entertain ourselves we invented a game. Actually, I invented it, but the other girls went along with it. The object of the game was this: While a nurse was working with a customer, you had to try to get her to break character by doing something horrible to Baby Nubbins.

For example, I opened all the drawers to all the cabinets in the adoption center and while another nurse was doing an adoption, I carefully walked down the aisle and rocked Nubbins's head into the jagged edges of each drawer, while humming a lullaby.

My favorite form of torture involved chance. The orphanage was located around a corner, so if there were no customers in sight, and you felt like a floor manager wasn't going to be turning the corner anytime soon, you'd take a risk, scoop up Baby Nubbins, and make out with him full on the mouth. It was fun to torture Nubbins in front of one another. But it was even better when there was a crowd of people standing outside the adoption center. It took real comedic timing. You'd change Nubbins's diaper on the diaper-changing table, then you'd carefully lift him, and gently place him on your shoulder and burp him ever so slightly. At just the right moment, you'd drop the baby.

It worked every time. Everyone watching knew it wasn't real, but when the baby hit the floor, they still jumped and gasped. And the best part was that they did it in sync, so it looked like a minor earthquake had just occurred.

I had to be cautious when I pulled stunts like this. I could not under any circumstances get caught or I'd lose my job. A job that, in spite of its ridiculousness, I really appreciated. I was paying rent, I was technically an actress, and my parents were off my back.

FAO also provided me with a whole new group of friends. I met a lot of other people my age, other actors. Jeff was one of them, the only coworker of mine that I've ever kissed. Jeff was average cute—tall, thin, borderline gangly. He's the kind of guy you'd expect to play video games in online groups, and occasionally smoke pot. His job at FAO Schwarz was to play a toy soldier. He stood outside the store in a red-and-black uniform with shiny gold buttons. He wore a tall black felt hat, and there were red circles drawn on his cheeks. I noticed him on my first day at work and decided that since Christmas was approaching, Jeff would be my Nutcracker fantasy.

I'm not certain how our flirtation began. Actually, that's not true. It's just a little embarrassing, and not something I'd want my parents to know. During one of our breaks we played the game "I Never" in the employee lounge. It's originally a drinking game but, since we were at work, we played a modified version. If someone said something they'd never done and you'd done it, instead of taking a shot, you just held up a finger. When you had all ten fingers up—*Oh, my gosh* . . . you were out! Okay, so not as exciting as the drinking game, but still fun. I was actually the one who suggested this version. We'd played it this way at church once. Let me tell you, it was a thrilling game, people were offering things like: I've never been to Wisconsin, I've never tried Dr Pepper, I've never thought about getting bangs.

The FAO Schwarz employee version was much more racy.

"I've never been arrested," one of the shorter elves from Connecticut volunteered. Santa and a guy who did LEGO demos both held up a finger.

"I've never been caught having sex in public," Princess Pretty offered. A nurse, one of the piano dancers, and a security guard all put fingers up. By this point in the game most people had five or six fingers in the air—my hands were still in my pockets.

And then it was my turn. I had a good one, too, one I was sure would get everyone. "I've never been to second base," I said enthusiastically. (Regular-people second base, not the Mormon version—I've totally held hands before.)

"What?" One of the elves gave me a quizzical look. "In baseball?"

"No," I said. "You know, second base." I gestured toward my boobs.

The room burst into laughter. "No one has ever touched your boobs?" Jeff asked. "How is that even possible?"

"How old are you?" Santa interrupted.

"Twenty-one," I said.

"But she's Mormon," Karla, a nurse I'd become better friends with, blurted out.

"Mormons can't have their boobs touched?" Jeff asked.

"We're not supposed to."

"Why?"

"It can lead to other things."

"Like what?" Jeff challenged.

"I don't know . . . ," I said. "You're not supposed to be *aroused*."

Apparently using the word *aroused* was a faux pas. The group started laughing hysterically, and it was, "Oh, does this arouse you?" and "Have you been aroused lately?" spoken one to another in proper British accents.

In the midst of this, Jeff turned to me. "Don't worry," he said, "I'll touch your boobs."

"What makes you think I want to have them touched?"

"You do, I can tell."

"I hate to burst your bubble," I said, "but I'm doing just fine without it."

Jeff looked directly into my eyes. "By Christmas," he said, "I will touch your boobs," like it was part of "The Twelve Days of Christmas" or something. *On the twelfth day of Christmas, my true love gave to me: twelve ninnies nipping, eleven peaches peaking, ten knockers knocking, nine mammories mounting, eight maids a-milking, seven sandbags shaking, six pink-nosed puppies, five nipple rings, four fun bags, three French hills, two tittie jugs, and a partridge in a pear tree!* Normally this would be considered sexual harassment, but since Jeff was average cute, I let it slide. The whole "Attractive Boy + Sexual Repression = Ethical Hypocrisy" equation.

The group was still laughing when the bell rang, putting an end to our game. "I love the sound of that bell," the shortest elf announced. "Every time it rings, I get so *aroused*."

After that, on slow days at work, when no one was looking, Jeff would walk by me holding two plush pumpkins pressed against his chest. Another time he stole the letters *B, O, O, B,* and *S* from an alphabet puzzle and left them outside my locker. I told him that under no circumstance would he or anyone be touching my boobs. Then I took two light sabers from the Star Wars section, held them in an X across my chest, and pranced around the store. My reaction only egged him on, of course.

Again, I was cautious not to get caught. Losing my job for sexual misconduct would be even worse than losing it for inappropriate handling of a plastic baby.

We sent secret messages back and forth—a topless Barbie, a plastic cow with enormous udders, a breast pump from the maternity collection—for about a month. It was actually pretty fun—seeing as it was the most male attention I'd had all year.

After all the build-up, we both understood that there was bound to be some sort of follow-through. So one night, when Jeff and I happened to walk out of work at the same time, we didn't go to our respective subway stops. We lingered.

Since work was our only common bond, we talked about how we both thought that the elves were pretentious. And how we felt badly for the actor assigned to Band in a Box, because the demo kit was missing half the instruments. That's when Jeff asked, "You hungry?"

"Always," I said, and then immediately regretted it because it made me sound like I was *always* eating. Which, when you weigh two hundred fifty pounds, isn't the kind of impression you want to make.

We decided to take the subway to a retro diner near my house. I thought it was a good idea until we were on the train. I live really far from work. We'd already covered all the basic information: where we were from, why we liked acting. We had five stops left and we'd already run out of things to say. You know it's bad when you catch each other reading the subway advertisements.

When we got to the diner we ordered milk shakes, cheesy fries, and hot dogs and sat across from each other in a cozy booth, still scrambling for conversation. That's when I noticed, a few feet from our table, a chest full of board games.

"Want to play?" I suggested. Jeff pulled out Monopoly, Connect Four, and Boggle, but they were all missing pieces. So we ended up choosing the game Guess Who? That was when things got weird.

Jeff sat the Guess Who? board in the center of our table and explained the game: We both had to pick a card from the deck. This card would show us who our player was. The object of the game was to guess the other person's "player" by asking yes-and-no questions.

"I think I remember this," I said, and I picked a card. Just as I was about to turn it over, Jeff put his hand on top of mine. "Let's make a wager," he said. "You win, I won't touch your boobs; I win, I get to touch your boobs."

I thought it over. There really wasn't anything in it for me. If I won, my boobs would not be touched. I didn't exactly have to play a game to earn that. I could walk down the street and no one would touch my boobs.

I looked across the table and into Jeff's blue-green eyes. Then I asked myself the real question: *Do I want someone to touch my boobs?* Two different guys had tried to touch them before, both at college parties, but because they were drunk and clumsy, and I was sober and astute, I had pushed their hands away. Still, at that moment, looking at Jeff, I was intrigued. I wondered if a man would like my boobs. Did I have nice boobs? My boobs are big, men like big boobs, but then again everything about me is big, and men don't seem to like that. I decided that half of me wanted to be touched and the other half did not. Jeff's fifty-fifty wager matched my indecision.

"Okay," I said. "It's a deal."

Jeff and I shook on it, as if having someone grope you always involved an official handshake.

I turned my card around and looked at it. Ben Forrester was the name of my person. Ben had brown eyes and a round face with a dark beard and he was wearing a hat. I looked at him again. He looked like my dad. *Great.* The last thing I wanted to think about was what my dad would think if he knew about this wager.

"Does your person have red hair?" Jeff asked.

"No," I answered. "Is your person wearing a hat?"

We asked each other a dozen yes-or-no questions. I tried to apply all of my intelligence, but I couldn't focus. Why? What I call my "Mormon filter" kicked in. Every time I consider doing something wrong, this happens. I can't just make a bad choice. I analyze the consequences too thoroughly and I filter all the information through my religion.

For example, if someone offered you a glass of wine, you'd probably be able to reach out and just take a drink. Not me. Before my hand reaches the glass, I've asked myself, *Is it worth it to put yourself in the position of being addicted to something?* I've thought, *The entire purpose of life on earth is to make choices, and addiction limits your freedom of choice.* By the time my hand gets to the glass of wine, I've already talked myself out of it. It's exhausting.

As I sat across from Jeff, I could think only of the things that would happen to me if I did something impure like let a man touch my boobs. My body was a temple and I needed to respect it as such and not defile it. The things I did with other people before I was married would limit my ability to completely love my partner because it introduced an element of comparison. Sexual acts were supposed to make me feel unholy in the presence of God, like my light had been diminished. I thought about what Mormons call the "eternal consequences" of your actions: Sexual immorality is the second worst sin, the first being murder. And I was so busy analyzing these potential consequences that I wasn't at all focused on figuring out who Jeff's player was.

That's when Jeff said it—before I was ready, before I knew what I wanted to do.

"Is your person Ben Forrester?"

I looked down at my card; the man who looked like my dad smiled unknowingly. He had failed me.

"Yes," I answered.

Jeff smiled.

"I live around the corner," I said. "We can do it there."

It's weird how your senses heighten when you're about to break character. If someone asked me, "As a Mormon, do you let guys touch your boobs?" I would say no. But there I was, not ten minutes later, sitting on my couch across from Jeff, lifting up my shirt. I was wearing a black bodysuit. Once I discovered bodysuits I always wore them under my clothes. It's really a pain when you have to pee. But just when I was about to give them up, I'd look in the mirror. My body looked so much neater with a bodysuit; I couldn't give it up.

When I lifted up my shirt I was worried Jeff would ask me what I was wearing. He didn't, though; he just stared at my chest and shifted in his seat to get closer to me. "Under bra or over bra?" Jeff asked.

"Over," I answered. Under was too big a step. Jeff looked disappointed.

"Fine," I said. "Under." I hardly knew him, but I didn't want to be the cause of any major letdown. Jeff awkwardly placed one hand inside the bra of my bodysuit and around my right breast. His fingers were cold and bony. Then he took his left hand and placed it on my left breast. We sat there like that for five minutes, not really talking.

I thought about whether I really liked Jeff. I guessed I didn't. On the subway ride we hadn't had much to say to each other, and the conversation only picked up at dinner because of the thrill of possibly doing something wrong.

But this wasn't so different than any of the other guys I'd been with. At this point I'd been kissed four times. I kept a list in my journal documenting all of them. Not counting Wade, the horny twelve-year-old I'd kissed on the trampoline, it was a list of strangers, location-based instead of name-based: guy at Joe's Pub, guy at Katie's dance party, and guy at Grassroots Tavern. Each of these kisses happened like my rendezvous with Jeff, behind closed doors, feeling somehow wrong. The major difference between Jeff and the other guys was that they'd all been drinking first. With thick beer goggles on they'd led me to a corner and tried to stick their tongues down my throat—not to romanticize it or anything. I guess I allowed these experiences because they made me feel like I was, in some way, part of the game. At least when friends talked about romance or relationships I could honestly say, "I've kissed a few guys, and I think. . . ."

Remembering these past screwups made me feel better about Jeff. At least he hadn't been drinking. An average cute guy—who was completely sober—liked me. Sort of.

Jeff bent his elbows so that he could move closer to me while still keeping his hands on my breasts. We made eye contact and he moved in for the kiss. I hated kissing. I didn't tell Jeff this—or anyone—but I hated kissing because I had no idea how to do it. The few encounters I'd had were all so sloppy and brief that even though it'd happened four times, I still didn't know how to kiss. This left me feeling overly anxious. *If I don't kiss well Jeff will think I'm a terrible kisser,* I worried, *when really I'm only a bad kisser because I haven't had time to practice. With the proper teacher, I could very well become a connoisseur.*

But Jeff was about to kiss me whether I knew how to kiss or not. He looked up at me and asked, "Is this okay?"

I nodded my head, but it wasn't okay. It wasn't okay to have his fingers on my breasts and it wasn't okay to kiss him. But it was what it was, and it's probably all it would ever be. I'd learned years earlier that the men I actually liked would never be attracted to me and I accepted it.

I let Jeff kiss me several times just on the lips, and then he stuck his tongue in my mouth. I never know what to do when a guy does this. *Do I put my tongue on top? Do I suck his tongue in? Will somebody cut me a break and just give me the answers?* For lack of a better response I decided, *Just play dead*. I flopped stiff to one side and let Jeff's tongue sit in the center of my mouth. I let it move back and forth, and then I let it retreat.

This was obviously not the right choice. Jeff stopped kissing me. He took his hands off my chest and sat up. Our make-out session was officially over. I immediately started to overanalyze. *Did he sit up because I'm a horrible kisser, or was he getting a kink in his neck? Should I have flicked my tongue? Oh, no . . . do I have hot dog breath?* Neither of us spoke. I thought of a few things I could say, but I couldn't figure out how to begin the conversation. *So how were my boobs?* just didn't sound right.

After a few moments, Jeff broke the ice. He stood up, walked over to my DVD collection, and said, "*Old School*'s a great movie. Do you mind if I borrow it?"

I could see we were just going to pretend it didn't happen.

"No problem," I answered, pulling my shirt down as he turned to face me. With the DVD under his arm he said, "Well, mission accomplished," followed by, "I really should be going."

Mission accomplished. I thought about his choice of words. What a stupid thing to say. Was he some sort of spy trying to touch virgin boobs all over the city?

"Do you work tomorrow?" I asked, walking him to my door.

"No, do you?"

"No."

"Okay, well, I'll see you on Monday."

"See you on Monday."

I unlocked the front door and opened it. Jeff took a step forward and then paused. His lips were slightly open and he looked like he wanted to say something more. So I waited. *Is he going to ask me out? Does he want to date me?*

He took a deep breath. "Don't tell anyone at work about this, okay?"

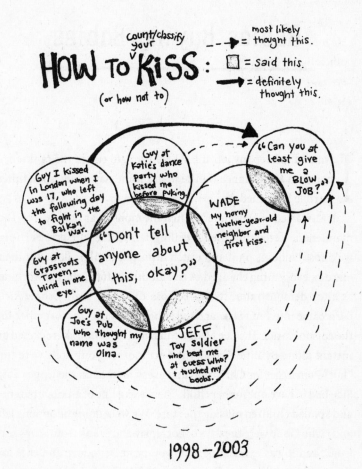

Babies Buying Babies

I wanted to keep my job at FAO Schwarz, to rise in the ranks, become an elf or dance on the piano some day. Only, something terrible happened.

It all started in November. At first the month was slow as ever. The maintenance crew installed a ceiling fan in the nursery. For fun, we'd toss Nubbins on it and watch him spin until he flew. But then one day, everything changed. A few months before I started working as a toy demonstrator, two girls from the MTV reality show *Rich Girls* came into FAO Schwarz and adopted a baby. On November 15, the episode aired. The Lee Middleton Doll Collection skyrocketed to instant fame. By nine o'clock the next morning our dolls were the "hot" item to get for Christmas and every mother on the Upper East Side had to have one for her child. There was a line of anxious parents and spoiled children outside the store. We were doing adoptions left and right. Gone were the days of horseplay and pranks—this was real work, and it was exhausting. "Do you promise to love and care for the baby?" "Will you read to the baby?" "Will you change the baby's diaper?" "What do you want to name the baby?" Fill out birth certificate. Repeat.

Business was so good that no one saw it coming, until it was too late. Within a week of the episode's airdate, we sold out of all the white babies. All we had left were incubators upon incubators of minority babies.

The manager of FAO Schwarz had a conniption fit. With Christmas only five weeks away the Lee Middleton Factory was already on back-order. There was absolutely no way to get a new shipment in until mid-January.

Day after day after day, the same scenario repeated itself.

Eager mothers would rush to the adoption center. "Is this the Lee Middleton Doll Collection?" they'd ask. Then they'd stop, dead in their tracks. I'd watch their heads go from incubator to incubator—they'd pause briefly at the Asian baby. "Oh wait—no. . . ." Then, trying as hard as they could to be politically correct, the mothers would look at us and say: "I'm sorry, but do you have any other shades of babies?"

Chad, the toy demo manager, had prepped us with a response. He'd taped a memo in the women's locker room reading: "If the mothers express a disinterest in the babies due to ethnicity kindly inform them that while these are all the babies we have in stock, there is a wider selection available online and they are more than welcome to order online."

But this was not what the mothers wanted to hear. They went on and on about how their child had to have a Lee Middleton Doll. Meanwhile there were dozens for sale behind them. Only they were the wrong color. "These dolls don't look like my little Susan," they'd explain, pointing to their child. "I want something that looks like Susan *(wink, wink)*."

We nurses decided to make the most of the situation and invented another game. Here's how it went: If a mother didn't want to adopt a doll because of its ethnicity, we worked on her child. It was pretty easy. First we would ask the little girl if she wanted to hold one of the babies.

"Wow!" we'd exclaim. "This baby has really taken to you! You would make an excellent mommy for this little one." The girls would gently stroke the babies, while the mothers would look at us in a state of panic. You could practically read their minds: *Why are you doing this to me? What did I ever do to you?*

The other game we invented stemmed from Chad's memo. Instead of saying, "There's a wider selection available online," we had to try and say, "There is a whiter selection available online," without getting caught or breaking character.

In spite of these games, the situation still depressed me. I remember one mother in particular. She was in her midthirties, with blond hair and a pinched face. When I offered her a Hispanic baby, she looked at me and said, "Oh, come on, we don't want a dark child—what would people think if Jessica was carrying a dark baby?" She touched my hand and looked into my eyes. "You know what I mean."

I knew what she was trying to imply: She was saying that since we were both white, I understood her. But what she didn't know is that while I'm fair-skinned, I'm actually half Mexican and that that doll looked exactly like my sister Tina and my brother Britain. And besides, did she honestly think that if someone saw her daughter carrying a Hispanic baby doll they would think that Juan the gardener had knocked her up?

There were so many things I wanted to say to these mothers. But I needed to keep my job, which meant I had to follow FAO Schwarz's policy: The customer is always right. So instead of speaking up, I took my hand out from under the pinched-faced woman's and said, "You are more than welcome to order online, where there is a whiter selection available."

But this was only half the story.

Technically we hadn't sold out of all the white babies; technically we still had one left. Nubbins. As a result, when mothers rushed to the adoption center and realized there were only minority babies, they'd immediately notice Nubbins. They'd spot him in our arms, round and pudgy with a head of red hair. He was the answer to their prayers. In their minds they had gotten there just in time—in their minds they were just that lucky.

"Can I see that baby?" they would insist.

All we ever had to do was turn Nubbins around. His head would flop back, his flippers would flip up, and the mothers would quickly say, "Never mind."

This happened so often that eventually we nurses decided to make a bet: "Who do you think will go first? Baby Nubbins or all of the minority babies?"

To be honest, when I've told this story in the past, and I've told it a number of times, I've said that I bet on the minority babies, because I thought Nubbins would be the last to go—if he'd go at all.

And then what I'd say happened was that Nubbins sold first, leaving behind an entire toy nursery of minority babies. And isn't that crazy!

But that wasn't exactly true. What actually happened was much harder to admit. It was this: The minority babies did start to sell. Slowly. First we sold out of all the Asian babies. Then we sold out of all the Hispanic babies. And finally, all we had left was Nubbins . . . and incubators of black baby dolls.

This just made us all feel worse. Inadvertently the bet had become: Who do you think will go first? Nubbins . . . or every black baby in the nursery?

I stood by my initial bet: "We'll never sell Nubbins," I insisted.

And then, a week later, a mother marched up to the adoption center. "Nurse," she yelled, "is this some sort of a joke?"

Her face was frozen in disgust. In one hand she was holding a Bergdorf shopping bag; with the other she was dragging a very solemn child.

"Where are the white babies?" she demanded.

I wasn't used to mothers being quite so direct. "We're all out," I said.

"You have got to be kidding. . . ." she began, then her eyes focused on Nubbins, who was nestled in my arms. "What about that one?" she asked.

I turned Nubbins around slowly for full impact, his head flopped back, his flippers flipped up. I waited for her horrified response.

"We'll take it," she said.

"What?" I thought, *Nubbins? You want to adopt Nubbins?* Was Nubbins even up for adoption?

I opened the white picket fence and escorted the mother and her daughter over to the rocking chairs. I set Baby Nubbins in the solemn little girl's lap. "Do you promise to love and care for this baby?"

The little girl looked up at me. "No."

I didn't know what to do. I had been doing adoptions for two months now, and I had interviewed hundreds of little girls. No one had ever answered no before. Technically she had just failed the adoption interview.

"Okay. . . ." I said, moving to the next question.

"Will you read to the baby?"

She looked at me, her eyes like ice. "No."

"Will you change the baby's diaper?"

"No."

"Okay . . . ," I teased, "but you're going to have a stinky baby." I mimed plugging my nose—when the little girl stared blankly, I felt like an idiot. I moved on to the last question:

"What would you like to name the baby?" I asked.

"Stupid," she said.

Again, not what I'd expected, and while I wasn't exactly Nubbins's best friend, I wasn't about to name him Stupid. "Why don't we try calling him . . ."

Her mother interrupted me. "Just name the baby Veronica."

"Veronica?" I asked. I couldn't tell if she was being serious, because while I knew the dolls weren't anatomically correct, Nubbins was clearly a boy. I scribbled "Veronica" in the "Name" sections of the baby bracelet and birth certificate, and then handed the paperwork to the mother.

I took Nubbins from the little girl, opened the picket fence, and pointed to the far-off register. "Now all you have to do is pay the adoption fee (*wink, wink*)."

As they walked away, I laid out a pink blanket and set Nubbins in the center. For the last time, his head flopped back, and his little flippers flipped up. That's when it hit me. *Nubbins has been adopted. . . . There will be no more Nubbins.* A little montage in honor of the doll began to play in my head. There Jenny was tossing him across the adoption center; there was the time Karla had "accidentally" rocked over him with the rocking chair. There was the sweet taste of his plastic kiss, and a crowd gasping as he tumbled onto a marble floor.

It had never occurred to me, but I loved Nubbins.

And if I sold Baby Nubbins, what it meant was just too depressing. After all the weird comments from customers about our less-than-desirable baby inventory—the rolled eyes and the frustrated glares—I still didn't want to face what it meant if a factory reject monster baby was adopted before a whole nursery of perfectly cute black babies.

I decided I couldn't let this happen. I thought about lying and telling them Nubbins had already been purchased. I thought about buying Nubbins myself. I imagined what I'd say to my dad when I called him to borrow the $120 it would take. "Um, Dad," I'd say, "there was this baby at the adoption center and he was about to go to a bad family and I think I could be a good family for him."

And then I looked up. The woman and her daughter had returned with their receipt. Reluctantly I placed Nubbins in the little girl's arms.

"I'm sure baby Veronica is going to have a wonderful home," I lied.

The little girl stared at me with her strange cold eyes and took the doll. As she and her mother walked out of the store I watched Nubbins's head bobbing on her shoulder until I couldn't see him anymore.

I'm sure baby Veronica is going to have a wonderful home. Long after they were gone, this line stayed with me. I was just acting. But this lifelong ambition of mine suddenly seemed misguided. In the end, I didn't like acting. I liked speaking my mind. Only I'd stopped doing it for the job.

Without really thinking it through, I unfastened the white picket fence, marched to Chad's office, and knocked on the door. He opened it wearing a Nerf hat with a target on it.

"I can't work here anymore," I explained. "I just sold Nubbins."

Chad had no idea who Nubbins was. In fact, if Chad knew half the things I had done to Baby Nubbins, he probably would have fired me. But he didn't, so instead he tried to get me to stay.

"I didn't want to tell anyone this," he whispered, "but I pulled some strings and it looks like we'll be getting a shipment of white babies in sometime early next week. If that happens, we're gonna need all the nurses we can get."

Any guilt that I had over quitting—dissipated.

"I'm sorry," I said, "but when the white babies arrive, I won't be here."

The Wookey Mirror

Every New Year's Eve I make extraordinarily unattainable goals and immediately forget them. And 2004 was no exception. I was twenty-one, recently unemployed, and sleeping on the couch of my parents' home in London. With nothing better to do, I took out my journal and wrote *What do I want?* on the top of the page. I proceeded to make a list of everything missing from my life. You know, to cheer myself up. There were easily forty or fifty things written down, but it all boiled down to two: *I wanted a job and I wanted a boyfriend.*

I was about to turn twenty-two and I still didn't know how to kiss. The "job" goal wasn't looking any better... I'd just quit FAO Schwarz, my lifelong ambition to be an actress was in question, and I didn't know what I was supposed to do with my life.

2004: Get a job. Get a boyfriend. I rewrote my two major goals and turned out the lights.

The next morning, January 1, 2004, I woke up to the sound of my father blasting Bob Marley and dancing. He was restless. He has a tendency to do this when he's on vacation and we're sitting at home. One Christmas he told us to get in the car and drove us to the airport. When we got there he handed us our passports. "Whoever finds the cheapest flight wins, and we'll go there," he said. Julia found a round-trip ticket to Rome for under $150. All seven of us, with just the clothes on our backs, went to Rome for three days. It was fun until we realized we didn't have clean underwear and all the shops were closed for the holidays. But that's the price you pay for adventure.

This year wasn't as extravagant. Instead, my dad took out the *Reader's Digest* guide to Britain. "Line up shortest to tallest," he yelled.

Even though Tina's no longer the tallest, we still keep our original age-based order. With our Christmas stockings still hanging on the wall behind our heads, we scrambled into a line: Tina (the pretty sister), Elna (the funny one), Julia (the sarcastic sister), Britain (the boy), and Jill (the baby).

My father opened the book and started listing off cities. "Pick a place," he said, "and we'll go there." We've played this game many times before. And we have a tendency to pick only cities with weird names. While most people visiting the United Kingdom travel to Bath or Stratford-upon-Avon, my family has been to Flash, Worm's Head, Knockin, Little Horwood, Snig's End, Dorking, Boysack, and Willey. This year was no exception. "Appleby, Birmingham, Harrogate, Liverpool, Stowmarket, Tiverton, Wookey," my father read. We stopped him. *Wookey.* We had to go to Wookey.

Reader's Digest described Wookey's picturesque scenery and quaint shops. But because of the holiday, only one attraction was open, an amusement park from the 1920s. We piled out of the van, split up, and started to explore.

I can now officially say that I have empathy for the people who lived in the 1920s. They must've had it pretty bad, because the things they found "amusing" are pretty dull by today's standards. The highlight of the entire park was an old machine that, when switched on, spun out a row of lions and a lion tamer on a track system. Thirty seconds later, the lions and lion tamer retreated into their cage. Thrilling. There was also a large wooden panel with a pirate ship and pirates' bodies painted on it. If you went behind it you could stick your head out and pretend you were a pirate, *Arrrrr!*

I was passing the "World's Largest Bucket" when I came upon a dimly lit corridor with a sign above it that read: HALLWAY OF MIRRORS, ILLUSTRIOUS ILLUSIONS. I've always liked funny mirrors. You don't feel bad about yourself when you've seen how much worse it could be. I lifted the thick red curtain and watched my reflection as I passed each mirror, my body shrinking and expanding.

I was in the process of making a goofy face in a stretched mirror when I noticed someone standing in the corner looking at me. It was a girl, a very pretty girl. She looked familiar—she was thin, she was tall, she had long golden hair, and these amazing big brown eyes. I smiled at her politely; she smiled back. It took a second to register. It was me! Me, in a mirror that made me skinny!

No way. I cautiously approached the mirror, worried she'd disappear if I wasn't careful. I'd seen distorting mirrors but never anything like this. I was perfectly proportional, but I looked nothing like myself—I was thin. My jaw dropped open. I'd spent so much time convincing myself that how I looked was just the way I looked that it never occurred to me I was capable of this kind of beauty—the outer kind. It was mesmerizing.

For the next ten minutes, I stood there playing with the mirror. I turned to see my profile. I put my hand on my hip, made flirty eyes, and blew myself a kiss. After that I tried walking in place; I waved; I curtsied—no matter what position I chose, it was a novelty. I thought of the movies *Big* and *Trading Places*, movies where people made wishes or swapped bodies. I imagined stepping through that mirror and coming out the other side as a thin person. In that universe I was a size 6; in that universe I lived happily ever after.

I stopped myself midthought. The notion that she was happier than me contradicted years of hard-earned self-acceptance. I had a mantra, *I am what I am.* I'd prayed and asked God to help me love myself—I didn't need to be thin. But in that moment, looking in that mirror, it wasn't just about size. For the first time, I had a sweet spirit and a sweet ass. And so, even though it was totally cheesy, I faced the mirror head on and I made a wish.

"I wish I looked like you," I said.

"Elna," a voice interrupted. I jumped. It was my father. He was standing a few feet behind me. "We're leaving," he said. My face turned red. I didn't know how long he'd been there. I'm pretty sure it was only for a second, but either way it's not the sort of thing you want to get caught doing—wishing on your thin reflection.

"I'll be right there," I said.

When I looked at him I noticed a sadness in his eyes that wasn't usually there. "See you outside," he said.

Alone, I turned back to the mirror and took one more look at myself—long legs, a waist, a neck, a thin face. I lifted my right hand and touched the glass. My fingers rested on the cold, flat surface. I examined them. On one side of the mirror they were thick and pudgy; on the other, the same fingers were longer, thinner—better.

Later that night I found the list of what I wanted for the year. *I can't control getting a job,* I thought, *and I can't control finding a boyfriend. But I can control my weight.*

I crossed out the old goals and wrote a new one: *I want to lose 80 pounds.*

Every time I'd lost an eyelash or caught a willow floating through the air I'd wish for the same exact thing: *I wish that I could lose weight.* When you wish for something over and over again and it doesn't come true, something else happens; not only do you give up, but you resent your wish and you resent wishing.

I didn't know how to lose weight. So I did what I always do when I need advice. I flipped open my scriptures and read the first verse I saw:

". . . I give unto men weakness," I began reading, "that they may be humble; and my grace is sufficient for all men that humble them-selves before me; for if they humble themselves before me, and have faith in me, then will I make weak things become strong unto them."

The word *grace* stuck out. I was only really familiar with it because of the song "Amazing Grace." I didn't know what it meant exactly, and so I looked it up. According to the Bible, grace is an enabling power given to men to help them accomplish things that, if left to their own devices, they would never be able to do.

Grace was my answer. I knelt down next to my bed and prayed. I told God I'd given up on me, that there was no way I could do this alone, and that I needed His grace to take over and go on a diet for me.

When I finished this prayer a vivid memory popped into my head, a wall covered in "Before" and "After" Polaroids. And okay, so I never told anyone about this, but I'd actually considered going on a diet three years earlier. My sophomore year in college, my friend Kim went to a doctor in Philadelphia and he helped her lose forty pounds. I asked her a lot of questions about it: "What do you eat? Are there pills? How much does it cost?" Kim got so sick of answering my questions that she offered to bring me to the clinic so I could see it for myself.

I wasn't sure what to expect. We pulled up to a town house in a run-down part of Philadelphia. A small plaque read PHILADELPHIA WEIGHT MANAGEMENT CENTER, HARVEY LEVIN, M.D. Kim opened the door and led the way.

The walls of the office immediately struck me. Every inch of free space was covered with before-and-after pictures, like a giant messy collage. I stared at all of the people, the women with perms and the men in sweatpants. They didn't look like the before-and-after people I was used to seeing in subway advertisements: Whale of a woman becomes gorgeous blonde with phenomenal breasts (clearly two different people). Instead, the "Before" Polaroids were of men and women who you'd expect to see working at FedEx or State Farm Insurance—real people—and the "After" Polaroids showed the same exact FedEx and State Farm employees, except they'd lost some weight. It gave me hope. *Anyone can do this*, I thought.

Later that night I took the train back to New York, my mind buzzing. *I can start immediately. I'll enroll, I'll commute to Philadelphia, I'll change!* The following morning I woke up to my life and my routine, and laughed at the naïve idea that I'd ever be anyone different than me.

Three years went by and there I was, New Year's Day, with the same desire to change. I went into the computer room and looked up the Philadelphia Weight Management Center on the Internet. It was still there. I made an appointment, January 14, 2004.

I remember being incredibly nervous the night before my appointment. I couldn't decide what to wear for my "Before" Polaroid. I laid my final choice out on the floor in the shape of a body, just as I had done every year on the first day of school: jeans, a polka-dot black-and-white blouse, a red cardigan, and red flats. When I stood up to look at it, I noticed that my clothes looked so much bigger than me, but if you hold your clothes out in front of you, they always look bigger. (Which is why I've never bought into those Weight Watchers commercials—you know, people holding their old jeans, indicating how much weight they lost. All jeans look huge if you hold them a few feet away from your body, weight loss or not.)

The next morning I took a train to Philadelphia. Michelle, a friend of my mother, picked me up at the station. It was embarrassing. In order to go on the diet, I had to tell everyone—my parents because I needed help paying for it, my friends because I needed their support, and near strangers like Michelle, because I needed a ride.

She dropped me off in front of the clinic. As I climbed the steps I repeated my father's advice: "You're either going out of your way to fail, or you're going out of your way to succeed. Either way, we still love you."

When I opened the front door and saw the Polaroid-covered walls, relief swept over me. Sometimes when you let an opportunity pass you by, you worry that you've closed that door forever. But here it was, a second chance. I took a deep breath and walked up to the front desk where a blond girl sat reading *People* magazine.

"Just sign your name on the clipboard," she said. I wrote down my name.

An older nurse with dyed-brown hair and cat's-eye glasses poked her head out from a doorway down the hall. "Ms. Baker? Right this way," she said.

I took an even deeper breath. *There's no turning back; it's now or never.*

"You're the patient coming in from New York, right?" the older nurse asked as I approached.

"Yes."

"Doctor Levin doesn't take out-of-state patients, so you'll have to talk to him before we authorize anything."

"They mentioned that over the phone." I tried smiling, in hopes that'd help my cause.

"Step up onto this scale," a nurse said abruptly.

I looked at the high-tech scale in between us. It had a diagram identifying height on one side, weight on the other. In different shades of red were the words *underweight, normal, overweight,* and *obese. Obese* was written in the darkest color, almost a blood red.

"I should take my shoes off," I said, kicking off my flats, "and my belt."

The nurse tapped her chart with a pencil and let out an impatient sigh. Apparently she'd been through this post-9/11-airport-security-ritual before.

I stepped onto the scale. Two horizontal red lines flashed in a quick sequence. And then the numbers 2-3-5 appeared. I hadn't weighed myself in years. It was better than I thought—at one point I weighed 260 pounds. I matched my weight and height (5' 10") with the chart and I fell into the bloodred category. *Obese*, I read. *Okay, so it's still not great.*

The nurse scribbled, closed the file with a neat slap, and then opened the door.

"You're just in time for the New Patient Orientation." She gestured to a room at the end of the hall. I walked forward tentatively and peeked through the door. Seven overweight women were sitting on folding chairs in a plain room.

When I didn't immediately enter, the nurse nudged me. "Go on," she said. "They won't bite."

A different nurse—thin, young, dark hair—was conducting the orientation. She handed me a laminated packet.

"Take a seat," she said.

I looked at the circle. The chairs were set up without consideration for the incoming guests—they were set so tightly I noticed one woman's leg was practically glued to her neighbor's. I squeezed into an opening.

"Welcome," the nurse began cheerfully. None of us looked that cheerful.

"Before each of you meets with Doctor Levin, I'm going to explain the diet."

She reviewed the laminated packet, a list of all the foods we could eat: veggies, protein, and more veggies. Then she stressed the importance of drinking water, and of exercise. As she spoke, my mind wandered; I found myself looking at the bodies of the other women in the circle. Next to me, across from me, diagonally: the pouches, the elastic-band jeans, watery full faces, somehow softer, somehow kind.

I considered my position in relation to them. *We are the same*, I thought. *We're the big girls.*

And yet, I'd always made it a point not to hang out with other fat people. Not because I have a prejudice against them per se. I guess I was just secretly worried that if someone were to see me with another overweight person, then it'd suddenly occur to them that I was fat, too. Guilty by association.

But I am like them, I thought.

"You need to record everything that you eat in this Food Journal," the nurse continued. "Don't hide what you eat," she said. "Admit everything." Everyone nodded.

You hide it, too? As far back as I can remember I'd sneak chocolate chips from my mother's pantry. I'd fill my pockets with them, and then go to the bathroom and eat them, a handful at a time. Inevitably, I'd forget a chip or two, and end up with dark brown stains in the pockets of my clothing—something that was hard to explain.

"It's time to love your bodies," the dainty nurse emphasized. I felt us all collectively roll our eyes. It was church all over again: *God sent you to earth, and God gave you the greatest gift, your body.*

I looked down at my body, surveying the outfit I'd set out on the floor the night before. It did not look big on me. It fit. *I hide behind my clothes*, it occurred to me. *But what do I look like naked?* I searched my brain for an image of my body—not the one I saw in pictures, my real body. Nothing. My mind was blank.

Oh, come on, Elna. You must remember something. Nope, nothing. *Oh, wait.* I vaguely remembered a bath I took once, after I got really heavy. I immersed myself in the water, but the tub wasn't deep enough. That's when I realized that no matter how high I filled it, I wouldn't be able to completely cover myself. I tried to compensate by pushing my back against the ceramic bottom of the tub. It almost worked; the soapy water hid most of me, but there was a portion of my stomach that was still visible. It floated above the water like a soft white hill. I looked at it and decided it was not part of me.

I called it an island.

After orientation I met with Dr. Levin, a kind man with glasses and white hair who reminded me of someone else's favorite grandpa.

"What's your goal weight?" he began.

"Eighty pounds."

He looked up, startled.

"I want to lose eighty pounds," I rephrased "not weigh eighty pounds, although that'd be nice."

Apparently anorexia jokes aren't big at weight-loss facilities; he didn't even laugh. Instead, he reached into his desk and began removing different bottles of pills.

"Your diet will be aided by medicine," he advised. "Potassium, serotonin, dopamine, a multivitamin, and phentermine, which will help suppress your appetite."

I looked down at the little circles of color. *Skittles*, I thought, *only the opposite.*

"Sometimes patients react negatively to the medication," he continued. "If I do take you on, I need you to come in once a week so that I can monitor your heart."

"Absolutely . . ."

"And like I told you before, I don't normally have patients who live out-of-state."

"I understand." I was about to make a case for myself, when he continued.

"But you have a certain look about you. Determination. So I will make an exception if you agree to do one thing for me—"

"*Anything.*"

"Do everything I ask you to do, word for word, and this diet will be a success."

I sat there for a moment and pondered his request. It was the same thing I'd always struggled with, only at church: *How do you do everything someone else asks you to do word for word? I mean, can you ever really trust that someone besides you has your best interests at heart? (Especially if their guidance could result in coronary thrombosis.) Or can you only ever trust yourself? But then again, I've trusted myself and screwed up over and over again and where has that gotten me? To the bloodred section on the scale.*

I took a deep breath. "I will do everything that you ask me to do. Word for word." I stuck my hand out, in an effort to be official.

The doctor smiled, took my hand in his, a firm grip, a shake, and the deal was sealed.

"Now stand against that wall and let me take your photograph," he said, pointing to the only blank wall in his office. I stood in the center of the empty space awkwardly, my hands placed unevenly at my sides. *This is it,* I thought. *My "Before."*

He clicked the camera and then handed me the Polaroid. "Do you mind shaking it for me while I put this away?" he asked.

"Of course."

I like watching Polaroids develop. The way they go from murky gray to a ghost version of you to a solid you is so cool; it's like watching your own resurrection.

As the solid Elna came into form, I was surprisingly pleased. I looked really cute. My outfit was an excellent choice; I looked like Betty Boop.

Dr. Levin leaned over me to look at the developed picture, and I felt him place his hand gently onto my shoulder. "Don't worry," he said. "It will get so much better."

Pooping Out a Fourth Grader

I celebrated my twenty-second birthday the same week I started my diet. Tina made a cake and invited a bunch of people over to celebrate. I don't know why she made it, seeing as I obviously couldn't partake. But she did. Not to sound like a Kathy cartoon, but the cake looked *so good*. It was chocolate and said "Elna" on it in white bubble letters.

It has my name on it—it clearly belongs to me, I thought as I stared at it. *NO.* I walked away. I tried to socialize, but no matter where I was in the room, I kept looking back at that cake, drool forming in the corner of my mouth. It was like we were having a showdown. And for the first time since starting the diet, it hit me. *How realistic is this? Can a person really change?*

I'd already lost seven pounds in one week, but most of it was water weight. I started to think about the goal: eighty pounds—it was so far away. *I am a person who eats cake,* I rationalized. *That's just who I am. I like cake.* But then I remembered the catalyst for going on a diet, the Wookey mirror and the possibility of becoming the girl I'd seen in it.

You're strong, I felt a force within me say. *You can do this.* And so, on my birthday, I ate celery and blew out a candle held between my fingers. At the time I had no idea how important this decision was. But now I realize it was my saving grace. Afterward, when someone offered me a mini–candy bar or a donut hole I'd think, *I didn't even eat my own birthday cake. Why would I break my diet now?*

When you're trying to change, every good decision you make adds up, and saying no gets easier because each day you have more evidence that you can. After three weeks of dieting, I went back to Philadelphia for a checkup. I'd already lost sixteen pounds. Before going on this diet I'd never lost more than two or three. It got me thinking: *How long does it take to lose weight?* On my way out of the doctor's office, I took a look at the numbers on the Polaroids to get a better idea: *Fifty pounds, forty-three weeks,* I read. *Seventy pounds, fifty-eight weeks.* I looked at hundreds of faces. All the numbers were roughly the same. It took most people a year or more. But there was this one woman, a pear-shaped, mousy brunette in a purple tank top and she'd lost *forty pounds* in *eight weeks.*

Is that even possible? I compared her stats to all of the other Polaroids. *No, this woman is by far the fastest.* The next closest contender was a man who had lost *thirty pounds* in *seventeen weeks.* That's when it hit me: *If a person is physically capable of losing forty pounds in eight weeks, who's to say that I'm not physically capable of doing the same exact thing?*

I went back to the forty-pound, eight-week woman and stared at her "After" picture. The same mousy pear-shaped woman, this time a few sizes smaller, innocently looked up at me. Sure she looked nice, sure she'd done something admirable, but she was about to be *destroyed.*

"You're going down," I said.

And just like that, I found my mission. I was going to beat the record. I was going to lose forty pounds in less than eight weeks and forever hold the title: Fastest Weight Loss Ever. Which meant in the next three and a half weeks I had to lose twenty-four pounds. Game on.

It wasn't easy. I'd already limited my caloric intake to one thousand calories a day. Now I was going to go against the doctor's recommendations and cut it down to seven hundred. In order to do this I'd take out three spoonfuls from my yogurt container and dump them down the drain before having the other six ounces. I'd also throw away a quarter of my protein bar, and cut out all carbohydrates. In addition to this regimen, I did extra credit. *Be sure to drink lots of water.* As soon as I woke up, I drank sixteen glasses just to get it over with. It was disgusting. I'd spit it up even as I gulped it down. But anytime I wanted to stop, I'd imagine the smug face of the purple-tank-top lady. Just knowing I could beat her reenergized me.

Exercise for at least thirty minutes a day. I exercised for an hour and a half. In February, Manhattan was practically shut down because of a huge snowstorm, but I didn't want to skip my morning jog. I'd made a chart, and if I skipped I couldn't put up a sticker. So I went jogging anyway. When I got back to my apartment I was shaking so badly that Tina was worried I had hypothermia. She made me sit in a hot bath until I stopped shivering.

Sitting there, soaking in the water, I looked at myself. It was hard to tell, but I was pretty sure I looked smaller than I'd ever looked. The next morning I took the train to Philadelphia for my weigh-in. It'd been seven and a half weeks since I'd started.

And guess what? *I beat the record. I lost forty pounds and six ounces in seven and a half weeks.* Which meant, according to the diagram, that I was now officially overweight. *I'm not obese anymore. I'm overweight!* I don't think anyone's been happier to be overweight in the history of the world.

On my way out of the doctor's office, I stopped in front of the Polaroid of the purple-tank-top lady to declare my victory. *I beat you . . . sucka!* Then I pumped my arms in the air and did a karate kick. *LOSER!* I pointed at her. *WINNER!* I pointed at myself. "I beat you, I beat you . . . ," I chanted. "Forty pounds, eight weeks," I reread, "I beat you . . . I beat you—" I stopped midsentence. *Oh, no,* I reread her numbers . . . *Forty pounds . . . that's all she needed to lose. I have to lose eighty pounds . . . I'm only halfway there.*

My legs gave out on me and I slumped down into one of the lobby chairs. *I can't do everything I've done all over again,* I thought. *I'm tired, I'm hungry, I'm sick of jogging, sick of baby carrots, and sick of drinking sixteen glasses of water and burping it back up.*

Bing, the door chimed. I looked up. It was one of the nurses coming back from her lunch break. "You finished?"

No, I'm not finished, I'll never be finished. "Yeah," I managed.

"Are you alright?"

"I'm *fine.*"

"How much did you lose?"

"Forty-one pounds."

"Wow. That's incredible."

And it's funny, because it was incredible for like two seconds, until I realized what it meant. *Can a person really change?* This echoed in my mind. *Yes,* I thought. *Yes, they can.* But it was too hard for me to finish.

On the train ride home, I made a pathetic attempt to rev myself up. *You can do this,* I said. *Eighty pounds, you go girl.* It was pointless. I couldn't even lift my arms. I needed to raise my blood sugar before I could raise my spirit.

And also, I knew—now that the purple-tank-top lady was out of the way, I had to face my toughest competitor: *me.* And when you're competing against yourself, it's so much harder—because you know exactly who you're up against. I thought about the logistics of quitting halfway. If I'd never tried to lose weight, I could've lived in blissful ignorance, blaming my condition on bad genes and big bones. But now I recognized: There is a way, only I was incapable of it. I'm not strong enough; I don't have that kind of willpower. I'm a failure.

The train wheels clanked as we crossed the bridge between New Jersey and Manhattan. I looked out at the city skyline and noticed something I'd never seen before: a billboard, a giant one, at least fifty stories high.

"Impossible is Nothing," it said. "Impossible is just a big word thrown around by small men who find it easier to live in the world they've been given than to explore the power they have to change it. Impossible is not a fact. It's an opinion. Impossible is not a declaration. It's a dare. Impossible is potential. Impossible is temporary. Impossible is nothing."

It was a sporting goods ad and, while I knew this sign was created by people who probably employed Ecuador's children to make a profit, I didn't care. I practically stood up in my seat and threw my arms in the air like Rocky. It was a sign—literally.

"Impossible is Nothing," I said. "Impossible is Nothing."

You can do this, a voice spoke to me. I felt a warm feeling in the center of my chest. *Just keep doing everything your doctor tells you to word for word and let time pass. Change is a combination of effort and time. Keep going.*

It's hard to describe what it feels like when God speaks to you. It's peaceful; every little bad thought and feeling is instantly washed away and your mind feels clear. There's a scripture in the Bible that puts it better than I ever could. Basically it says that there was a strong wind that broke the rocks into pieces, but God wasn't in the wind, and after the wind an earthquake, but God wasn't in the earthquake, and after the earthquake a fire, but God wasn't in the fire, and after the fire a still, small voice, and God was in the still, small voice.

Thank you, God, thank you, I prayed. *We can do this. I know we can.*

* * *

It took me three and a half months to lose the rest of the weight. But I did it. In five and a half months I lost eighty pounds, which is the equivalent of pooping out a fourth grader. It wasn't until Dr. Levin took my "After" Polaroid that I realized I had finished. I shook the Polaroid, murky gray, ghost version, solid—and suddenly there it was, evidence: *Impossible is Nothing.*

Kissing, Take Five: Shannon

The same week that I lost forty-one pounds and beat the Fastest Weight Loss Ever record, I was invited to a Saint Patrick's Day party at a bar on Houston Street. I'd been so focused on dieting, I hadn't been out in two months. *Will people notice that I'm getting skinny?* I wondered.

At first it was like any other night: The bar was overcrowded, I pined after several different men, none of whom noticed me, and a drunk girl threw up on my shoe. I was in the process of cleaning it up when I suddenly felt very pathetic, like when you're in the middle of talking to yourself and you realize you're talking to yourself.

I looked out at the room, city streetlights glowed through the checkered windows, lighting rows and rows of heads, people. There were drinks being passed around and in one corner there was dancing. It looked fun—if glazed-over eyes, puking, and general zombie behavior can be labeled fun. But still, I wasn't a part of it—I was moving in the opposite direction of everyone there, and in spite of how easy it was to do, I couldn't get myself to turn around. *What am I doing here? I'm sober—it's Saint Patrick's Day—everyone else is wasted.*

And it's not that I mind when people drink, but when it gets to the wee hours and everyone but me is trashed I start to feel like Will Smith in *I Am Legend*, only without the dog.

Just go home. I pushed my way through the crowd toward the exit. "Harry Potter here I come," I said as I swung the door open. And that is when it happened: Stepping onto the street, I practically collided with a tall, brown-haired man. We both stopped. *He's so beautiful!* I felt a jolt in my chest.

He looked at me. I waited for him to brush by, or make an annoyed face, or yell. Instead, he held my gaze and did something no man had ever done: *He nodded his head.*

I nodded back. And then, assuming this was the extent of our exchange, I continued outside. *But wait*, I felt something—a hand on my wrist—and then, *oh, my*, I was being spun around.

"You can't leave now," the gorgeous man said. "I just got here."

"Okay!" I shouted.

It was an easy sell. The beautiful man gripped my wrist, swung the door open, and pulled me back inside.

"I'm Shannon."

"I'm Elna."

"Let's dance," he yelled above the noise.

I smiled nervously and followed him to the dance floor. The song "Macarena" was playing, which I hate, but I know the dance (they teach it every year at the Mormon Halloween thing).

"You remember this?" he shouted.

"Sure," I answered.

"Teach me." He took a step back and waited for me to begin.

"Okay." I put my arms out straight, flipped them over, and then crossed them tentatively. Several people were struggling to remember the moves; when they saw me, they immediately copied.

I moved my hands behind my head, I placed them on my hips, I shook my butt, I jumped, I turned, I started from the top again—everyone followed.

"You're leading," Shannon yelled.

"I *KNOW*," I said in awe. We were back to the part where you turn and shake your hips. This time, when I turned, I caught him looking at my butt. Not just looking, okay, he was making a face no man had ever made—it was as though he wanted something from me.

¡Olé! I did the Macarena jump and turn. As I did this, a strand of hair fell from my ponytail and landed across my face. Shannon reached over and moved it back with his hand. It was a simple movement. Yet something about the way he did it made me feel like he was waking me up.

Anda tu cuerpo alegria Macarena. I held my hands out again, only this time I was more aware than ever that this was my body and that people could see it. I spread my fingers and looked at the space in between each one, I flipped my wrists, *mine*, I touched my hips, *hip bones!* I felt faster, fluid, almost like I was floating. I jumped. Fifteen people jumped with me. At the same time, someone at the bar tossed a wad of bar napkins into the air. I looked up at the swirling white napkins, raining down on us like confetti, listened to the eerie, "HAHAHAHAHA" of the Macarena girl, and thought, *Oh, my gosh— it feels so good to be me!*

The song ended. Shannon took my hand and led me over to the bar. Without music, without dancing, I suddenly felt very nervous. I'd never made it this far and I didn't know what to do next.

"You're a good dancer," he began.

My mouth was dry and red blotches started appearing on my neck and on my chest.

"Thank you."

"And you have beautiful eyes."

"My dad calls them my root beer eyes!" I blurted out, immediately cringing.

"Your lips are beautiful, too."

"What?" I couldn't quite hear him.

"I said . . ." He stopped midsentence and leaned in for the kiss.

It totally caught me off guard. *Relax your jaw muscles, ease into using your tongue, flick the tip of your tongue against his.* I tried to remember all the advice I'd ever read. *Create a slight suction . . . and whatever you do, don't screw this up!!!*

He clutched the hair at the base of my ponytail and pulled my head toward his. I wish that I could say losing forty pounds automatically gave me the ability to kiss. It didn't. *Boy likes me! No way! Relax your tongue? No, relax your jaw. Ughhh. What the hell does any of this mean?* His soft, slightly wet lips reached mine. I froze. *Just play dead,* I decided.

My body went limp, my eyes rolled back in my head. Shannon might as well have been kissing a cold cement wall.

"Sorry . . ." He stepped back. "I didn't mean to scare you."

You didn't scare me, I want to kiss you, I thought. Only that's not what came out. "I have to go!" I shouted.

"What, why? What's wrong?"

"Nothing," I answered. "It's just . . . here," I grabbed a bar napkin and wrote my name and telephone number on it. "Call me and we'll go out, and it'll be *just great.*" (By "just great" I meant that somehow in the next few days I would research kissing and learn how to do it, and then I'd be prepared.)

I handed the napkin to Shannon and ran to the nearest exit. On my way out the door, I couldn't help it; I looked back. He was still standing at the bar. Smiling, Shannon took the napkin out of his shirt pocket, pressed it against his heart, and blew me a kiss.

If it were possible to choose a moment to come back to on my deathbed, I would've chosen that one. I mean, I know I'm young and I haven't gotten married or had my first kid, so I might regret picking a moment early in the game, but I didn't care, it was the greatest feeling in the world watching him press that napkin to his heart and promise me, in an air kiss, that we would be together.

Shannon never called.

Cyprus

_____

Every member of every family plays a specific role. I've mentioned it before, but just to refresh your memory, this is the rundown for my family: Tina's the pretty sister, I'm the funny one, Julia's the sarcastic sister, Britain's the boy, and Jill's the baby. (We're all capable of being many different things, but for the sake of simplicity this is how I classify us.)

I didn't intend being the "funny one"; it was a matter of survival, and after years of wearing this label, I identified myself with it. However, after I lost weight, I didn't have to work the room to get noticed. I'd enter a room, and people would see me. While I liked it, it was unnerving. I remember one night in particular. After grilling me on diet tips for over an hour, a girl I barely knew said something that really got to me: "You look so great," she said, "but remember, Elna, you used to be so funny. _Don't lose that._"

Don't lose that? As if to imply that I already had. _You don't know me. You don't know my life._ I tried to shake off the comment, but for the rest of the night I was left with a strange feeling. If you've lost a ton of weight, then you know what I'm talking about. I felt unsettled. Like I'd gone to Paris and forgotten to turn off my stove. Whatever it was, I'd left something important, something I could not quite place, behind.

I didn't want to listen to myself, or to confront what was happening to me. So I pretended that nothing had changed. I looked at my new body and thought, *This doesn't make a difference: I am what I am.*

But it made a HUGE difference. The first thing I noticed was when I walked down the street attractive people would do something to me they'd never done before: They'd look me up and down, and then nod their heads. It was the same gesture Shannon had used, only now both men and *women* were doing it. That's when it occurred to me: *There is an attractive people club and the nod is their secret handshake.* They were letting me in on a trial basis. It was exciting. More exciting than I thought it'd be. It was like a point toward being pretty.

And then I went to get new clothes. I had been a size 18/20, now I was a 4/6, and that was also more exciting than I thought it'd be: It was two points toward the idea that I was actually pretty. And then I met someone who didn't know I had ever been fat and they said, "I bet you were a cheerleader in high school?"—and that was way more exciting then I thought it'd be—ten pretty points.

Gradually I stopped writing and performing, and instead I spent all my time going to clubs, wearing tiny outfits, and trying to get as many points as possible for being pretty.

Soon I was afraid of telling people that I'd ever been heavy for fear that this would repulse them. I tried to destroy any evidence of my former self. I threw all my old clothes away and every picture taken of me when I was chubby. If I ever get married, the wedding slide show will be amazing: my husband as a baby, me as a baby, my husband in kindergarten, me in kindergarten. My husband graduating from middle school, high school, backpacking through Europe, drinking at college party—me, at twenty-two, looking skinny!

Another bizarre aspect of this transformation was that, aside from Tina, no one in my family had seen me. I was living in New York at the time and they were still in London. My mom asked me to send her pictures, but we had a family vacation planned for August, so I decided to wait and make an entrance.

After three months of being officially thin, it was finally time for them to see me. Tina and I flew to Cyprus for our family trip. *What if they don't recognize me?* I spent the entire six-hour flight going over their potential reactions. In some versions they screamed, in others they fainted. There was the possibility that they'd pick me up over their heads while chanting my name. Or the embarrassing prospect of them kneeling on the ground and worshipping me. I couldn't figure out why none of these scenarios seemed right until we were nearly landing. *I don't want my family to change like everyone else has. I want them to treat me like they always did.*

When the glass doors to the arrivals area sprang open, I immediately spotted my family. They were behind a metal railing. Julia was looking to her left, my mom and Jill were looking to their right, my dad was looking at his BlackBerry, and Britain was looking directly at me, only he didn't know it yet. I lifted my hand and waved.

"Elna?"

When Britain said my name, they all turned and stared at me, their mouths hanging wide open. *Boom,* they came back to life and started overreacting. My mother and Jill screamed. My brother picked me up and hugged me. "You did it, girl," my father said, giving me a high five. The only person who didn't react was Julia, and that's because, as a rule of thumb, Julia, the sarcastic sister, never reacts to anything. "Hi, Elna," she said deadpan.

For the next half an hour, I watched them watch me at a distance. It was as though they knew that I was Elna, their daughter, their sister, but every gesture I made was being put into a replacement file. Old Elna laughed like this . . . new Elna laughs like that.

I reveled in the attention, but as thirty minutes turned to forty, the novelty wore off. I pulled a water bottle from my bag and started drinking. I have this terrible habit of drinking loudly. I can't half drink anything. When I drink I throw my head back and gulp so that little bubbles of water shoot back into the bottle and make loud gurgling sounds.

"You sound like a fish," my dad said.

"Whatever." I rolled my eyes and took another gulp. Just as the bottle reached my mouth, my dad purposely pressed forward on the gas and then the brakes. Water spilled down both sides of my chin.

"Rude!" I yelled.

They all started laughing. My dad, my mom, Tina, Britain, Jill, even Julia—everyone was laughing. And just like that, the spell was broken. I was Elna—eighty pounds heavier or eighty pounds lighter, it didn't matter. I was the same person I'd always been, which is what I thought I wanted.

Until the first night of our vacation: We were eating dinner when the owner of the restaurant came up to my father and said, "Your daughter is so beautiful."

For a second I thought he was talking about me, but then I followed the direction of his outstretched fingers ... *Tina.*

He spoke to my sister in Greek. Tina served her mission in Greece, so she's fluent. A minute later, he excused himself, saying something excitedly.

"Where's he going?" my mother asked.

"He says he's going to get me a *present!*" Tina said this like it was crazy and unexpected, when really this sort of thing happens to my sister all of the time. Case in point: her expensive bottle of perfume that she yells at me for borrowing. It was a gift from a forty-year-old married man who sat next to Tina on an airplane. According to Tina, the man just needed to spend some of his British pounds before going back to the States, so could he please buy her a bottle of perfume. Tina's an idiot.

The owner of the restaurant came back to our table holding a red velvet box and grinning like the Cheshire Cat. He presented the box to my sister.

"*Os di mo,*" Tina said.

I craned my neck so that I was looking directly over her shoulder as she opened it. Inside the box was a gold necklace with an oval purple stone.

"Ooooh." Tina gasped. It was hideous. I mean, absolutely hideous. Tacky, gaudy, definitely fake. And still, I felt a rush of envy sweep through me. I wanted to be the pretty child now. *Mine!* I wanted to scream. *That necklace should be mine!*

We left the restaurant shortly thereafter. Tina posed for pictures with the owner, and everyone said good-bye like we were old friends. Everyone except for me—I stalked off ahead of the group. I was still fuming when Julia caught up with me.

"Well," she sighed, "I guess *Tina* will always be the pretty one." Julia wasn't saying this to make me mad; she was just being sarcastic.

Unfortunately, I was in no place to receive this information. My face contorted hideously. "NOOOOO!" I yelled (in a voice that resembled Frankenstein's monster). "ME PRETTY NOW!!!"

It only got worse from there. The next day of our trip we drove to the beach. On the way there, my dad said something about Alexander the Great and elephants.

"Elephants are *ele-funny,*" I piped in. Everyone stopped talking and looked at me. I'd interrupted play time with the unpardonable, a bad joke. And okay fine, it wasn't the brightest line in my comedic repertoire, but sometimes you say stupid things.

"Elna," Julia said, point blank, "*you're not funny.*"

She's right, I thought. *I'm not funny. I traded being funny for being pretty, and Tina is still prettier than me.* I completely lost it. Pretty soon I was sobbing audibly. "I'm not funny," I kept saying through bouts of tears. "I'm not FUNNNNNNY!"

My family sat in stunned silence. Soon I was crying about everything all at once, but mostly I was crying about change and how when you change in one area of your life you open yourself up to changing in all the others. *I didn't sign up for this.*

"Elna," my dad said, trying to calm me. *"Elna."*

I looked up at him. *Say something to make all of this better,* I thought. *Fix me.*

"You're not funny. . . ." he offered, "you're hys*ter*ical."

"Noooo," I wailed.

The tone was set for my final meltdown. Three days and another dozen misunderstandings later, we took a day trip to the Turkish side of Cyprus. We were approaching the green zone, a U.N. patrolled area in between the Greek and Turkish border, when it occurred to me that it was already twelve forty-five and that I usually ate lunch at one. Based on my strict regimen, I'd eaten at one o'clock every day for eight months.

"Dad," I said. "It's almost one, I need to eat."

"You can get lunch on the Turkish side."

"But it's *almost one,*" I insisted. *"I eat at one."*

"There'll be plenty of places to eat once we're there."

Lies, total lies. When we got to the Turkish side every single shop was closed.

"We'll find a place," my father said.

"It's siesta! Everything's shut down." I held my hand to my head. "I'm going to pass out." Truthfully, I don't think I was in any danger of passing out. I was just a little hungry. But I decided to play up my symptoms.

Once again, the family focus shifted from "sightseeing" to "fulfilling Elna's needs." We started roaming the streets looking for food.

It was pointless; not a single store was open. To make matters worse, I was acting the part so convincingly that I started to believe it. Every corner we turned caused my blood sugar to drop lower and lower. Soon I was twenty paces behind the group.

I was hoping they'd stop and wait for me. On the contrary, all six of them turned a corner and disappeared. I waited, my breath held, for someone to realize and come racing back. No one did.

Six people, six chances to glance back, and no one did. *I could drop off the face of the earth and they'd never even miss me!* It was then that I got the idea to fake pass out. That way when they found me, they'd feel really really bad. I walked over to an abandoned building, dusted off the stoop, sat facing forward, and dropped to the side.

They'll come running, I imagined. *They'll shake me, I'll open my eyes and weakly say, "I don't know what happened, I felt faint and then it all went black . . ."* Brilliant. After Paul Stowe, I should know better than to act anywhere but onstage. But my mistakes rarely lead to learning.

I waited in this position for at least fifteen minutes. Occasionally I'd open my eyes and peer down the street. Each time I expected to see my family, each time the street was empty. It was depressing. *My family left me, no money, no passport, on a bombed-out street in the middle of nowhere.* Just then, I heard a noise. I shut my eyes tightly and waited for whoever it was to come running.

Only, they didn't. *Scrape, scrape, scrape.* I heard slow, dragging steps. *Scrape, scrape, scrape.* The footsteps stopped a few feet from where I was lying. I could feel someone watching me. *They probably think I'm faking it,* I thought. *Well, I'll show them.* I let my eyelids flicker weakly and I was about to limply hold my hand to my head, when my eyes came into focus. Standing directly above me, one arm outstretched, was an emaciated woman wrapped in rags. I screamed. She stumbled backward.

"I'm sorry." I sat up frantically. "I thought you were . . ."

She stretched out her arm palm facing up and said something to me in another language.

"Oh." I reached into my pocket. "I'm so sorry, I don't have any money."

She moved her palm closer to my face, and shook it. This time she spoke rapidly, almost yelling.

I mimed that my pockets were empty and said, "Nothing."

She stopped speaking and looked at me. Her expression was neither angry nor kind. *You have so much,* it said. *Why aren't you helping me?* With that, she turned around and walked up the street. *Scrape. Scrape. Scrape.* One of her legs was dragging behind, her shoulders hunched as though with osteoporosis. While her skin was leathery from sun damage, I could tell we were about the same age.

You're hungry because you're on a diet, I thought. *She's hungry because she's starving.* I considered all the food I'd been giving up. The three spoonfuls of yogurt I dumped down the drain each morning to save on calories. Or the trick I use at restaurants: If you don't want to overindulge, take two-thirds of your meal and cover it in salt.

You're an asshole. I felt genuinely bad, upset, disappointed with myself. But at the same time, the whole encounter pissed me off. *Okay, God, I get it.* I thought, *Thanks for laying it on real thick. Can't I just wallow in self-pity for a few minutes? No. Cue the emaciated Turk who is actually starving. Thanks a lot. I really appreciate it.*

Just then, I heard someone coming. I turned; it was my brother. *Crap.* It was too late to get back into my position. So instead, I put my elbows on my knees and rested my head in my hands.

"We found a restaurant," he said as he approached me.

"Huh?" I looked up weakly.

"Are you okay?"

"I felt really dizzy," I answered, "so I put my head down. I think I passed out."

It wasn't as believable now that I was awake. Plus my family's used to my antics. Britain waited for me to finish. "Let's go," he said.

I stood up, exaggerating my frailty. Taking a few steps, I decided to use the encounter with the beggar woman to my advantage, and I mimicked her.

Scrape. Scrape. Scrape.

"Can you please walk like a normal person?" my brother said.

"I'm in pain!" I yelled.

Scrape. Scrape. Scrape. A few blocks later, this faux-cripple walk was starting to wear me out, so I stopped it. I tried to be subtle, but it looked kind of like the ending to *The Usual Suspects*. And while Britain didn't say anything, I could tell he noticed.

"This is it." Britain stopped in front of a fluorescent sign: AMERICA FRY CHICKEN. "It's just like KFC," he said.

"Great," I muttered, "because the best thing for weight loss is deep-fried chicken, gravy, and biscuits."

We walked inside. My family was sitting around a circular table, waiting for me. A single plate of food was set in front of an empty seat. My mom handed me a fork. I sat down. Fried chicken, saffron rice dripping in an orange-colored oil, and French fries. I picked at the chicken, searching for the white meat. Then I took my napkin and pressed it on the rice.

"Good job," my father said.

I stopped midbite. According to him, he meant: *Good job trying to stick to your diet even though you're starving.*

But that's not what I heard. What I heard was: *Good job, you throw a fit, the world stops, and you get whatever you want.*

For the third time in a row, I lost it. Pushing the plate of fried food across the table, I yelled, "If you listened to me this would have never happened! No one listens to me! You just want me to be the same, but I've matured. I'm a grown-up now and when *I say I eat at one, I eat at one!*"

I've never seen my dad look more upset. He started to say something, but held his tongue and walked out of the restaurant. The rest of my family sat in silence.

"Elna"—my mother took the plate of food and moved it back in front of me—"we are not leaving this restaurant until you eat every single thing on this plate."

"Mom," I whined, "it's unhealthy."

"I don't care. Eat it. *All of it.*"

It took a while. I used over fifty napkins, one for each French fry. But as soon as I finished, I felt better. It was like I'd just come out of a coma or something. I looked up. Everyone was there—my mother, my sisters, and my brother.

"Is there anything fun to do in this town?" I asked brightly.

They collectively clenched their teeth.

"Hey." I looked around. "Where'd Dad go?"

They could've killed me right then and there.

By the last day of our trip everyone had had enough, except for my mother. She woke us up early and announced that instead of just hanging out by the hotel pool, we'd spend the day driving to Aphrodite's Rock, a rock on the Mediterranean Sea that was shaped like a Goddess. Reluctantly, we crammed into the rental van and drove toward the sea. Only instead of leading us to Aphrodite's Rock, my mother, who was navigating, accidentally followed the wrong signs. By the time she realized her mistake we were two hours into the journey.

"Shoot." She smacked her head. "We're going to *Adonis's Bath*, not Aphrodite's Rock."

"What's Adonis's Bath?" my dad asked.

"*I don't know.*" She opened *Rick Steves' Guide to Cyprus* and started flipping through it. "It's not in here."

"It has to be in there."

"Well, it isn't."

"Let me see." He pulled the guidebook away from her.

"It's not in here," he concluded a minute later.

"I know." My mother smirked. "But we're almost there, so we might as well go."

"I didn't want to go out in the first place," my father said.

"*We're going there.*" When my mother makes up her mind, there's no discussion.

We headed up the mountain—full speed. Everyone was silent. They say one bad apple can spoil the whole bunch. Well, one bad Elna can spoil the whole family. And over the course of our trip, tension had built up among everyone. Julia was mad at Jill because she stole her earrings, Tina was mad at my mom for saying she was willfully unmarried, and my father, who was paying for the trip, was annoyed by his entire ungrateful family.

"The origin of the word *Adonis* may not actually be Greek." Tina tried to clear the air by sharing a meaningless fact. "*Adonis* is often associated with a woman's need to express unbridled emotion."

I caught my brother and father exchanging looks in the rearview mirror. *Women: expressing unbridled emotion? Impossible.*

"We're supposed to turn soon." My mother interrupted Tina's lecture.

"Where?" my dad said. We were driving alongside a cliff and there was clearly nowhere to turn.

"*I don't know.*"

"Damn it, Christine." He yanked the steering wheel to the right.

"*Gary, NO!*" she shouted.

From the back of the car, all we could see was the sky and the edge of a cliff. From the driver's seat my father could see a sign that said

Adonis's Bath, a steep drop off, and a dirt road. We didn't know this. Instead, we collectively thought *Dad has finally had enough and he's driving us off of a cliff.*

"*Don't do it!*" we screamed at the top of our lungs.

We landed on the dirt road a second later, our hearts beating fast, each of us genuinely relieved to be alive. Both my parents started laughing. *They thought we were going to kill them.*

It felt so good to scream that, even though we were safe, we kept doing it for fun. This only encouraged my father. He whipped around corners, and zoomed past goats until we reached the mystery destination, Adonis's Bath. It was the most beautiful place I'd ever seen. Two waterfalls dropped from a cave into a fresh pool of water where hundreds of pink flowers were floating. There was a willow tree with a rope swing, a hammock, and rocks covered with bright green moss and ivy.

We spent the rest of the day playing in the water. Britain and my father dove off the highest waterfall into the pool. My mom, Tina, and Jill made floral wreaths, Julia sat in the willow tree, and I—I stopped taking myself so seriously and had fun. The funny one, the pretty one, it didn't matter, I could be anything. Nothing was missing, I hadn't left anything behind, I was still me.

On our way back to the minivan, we passed the owner of the bath.

"You should really put this in the guidebooks," my dad told him. "It's the highlight of our trip."

"You can't put paradise in a tour book." He shook his head. "You have to discover it."

We flew back to London the following day. When we got home, my brother, with total purpose in his eyes, took out a Sharpie and walked downstairs. In our den we have a white leather couch called the "Sharpie couch." The couch was supposed to go to the dump years ago, but before we threw it away, we took Sharpies and decorated it. My dad liked it so much he decided to keep it. Now, when we think of good one-liners or inside jokes we write them on the couch in Sharpie.

TOP THREE THINGS NEVER TO SAY TO ELNA, Britain wrote in the center of the couch:

1. TINA WILL ALWAYS BE THE PRETTY ONE.
2. YOU'RE NOT FUNNY.
3. GOOD JOB.

The Blue Slip

In spite of the fact that I'm religious, there's a huge part of me that wants to be considered sexy. But if you're not selling sex, you really shouldn't advertise, so I don't. To keep things safe, I present myself as cute. I own tights in every color and, for most of my adult life, I've worn my hair in a bob.

But one day, shortly after losing weight, I was walking through the East Village when I happened upon a lingerie store. I'd never owned lingerie before. *Why not?* I thought, walking in.

"Our thongs are half off today," one of the women behind the register said. Her smile seemed creepy until I realized she meant, *We're having a sale.*

I walked over to a rack of matching bras and panties and started rifling through the options. Mormons aren't big on lingerie. As far as I know my mother doesn't own any: She wears garments. Eventually I will, too. When I get married I'll go into the Mormon temple and make a further commitment to my religion. I don't know what the ceremony entails, because it's sacred and no one talks about it. All I know is afterward I have to wear special underwear called garments. People who aren't Mormon make a big deal about it and sometimes they ask questions like, "Do you wear magic underwear?"

Garments don't have magical powers; at least I don't think they do. Basically they're a set of long boxer briefs and a camisole top. You can't wear sexy clothes and expect them to cover your garments, which is why I'm not looking forward to the transition. But they're supposed to remind me that my body is sacred, like a temple, and that I should dress modestly. I expect to own them one day. In the meantime, I'll wear miniskirts as often as I can.

Now, back to the lingerie store. I was moving from bra-and-panty sets over to a rack of vintage lingerie, when I stopped. In front of me was a slip so mesmerizing that it looked as if it was hanging from an invisible Lauren Bacall. It was literally the sexiest item of clothing I'd ever seen: dark navy blue, with thin straps, a see-through lace top, a silk body, and a slit up the leg. I read the price tag, "Vintage 1940s," and imagined a whole history: It once belonged to a woman, possibly a World War II spy, possibly a bored housewife in thigh-high stockings and brilliant red lipstick.

"Can I get you a dressing room?" the cashier asked.

I couldn't help it. I had to try it on. "Yes."

She led me into the back, and opened a pink patent-leather door with gold buttons that reminded me of Barbie's dressing room.

"Let me know if you need any help," she said before leaving.

I shut the door. Alone, I took off all of my clothes, bra included, and pulled the slip over my head. The fabric felt cool against my skin, and it smelled of something—maybe lilac, I wasn't sure. I adjusted the straps and took a step backward so that I could see my reflection in the mirror.

Oh, my gosh. I stared.

I was the spitting image of the girl in the Wookey mirror. Stepping forward, I touched the glass. This time my fingers were the same on both sides of the mirror.

"Hi," I said.

"Hi," she answered.

I stood there for a moment, examining her. I touched my collarbones and neck, which looked like it had grown a foot since my weight loss. Then I looked at my long arms and slender fingers. I instinctively ran my right hand through my hair, admiring the S my body made when I had my elbow bent in the air and my butt pushed back. *Wow.* There was an aspect I'd failed to notice about her before, something only this slip brought out.

I'm sexy, I thought for the first time ever. *Who knew that I could be sexy?*

It was too fun not to play with. Soon I was posing with one leg kicked up. I turned my head away, and then quickly back. I pouted, I bit my lip, I puckered. With each move the slip clung to my hips and I noticed that while the fabric was dark, you could make out the space between my legs pretty clearly, which was hot. I leaned in and studied the lace against my breasts. My skin brought out the shape of the intricately woven flowers. I looked closer. *Oh, my goodness, you can see my nipples!* I let out a squeak.

Someone tapped on the dressing room door. "Is everything okay?"

"Yes," I quickly said. "It's fine, I mean great, *it's great.*"

"Do you need help with your size?"

"No, *I like my size!*"

"Alright, just let me know if you need anything."

"Okay."

I turned back to the mirror and took one more look at myself. I thought about all the times I'd seen a woman's body and wished that it was mine. Now I didn't know quite what to do—*should I hold my breath and wish to become her? Or is this already me?*

I bought the slip. I knew it was pointless. I mean, it's not like any guy would ever see me in it. Not until I'm married, at least. Or actually not even then—a sexy slip over Mormon garments would just look tacky. But still, it was just too amazing not to buy.

Kissing, Take Six: Christian

Now that I had racked up enough pretty points, I decided to do something about the "You used to be so funny" comment. I got an internship at The Peoples Improv Theater. During my first week there, the guy who ran the theater noticed I had good penmanship. He turned me into his handwriting slave. Instead of doing comedy, I spent all my time making signs.

One Tuesday night in April, I was making a sign to go above the office that said, THE WORKSHOP. Naturally, I got overambitious I painted a huge canvas with camouflage designs. Then I wrote *THE*, and I started to write *WORKSHOP*, but I centered it wrong and by the second letter I already knew I wouldn't have enough room to fit the entire word. It was already eleven thirty; my shift was over. But I'm like my dad. If I start a project, I have to make it big and I have to finish it.

Which is how I ended up walking down Fourteenth Street, at midnight, with a giant dripping sign.

I was focusing on this predicament, trying not to get paint on my jeans, when I heard a man's voice ask, "What's the WU?"

I looked up and practically squealed. It was *him*, Shannon, the love of my life from the Irish bar, standing there in the middle of the sidewalk, Fourteenth Street, Second Avenue—the missing man of my dreams.

"Shannon?"

"No," he said.

"Oh . . ." I paused. On closer inspection, he was right. He wasn't Shannon, he just looked like Shannon, a little different, but beautiful just the same—chiseled jaw, almond-shaped brown eyes, and dark hair that flopped loosely to the side. He belonged on the cover of a men's magazine.

"I'm sorry," I said. "You look just like someone I know . . . or sort of know, or actually don't know at all. . . ."

"You look familiar, too." He smiled and brushed his hair out of his face. As he did this I noticed that his fingers were covered in blotches of black ink.

Oh, I can't take it, you're even prettier when you smile.

"Are you an artist?" he asked.

"Huh?"

"Or just a big fan of the Wu Tang Clan?"

I laughed. "No, I just painted this sign and it was supposed to say 'The Workshop,' but I ran out of space, and then it started dripping, and 'The Wo' became 'The Wu' and sorry none of this is interesting, why, are you an artist?"

"How could you tell?"

"Your hands." I pointed to his fingers.

"Oh, that." He laughed. "I painted my coat today." He lifted the base of his beige Burberry coat so that I could see the bottom. A woman with black hair and big sultry lips looked back at me.

"Nice," I said.

"Hey, check this out." He held his hand next to mine—we had ink on the exact same fingers.

I laughed . . . and then, *Crap*, there it was, that feeling all over again, like the world had become small and we had grown big, or vice versa. In an instant, I forgot all about Shannon.

"I'm Christian," he said.

"Me, too!"

"What?"

His name is Christian, not his religion, idiot.

"I mean, I'm Elna," I quickly corrected.

"That's a cool name."

"Thank you . . ."

"I was just heading to Café Pick Me Up," he said.

"Oh, okay." I wasn't sure how to respond. "Have fun."

He laughed. "No. Do you want to get a cup of tea?"

"Yes!"

Minutes later, Christian and I were sitting across from each other at a twenty-four-hour French café.

"Has anyone ever told you you have beautiful eyes?" he began.

"My dad calls them my root beer eyes!" I repeated verbatim. *Oh, no, it's happening again.*

Christian changed the subject. "I went to the new MoMA yesterday. Have you been yet?"

I nodded my head yes.

"What did you think of it?"

A fair question; what did I think of the new MoMA? I searched my brain for a response, and instead of the sharp, quick thought bubble that usually formed, all I could get was a fuzzy haze.

"It's super cute," I said, followed by the thought, *Wow, this is what it must feel like to be stupid.*

"That's exactly what the review in *The New York Times* said." He nodded.

Right on cue, I started to giggle. Everything Christian said was funny, even if it wasn't.

Why is this happening? I glanced down at my chest; it was covered in red splotches.

"Excuse me," I said abruptly. "I have to . . . pee pee." I pointed to the bathroom and escaped from the table.

That was close. I entered the one-stall restroom and locked the door behind me. Alone, I felt my ability to breathe and think restored. I walked over to the sink, put my hands on either side of it, and looked up. . . .

Oh, no, I gasped.

Staring right back at me, in all of her splendor (as if a day hadn't passed since I first thought Paul Stowe was my boyfriend) was the semiretarded school girl.

You—I should've seen it the whole time. *She ruined my chances with Paul,* I thought. *She's the one who sabotaged Shannon, and now she's trying to take Christian from me.*

She smiled an evil smile. "He's going to be your boyfriend," she began to chant in a high-pitched singsongy voice.

Go away, I cautioned her.

"Go away," she mimicked like a child.

Look, I tried to reason with her. *I'm a grown-up now.*

"No, you're not!" She rolled her big eyes at me.

Yes, I am.

"He's gonna be your boyfriend!" She bounced up and down.

I'm being serious, I pleaded. *Please, if you ever felt any compassion for me at all, do me this one favor: Stay in this restroom and let me go back to that table, alone.*

"Boys have wee-wees, girls have vajayjays!" she squealed.

Stop it! I grabbed her by the shoulders and shook her violently. *Can't you hear me? Don't you understand? I want you to go away.*

Most people experienced this moment in middle school when they traded their imaginary friends in for dirty magazines and lessons on giving head. But I'd missed this aspect of my adolescence. I was a thirteen-year-old in a twenty-two-year-old's body. And lines like "super cute" and "I have to pee pee" weren't going to get me very far. If I wanted to take part in the world I'd suddenly landed in, I needed to cram ten years of life experience into a few minutes.

But first and foremost, I had to kill the semiretarded school girl. *Good-bye*, I said with finality.

She looked up at me innocently and a bubble that was attached to her chin by dribble popped. This made her smile, and as she smiled I couldn't help but notice that her eyes were the biggest, sweetest color brown—and that they were indeed the color of root beer.

"Buh-bye," she answered.

I turned away from the mirror, placed my hand on the doorknob, and took a deep breath. Christian was sitting where I left him. I walked across the café in a straight line, and sat back down. Draping my hands in a V across the table, I cleared my throat. When I spoke, it was with a woman's voice. "Have you read the latest issue of *The New Yorker*?" I asked. And in an instant I knew—*everything is going to be okay.*

An hour later we were standing in my courtyard laughing too loudly at each other's jokes and talking about art, our favorite books, and all the things that would indicate exactly how cultured we were.

"I *read* all the time. . . ." I said, like it was a really big deal, even though technically all I was doing was name-dropping literacy. That's when it happened, way sooner than I wanted it to: In the middle of my sentence, Christian leaned in and tried to kiss me.

You can do this . . . , I told myself. But it was like diving off a cliff into water: You either jump, or you don't. If you hesitate, you're screwed. *What if I mess up?* I thought. *Oh, no, I'm screwed.* His lips reached mine. I responded as usual—I tucked my head into my shoulder and I tried as hard as possible to be invisible. But I wasn't invisible. The whole time Christian could see me. And in his eyes I was probably very different from the real me. To him, I was the kind of girl who did cheerleading in high school, or at the very least went to senior prom with someone other than her gay best friend.

Christian pulled back. The look on his face was all I needed to assess the damage: *That sucked*, it said.

You've done it again. I immediately started to overanalyze. *You ruined it. . . .*

That's when I heard it, the same woman's voice that I'd used in the café spoke to me again: *Just act like you know what you're doing,* the voice instructed.

Just act like you know what you're doing, I repeated. *Yes!* In one swift movement I grabbed onto Christian's T-shirt, pulled him into me, and kissed him. He moved his tongue into my mouth. *Oh, no, this is the part where I always screw up. . . .*

I waited for it to feel weird. Only this time was different, it wasn't just a stranger's tongue, it belonged to a person I was eager to know. And so I kissed him, for real. I pressed my tongue against his, and as I did this I was amazed at all the things my tongue could make my body feel just based on the rhythm, speed, and pressure with which I moved it. It was amazing. *How have I had this tongue for twenty-two years and never realized its power?* I felt excitement in places I'd never understood excitement could be, other than in theory. I felt enlightened. I felt happy. I felt relaxed and held and loved. And I felt like I could be in control, too. And this feeling made me kiss him with confidence and urgency.

Ten, one thousand.

Christian came up for air. "You're an incredible kisser," he said.

"I know."

Kissing, Take Seven:
Home Depot

I waited for Christian to call. Waited and waited and waited. The weekend came and went—nothing. So I got desperate and sentimental and played Frank Sinatra's "Strangers in the Night" over and over again. And to make matters worse, my urge to kiss, which had been dormant most of my life because I didn't know how to kiss, was suddenly there at maximum intensity.

He called on Monday. I leaped up off the couch and twirled around my apartment while we spoke. "What are you doing today?" I asked, ever impatient.

"I have to go out to Queens to go to Home Depot," he said.

I didn't waste my time. "Can I come?"

We decided to meet at the corner of Forty-second by Grand Central Station so we could take the subway together to Home Depot. As I stood there looking at all the faces of people crossing the street toward me, I noticed how so many different men looked like versions of Christian. *It's him, no, that's not him. It's him, no, that's a woman. Wait. What does he even look like? Did I make him up? I made him up. He was too perfect and his lips were too soft, and I couldn't possibly have kissed someone so strong, so handsome. . . .*

And then, I saw him behind two Asian women; holding a red

umbrella, he looked up at me and smiled. I panicked. *What do I do? Do we kiss, do we say hello, do we acknowledge we like each other, do we shake hands . . . ?* Christian walked up to me, placed his hand on my lower back, gently pulled me into him, and kissed me like I always thought lovers would kiss. Softly, confidently, like a declaration.

The euphoria set in. We kissed on the subway platform, we kissed on the train, we kissed walking across the parking lot into the Home Depot. We kissed in the nuts-and-bolts aisle. We entered a display shower, shut the faded glass door behind us; he pressed me up against the wall and we KISSED.

And it was just kissing. Christian didn't try to fondle me, or get dirty, which I took as a great sign. The night of our first kiss I'd told him that I was Mormon and that I didn't have premarital sex. His response astonished me. "That's so refreshing," he said. "My last relationship was entirely based on sex; it'd be nice to have something where sex wasn't part of the equation."

I decided to hear the second part of the sentence, and not the first. It was a personal triumph, in my mind. I'd stood up for my religion, and he respected that and now we could have an entire relationship based on kissing. And I cannot tell you how happy that made me.

So happy, I just kept kissing him. We kissed while looking at saws in aisle ten, we kissed in line, and then Christian, his arms wrapped around my waist, said, "So even if you fall in love, you still won't have sex?"

He said it lightly like he was saying something normal and uninteresting, like "Kellogg's is a great brand of cereal." But I understood what he was really asking.

It took me a moment to answer. "No," I said, "I won't have sex. Not even if I fall in love."

"Cool," was his response, and he kept his arm around my waist, which I thought was a good sign. It turned out not to be so "cool."

From that moment on it was like I saw our date in rewind, Christian was backing up, pulling away, we were kissing in aisle ten, then in the display shower, then nuts-and-bolts, then the parking lot, the subway, the platform, the corner of Forty-second and Fifth, and then he was walking backward and away from me. Holding his red umbrella, he disappeared behind the two Asian women. Soon he was out of sight. (They were really tall Asian women.)

AGE 22

What I believe:	What I used to believe:
- My diet was a miracle!	- No matter what you look like, it's what's on the inside that counts.
- If you're thin you can have whatever you want.	
- Grace is a transformative power.	- People who act like they know what they're doing actually know what they're doing.
- God answers our prayers.	
- Impossible is NOTHING.	- No caffeine for me.
- In being honest-ish, true-ish, chaste-ish and benevolent.	- That kissing should involve a lot of flicking of your tongue and quick circular motions.
- In Diet Doctor Pepper—it's awesome.	- That it's easy not to have sex.
- Masturbation is Evil.	
- The church is true! (and all the other stuff I already mentioned)	

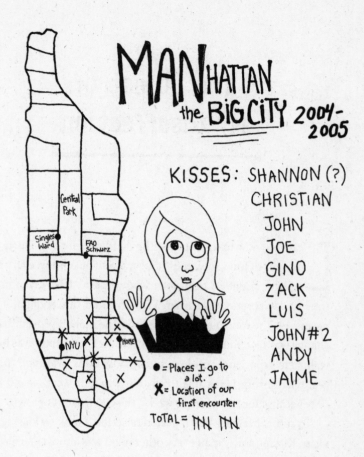

The Object of My Disaffection

Learning how to kiss opened the floodgates for me. During the months of June, July, and August, I went out almost every night and got attention from men who wouldn't have given me the time of day six months earlier. When you do this enough, it feels necessary. The more men that liked me, the more it proved that the change was real. But like with Christian, each encounter was brief. I wanted to experience true love, but because I was "waiting," the longest relationship I was able to sustain was four weeks—and that's only because for two of those weeks, the guy was out of town.

To compensate for this repeated rejection, I took up kissing with vigor. Kissing a new man every other night was almost like having a boyfriend. Only, the attention was addicting. If a tree is pretty in the woods and no one tells it that it's pretty, is it still pretty?

After a summer of flings, I flew to Seattle to visit my grandparents.

"You look so amazing, we're so happy for you—" my grandmother began.

"Enough small talk." I cut her off and headed straight for the closet. *The sacred dress.* I wanted to get into that thing now.

My grandmother lifted it out of her closet and handed it to me. I slid it over my head and zipped it up. It fit like a glove. My grandfather, who had carried that fabric all through the war, looked at me and started to cry. And my grandmother turned to me and said she wanted to give me this dress as a gift because she was so proud of me for losing all the weight.

I turned to look at myself in the mirror, and for the first time since going on the diet, I stood still and let all of my hard work sink in. I didn't need men to kiss me in order to prove that the transformation was real. It was real.

I'm beautiful.

I headed back to New York City the following day, the dress tucked neatly in my luggage. And that's when I remembered my daydream: *I'm all grown up* I thought. *I have the dress, I'm finally beautiful. Where's Brian Egbert, the most popular guy in first grade?*

Brian was living in Washington State, and he had a kid. And high school, or any system where I could enter and prove my popularity, was long gone. *But wait,* I thought, *what about the Mormon singles ward?*

I stopped going to singles activities two years earlier. But I thought, *I bet my new body will get me new attention.* And it wasn't just that. There's something I haven't shared with you about my religion that might illuminate some of my choices: When I was fourteen I went to a Mormon patriarch to receive a blessing. This is a tradition unique to Mormonism, and you can only do it once in your life. The patriarch, an old man I'd never seen before and never saw again, put his hands on my head and said a prayer in which he described my future. This blessing was later transcribed into a two-page letter and mailed to me. It sounds creepy but it was actually pretty cool, like Keanu Reeves visiting the oracle in *The Matrix*.

Over the years I've reread my patriarchal blessing at least a hundred times. It describes the life God intends for me, and it says that this life is not a guarantee; it's predicated upon my choices. I like it because it feels unique to me and at the same time it's obscure enough to be loosely interpreted. It does, however, say one thing that allows no room for interpretation. It says that I will marry a Mormon man who loves me dearly and that we will be married hand-in-hand in a Mormon temple and sealed for time and all eternity.

I'd think about this line every time I was in a relationship with a non-Mormon. *Am I going against my fate? Am I forfeiting the ideal future that God has in store for me?* Dating outside my faith was something I did for the fun of it, but I understood it couldn't lead to anything. I figured, best-case scenario, I'd find a Mormon who I liked and this would align my will with God's will for me. Which is why, in spite of my resistance, I went to Mormon singles activities, and ended up at the Halloween dance every year. I was supposed to marry a Mormon man. . . . I'd resigned myself to this fate.

And so, with my tail between my legs, I went back to the New York Regional Mormon Singles Halloween Dance, for the sixth time in a row.

Only, when I got there, the same scenario kept repeating itself: A guy would spot me in the corner and his face would light up with what looked like genuine interest. He'd start walking in my direction. As he approached, my mind would go a million miles a minute: *Maybe I was right, maybe this year will be different, maybe I will meet the one!*

And then, five feet from me, he would begin to drag his feet, and in his eyes I'd see what could only be recognition. "Wait"—he'd process it—"isn't that Elna Baker?"

He'd shimmy backward and bolt in another direction, like a car making a three-point turn.

Think positive Elna, think positive. I surveyed the pathetic scene. A man lingering near the doorway was wearing a baby suit with a bib saying, *Got Milk?* Two other men were dressed as competing kissing booths, each with a sign advertising a *twenty-five-cent kiss,* instead of a more accurate slogan: *undersexed and overage.*

I was halfway out the door when the most beautiful Mormon man I'd ever seen up close walked in.

His name was Brady. He was a recent addition to the uptown ward and he was by far the hottest male to ever frequent the Mormon singles scene. The music stopped, the disco ball exploded, and the women lost their shit. Myself included. I spent the rest of the night dreaming that this beautiful stranger would be mine.

Within a week, I was attending every single church activity. After three weeks, I exchanged actual words with Brady at a combined ward Linger Longer. (Every first Sunday of the month the church activities committee will set up refreshments for the congregation to eat after church services. They like to call this a "Linger Longer" or "Munch and Mingle" or a "Chat and Chew." It's all about the alliteration. If it were called "come and eat and talk," people wouldn't know what to do.)

At every activity, all Brady had to do for attention was enter a room. He pivoted from side to side while women introduced themselves, brought him dessert, and laughed too loudly at whatever he happened to say. They were baking him cookies and breaking their faucets for Brady to fix. Flirting in a way only Christian girls know how to do. That night at the Linger Longer, I watched them watch us, and that's when it hit me. *Brady is the Prom King and if he chooses me—I'm the Prom Queen.*

He would be mine. But while I was quickly become a kissing connoisseur, I'd never really dated anyone. I couldn't compete with these women. And by these women I mean one woman in particular: Amber Cunningham.

I hate Amber Cunningham. I completely utterly hate Amber Cunningham. For the record, the girl I've chosen to call Amber

Cunningham isn't actually named Amber Cunningham. Her real name is Eliza. And before Eliza she was Ashley, and before Ashley she was Jamie, and before Jamie she was Kelsey—my first archnemesis at church, dating all the way back to church primary school. If this were a biblical story it would go like this: Kelsey begat Jamie who begat Ashley who begat Eliza who begat Amber Cunningham. I lump these women into one because I resent them for the same reason: They're crazy dogmatic Christians on a quest to find celestial popularity. An Amber is like a Heather only she's attacking your spiritual worthiness and your dress size at the same time.

Our first encounter was in primary. We were in the same Sunday school class and as long as we were being reverent, our teacher let us play outside after church. One Sunday, Amber gathered a group of kids around her.

"Someone here hates me," she said. "It's not Christlike."

"Who is it?" we all asked.

"Elna."

Huh? My mouth dropped open. All the kids turned to face me.

"I don't hate you, Amber," I insisted. "I like you."

"That's a lie," Amber said. "You glared at me."

"It was the sun," I pleaded with her. "Sometimes I squint my eyes in the sun."

"If you are on the Lord's side," she said, "you will be my friend. If you are a follower of the dark angel, Satan himself, you will be friends with Elna." In retrospect it is easy to see that this sort of illogic can land you in a lot of trouble, like a war in Iraq. But to a second grader it was devastating. Naturally, Amber won this imaginary war in heaven.

It wasn't until returning to the States from living abroad that I encountered the remaining Amber Cunninghams. In the nine years I've been in the singles ward I've cycled through many Ambers. It's supposed to be a place where I go to receive spiritual enlightenment. Unfortunately, church is often a battlefield.

Since most Mormons believe you need to be married to make it into the highest level of heaven, every member of the congregation is operating with the same agenda: *If I don't get married to one of these people, I limit my eternal progress.* Only there's a major problem with this setup. In Manhattan, and in the Mormon community in general, there are far more women than men. If you do the math, it doesn't add up—at least one third of the women won't get a Mormon marriage. There's nothing a Mormon woman will not do for a handsome returned missionary. Add Amber Cunningham into this mix and my only advice is, *Step out of the way.* I repeat, *Get the fuck out of the way.*

At church, Amber's goal is to make all the other women feel bad about themselves. This way, when a new attractive guy moves in, Amber can easily move in for the kill, having already reduced the remaining female members of the ward into gibbering neurotics. *That's an interesting outfit?* She'll say, or *I noticed you didn't take the sacrament today; is it because you're not worthy?*

And do you know what the craziest part about all of this is? Amber's popular. I'm dumbfounded by it. Not because I'm jealous or want to be popular myself, but because she's insane. She raised her hand in church one Sunday and said that Katrina happened in New Orleans because sometimes God needs to "cleanse the world of sin." It's people like her that make damage control in the non-Mormon world a never-ending task.

Over the years there've been several occasions when I've wanted to stand up to Amber. Only, something happens to me when I am in her presence. I lose my ability to think; I'm afraid of her. And, even though we've known each other for years, Amber always pretends she's forgotten my name. That alone throws me off course. In fact, the only time Amber acknowledged that she was aware of my existence was after I lost weight.

"Wow, you look fantastic!" She stopped me in the hallway. "Did you get gastric bypass surgery?"

"No, I lost weight naturally."

"Really? I only ask because of your skin." She pointed to the excess skin under my arm. "Doesn't skin retract if you lose weight naturally?"

I thought of a million comebacks later that night, the "wit of the staircase" as the French call it. Like, *Doesn't it strike you as odd that your best feature is pointing out the worst in others?* Or, *Amber, go fuck yourself.* But in the moment all I could think to say was, "It depends on how fast you lose it."

I spent most Sundays brooding over Amber's comments and wishing awful things on her. That is, until 2004, when Amber moved uptown. Her new apartment was outside of my ward boundaries. The next year, we'd see each other every few months at combined church activities, but other than that, my life was Amber-free—that is, until Brady moved to town.

After our brief Linger Longer encounter, I wanted another chance to interact with him, and so I joined his family home evening group. Traditionally Mormons reserve every Monday night for family time. They call this family home evening, or FHE. You don't have to have a family to do it. There are several FHE groups for singles living in New York and each group has a fake mom and dad who coordinate the night's events. I never go. Why? It's totally boring and an offshoot of the singles ward. The evening begins with a prayer, then someone reads a *Chicken Soup for the Soul*–like cheesy devotional that they get too emotional to finish, followed by dessert and chatter.

As soon as I found out Brady was the "dad" of uptown FHE, I joined. There was only one problem: The "mom" opposite him was none other than Amber Cunningham.

For moral support I brought my younger sister Julia along with me. She was living with Tina and me for a few months while she was preparing to leave on her mission. When I told her about Brady and joining his FHE group she said: "I'd rather eat glass."

In spite of her resistance, Julia's a glutton for punishment. We headed to Amber Cunningham's penthouse apartment the following Monday night. When we got there, the door was propped open, so we went inside, only to find the place was empty.

"Hello?" No one answered. "Hello?"

"Are you sure this is the right apartment?" Julia asked.

I looked around the room. A set of scriptures sat on the kitchen counter next to a plate of freshly baked brownies.

"A New Yorker wouldn't be caught dead with scriptures," I said, "or food made with trans fat."

Not certain what to do, we both stood there fidgeting. "I have to go to the bathroom," Julia said.

"That's probably it." I pointed to a door on our left.

"Don't go anywhere without me," Julia said. I'm not sure if I mentioned this already, but in addition to being sarcastic, Julia's incredibly shy and prone to social anxiety.

"I won't."

As soon as she shut the door, I walked into Amber's living room. While I'd never actually lived in Utah, I'd spent enough time there to get a feel for it. Amber's living room looked like a Utah Home Catalog. *Ughh.* I cringed. On one wall there was a painting of Jesus. While Catholics usually paint the Savior suffering, Mormon artists tend to depict Him as a rugged Idaho mountain man—the kind of Jesus you wouldn't mind dating. In this particular picture he was healing a blonde child, because blondes were big in Jerusalem in 33 A.D.

I turned around. The other wall had a painting of a shepherd herding lambs. *Follow me,* it read. *No thank you,* I thought. Next to this there was a photo of the Salt Lake Temple. And then, last but not least, a picture of Amber's family.

I got closer so that I could count them. *One, two, three, four, five . . . eleven children,* sitting sideways on a long tree branch, all wearing denim, smiling and straddling one another. *Families Can Be Together Forever,* it said.

I felt a pain in my chest, and just like that, picture after picture piled up. The room got smaller, I felt crowded and overwhelmed.

Go. Now. Get Julia. Run, and never look back. And I don't know why I get this way, but sometimes I feel like I am being tied by invisible ropes and that I need to flail my arms just to prove my freedom. But then there's this feeling of impending doom because I know deep down that this is where I come from.

It is inevitable that I will be at a store some day, see a painting of Idaho Jesus, and think, *Well isn't that nice.* I'll hang it in my entryway and smile as I step back and check to see if it is straight.

"Hey."

I jumped. It was just Julia.

"Should we leave?" I asked her.

"I guess so . . ."

Just then we heard a giggle coming from behind a door at the end of the hall.

"Did you hear that?"

"Yeah." I started walking toward the sound.

"*Don't go in there,*" Julia whispered, as if we were in a horror film.

"Relax." I stopped in front of the door and looked through the crack. It was pitch-black inside the room. "Hello," I said. "We're here for FHE." When no one answered, I placed my hand on the doorknob tentatively and pushed it forward.

The lights flipped on just as I did this. "Surprise!"

Ten people between the ages twenty-five and thirty were crowded onto Amber's bed. I must've looked shocked because they were laughing hysterically.

"We totally got you!" Amber said.

"Huh?"

"The doorman said someone was coming up," Jonah, one of the guys, explained, "and we thought it'd be funny if we hid in the bedroom."

He was right, they thought it was hilarious. One girl had tears streaming down her face as if boys and girls sitting on the same bed is terribly risqué. I was about to do what I usually do in these situations—wonder: *What's wrong with me?* But then I looked at Julia, and her face was all the confirmation I needed: *Are these people retarded?*

It took about five minutes for the group to stop laughing. Once they did, I introduced myself. "I'm Elna, and this is my sister Julia." Maybe it was the fact that Julia's beautiful, and I was suddenly thin, but we didn't get a very warm response from any of the women.

"Aren't you in a different FHE group?" one girl accused.

"Yes," I explained, "I'm supposed to go to downtown FHE."

"Oh, so why are you here?" Amber asked.

"I work around the corner," I lied, "and this FHE is closer."

Just then, I heard someone walk up behind me. I turned; it was Brady—the real reason.

"Hey, sorry I'm late," he said.

Brady. Brady. Oh, Brady. . . . I hadn't seen him since the Linger Longer and I have an overactive imagination, so sometimes I remember things much better than they really are. This was not the case with Brady Owens. He was tall, he was dark, and he was handsome.

"What're you doing in Amber's bed?" he asked.

"One of Jonah's pranks," Amber explained. The group collectively made a face that said, *You know Jonah.* Brady smiled back, *Oh, yes, we all know Jonah.* There was more laughter and backslapping and recapping. But it didn't matter, Brady wasn't paying attention—he was looking directly at me.

"Hey," he said, "we met at the Linger Longer, right?"

"Yeah."

"Elena?"

"No, her name's Elna." Amber walked directly through us and linked her arm with Brady's. "She goes to the downtown ward, but she has to come to our FHE. Any who . . . shall we get this thing started, *Dad*?"

For FHE, Brady and Amber decided to give a lesson on talents. You know, *Don't Hide Your Candle Under a Bushel, But Set It on a Hill for the Whole World to See Because a Candle on a Hill Can Be Seen for Miles and Miles, and There's No Such Thing as Wind.* Amber stood at the front of the group. "Tell us what your talent is," she instructed, "and share it with us!"

I froze, as usual. When they ask, "Say your name and an adjective," inevitably I blurt out, "Eager Elna," and spend the rest of the night wondering why I gave myself a dildo nickname. But if my propensity to embarrass myself is a problem, it's nothing compared to what happens to Julia. I still remember her fifth birthday. We went to a Mexican restaurant, and when a bunch of waiters started to sing "Cumpleaños Feliz," Julia was so embarrassed she slid under the table and refused to come out for the rest of the meal.

I'm so sorry, I mouthed to her.

It was time for the talent show. Someone did the Mormon rap, a popular number at church talent shows. These are the actual lyrics: "Hey brothers and sisters, Listen to me, I'm talking to you religiously, My Mormon Rap will make you see, That I'm as funky as Donny and Marie. Mormon, Mormon Rap, Do the Mo-mo-mo-mo-mormon Rap. I'm a fine young man, I'm living clean, Don't smoke, Don't drink, If you know what I mean. Don't touch Soda Pop if it has caffeine, You might say I'm a good little Sunbeam. I didn't even date, Until I turned sixteen, I don't even know the meaning of the word obscene. Flipp'n, fetch'n, scruddle-dee-me, jimminy cricket, and fiddledy-dee!"

Afterward a double-jointed guy crawled through his linked hands, and then Amber impersonated a velociraptor from *Jurassic Park* because that's a talent that every untalented person does, and p.s. you know she's been doing this since junior high. Amber finished with a bow and then, *crap*, it was Julia's turn.

"I don't have anything to share," she said quietly.

"Oh, come on," Amber insisted, "everyone is talented at *something*. . . .

It was subtle, but the way Amber was looking Julia up and down, I could tell that she was trying to make her feel small, worthless. Amber'd been giving me this same look for years. And while I'd never spoken up on my own behalf, I jumped at a chance to defend Julia.

"She doesn't have to go if she doesn't want to," I said.

"She can speak for herself," Amber said. "Don't be shy. Talents get bigger when you share them."

"Leave her alone. . . ."

"I can sing," Julia interrupted.

We both stopped and looked at her.

"I can sing," she repeated. Which is true, Julia has an incredible voice. It's rich and sultry and every time it comes out of her, you wonder if she's momentarily possessed by Billie Holiday. Except for one problem: Julia lacks stage presence. She'll knock a melody out of the park, and then look at the crowd defensively: *I do not want attention. If you even remotely clap or acknowledge me, I'll kill you.*

Julia began, "Summertime, and the living is easy." The room went completely silent. "Fish are jumping and the cotton is high. . . ." Her voice was as haunting as ever. *Go Julia.* I was proud of her.

As soon as she finished, Julia made her usual "that didn't happen" face, and slumped back in her chair. Several of us, Brady included, cheered.

"Thanks," Amber said. "That was, um, *nice*." Julia had clearly violated the unspoken rule: *You're not supposed to share a real talent, this isn't a recital.* I watched Julia take Amber's words in, her shoulders slouching even farther than before. I wanted to punch Amber in the mouth.

"Elna?" Amber said. It was my turn.

"I can juggle," I blurted out, followed by the thought, *Why! Why do I consistently lie?* I can't juggle, *I do not know how to juggle.* I mean I sort of know how, but not well.

"Cool," Brady interjected. "Did you learn as a kid?"

"No, I took a clowning elective in college," I said, the truth this time. "We did a lot of juggling."

"Let's see," Amber said.

"Oh, I haven't juggled in years."

"When did you finish college?" Brady asked.

"Last May," I squeaked, "but I don't have any balls. . . . I mean, *ha, ha.*"

Naturally this made everyone uncomfortable. They avoided eye contact with one another—*Don't think dirty, don't think dirty.*

Amber stood up and walked over to the fruit basket that was resting on her mantel. She carefully selected three tangerines.

"Here you go." She placed them in my lap. "Juggle."

"Okay, fine."

While Amber sat back in her seat, I picked up the tangerines. I held two in one hand, and one in the other. *How hard can this be?* I thought. *You've done it before; access your inner clown.*

One, two, three, one, two, three, I mouthed to myself, each time I intended to throw the tangerines, but hesitated. *One, two, three, one, two, three . . .*

One, two . . .

Just then, I heard something I wasn't supposed to hear: Under her breath Amber said to the girl next to her, "You should really know how to juggle before you volunteer it as a talent."

It was an out-of-body experience. Without thinking, without even aiming, I threw the single tangerine in my right hand across the room. It hit Amber directly between her eyes. I could not have targeted it better had I tried.

Amber flew back in her chair. I looked down at my empty hand, my mouth wide open with surprise.

"What in the heck . . ." Amber began.

Everyone started laughing.

"I'm so sorry." I didn't quite know how to explain myself. "I thought you were asking for a tangerine," I managed.

"Yes," Julia agreed. "She was definitely asking for it."

After this fateful FHE, I was more determined than ever to win Brady.

I bought every manual ever written on landing a man, and I started reading them: *Mr. Right, Right Now!*, *Why Men Love Bitches*, and *Sex and the Single Girl* (which is totally pointless if you're Mormon).

And then I found *The Fascinating Girl*, a book my grandparents had given my mother in the seventies. "To our own fascinating girl," the dedication read. "Christmas 1972, Love, Mom and Dad." I read the pearly white book cover to cover. It was all about getting a man by reverting to the 1920s style of being submissive. There was an entire chapter called "Unlearning Your Efficiency," and another one on Angela Human. Half human, half domestic goddess, she was the ideal woman from a man's point of view. My favorite chapter, "How to Make the Most of a Picnic," encouraged the reader to "not just sit there" but to explore the path and get into predicament after predicament—allowing the man to assist her with his strength and cunning. When I finished the book I thought, *This can't possibly work.*

I decided to practice on Brady. "Compliment his masculinity: A man's most central need . . . is to be admired for his masculine traits—his strength, aggressiveness, idealism, manly courage and determination. Admire him by using words like: big, tough, brute, invincible and indominatable."

When I passed Brady in the hallway at church the following Sunday, I said, "You look strong and bearlike today." He beamed. *This has to be joke*, I thought.

It was the gateway drug. Once I realized that the methods—while seemingly outdated—worked, I shamelessly started using them.

I waited for FHE to make my second attempt.

Timorousness: "You can practice timorousness around men by first unconsciously performing some task, then when you realize that the man is noticing you, suddenly become self-conscious and confused."

I walked over to Brady and began, "Your tie is crooked; can I fix it?"

"Sure," he said.

Holding onto the knot, I delicately tugged at the base of the tie. Then I stopped suddenly, and held Brady's gaze. *I'm so hot for you,* my eyes said. *Oh, dear.* I looked down at the floor. *Now I'm shy.*

It left him speechless.

But this was nothing compared to the finale—the icing on the cake—"The Beauty in Distress Method." Similar to "Making the Most of a Picnic," this chapter explained that every man wants to be your hero, so you should create situations where you are a beauty in distress so the man can save you.

I was passing Brady in the hallway after a church activity. The usual flock of girls, Amber Cunningham included, surrounded him.

"I'm organizing a soup kitchen," I heard Amber say.

That's when the idea came to me: *beauty in distress.*

In one swift movement I emptied my purse upside down so that all the contents spilled out. As I did this I let out an "Oh, no!" and pretended to trip. It was more realistic than I expected. I forgot that my iPod was in my purse and, as it smacked against the floor and cracked, the "Oh, no!" that came out of my mouth was completely genuine.

Amber and a few of the other women started to laugh at me. When Brady didn't react, I started second-guessing myself. *I'm not a beauty in distress.* I crawled to my knees and started collecting my stuff. *I'm a scattered, pathetic fraud.* The laughter stopped. I looked up. Brady was towering over me.

"Don't worry, babe," he said in a firm voice, "I got you."

He put both of his hands on my elbows and lifted me off the ground. As he did this I caught a glimpse of Amber's face. *I know exactly what I'm doing*, I thought, as clearly as if it were written on a scoreboard above her head. *I'm slaughtering you.*

When Brady finally made his first move a week later, it was as though all of us Mormon women were standing against the wall holding our breath. And then it happened. He picked me. *He chose me.*

I did something I'd never done before. I turned around, and in a look I said to all those women—Kelsey, Jamie, Ashley, Eliza, and Amber Cunningham: *I WIN.* Or *Fuck you.*

The night of our date involved two hours of prep work: I exfoliated, I moisturized, I had the hair, the makeup, the shoes . . . and then I put on my grandmother's sacred dress.

And suddenly there I was on my dream date, sitting across from Brady in the candlelight. We were in the middle of a conversation about Brady being the captain of the BYU rugby team, when he stopped and looked at me.

"Let me guess," he said knowingly. "You were a cheerleader in high school."

No, I thought, *I weighed two hundred fifty pounds in high school.* Only I didn't say this. Instead, I took the pretty point, made spirit fingers, and yelled, "Gooooooooo Cougars!"

I could see by Brady's face that he thought it was adorable. I wasn't lying, I was insinuating. I got this technique from the book. If I wanted to make a relationship with Brady work, I didn't have to flat-out lie—all I had to do was pick up on what he wanted and pretend that this was me.

"Did you serve a mission?" Brady asked me.

I waited for him to tell me what he wanted to hear.

"Or were you more interested in starting a family?"

"Exactly." I smiled. "I just never met the right man . . . one who loves God and his family," I quoted directly from *The Fascinating Girl.*

Our date continued to go well. I'd looked up *masculinity* in the thesaurus before arriving. We were two-thirds of the way through our meal and I'd already used every word.

"I have to use to ladies' room." I excused myself. "Will you watch my purse?"

I was walking down a dimly lit corridor in an attempt to find the bathroom when I noticed a thin blond woman walking toward me. We looked each other up and down and at the same time we both did the nod. As we got closer, I guess I expected her to move. When she didn't, I thought, *She's kind of a bitch.* So whatever, I'm the bigger person, so I moved to the right. But she went right. So I moved left, but she went left. Finally I stepped straight ahead only to realize I was ten inches away from smacking into a full-length mirror. I looked at myself. Gaunt, with hollow-looking eyes. You don't realize that the little things you've been doing will add up or think that you're capable of behaving like anyone but you, until you've done it, every day, for a long enough period of time. *Oh my goodness,* my jaw dropped open, *I'm the blond bitch!*

I did the only thing I could: I put this information in a locked vault in my brain, and decided to forget it.

"You look like you've seen a ghost," Brady said as I approached our table.

"I have low blood sugar," I answered.

"Well then, we should go somewhere and get dessert."

Dessert? I don't eat dessert! Fifteen months of counting calories and I'd almost forgotten the word. But I didn't want the date to end, which is why I said, "Dessert sounds lovely." Technically not a lie.

As Brady led me toward Union Square, my mind was racing. *If we get brownies, that's 450 calories, and cheesecake is like 600.* Just then I saw it: fluorescent white, with pink and royal blue lettering, a beacon of light, a godsend, a Tasti D-lite. Fake frozen yogurt, no fat.

"We could go there?" I offered. "I hear it's good." I ate there every other day.

Brady pushed the glass door open and escorted me inside. "What do you recommend?"

"Well there are only three flavors," I answered, "chocolate, vanilla, and something I refer to as gray."

He ordered two vanilla-chocolate swirls, walked over to a table, and pulled out my chair for me.

"What do you think?" I asked as Brady finished his first bite.

"I guess I don't understand why women like this place so much," he answered. "It's not as good as regular ice cream."

"Well," I began—with authority (there are only a few topics I can legitimately call myself an expert on and this unfortunately is one of them). "It's probably because Tasti D has forty calories and no fat, whereas ice cream has two hundred fifty to three hundred calories plus twenty-eight percent of your daily fat."

"This is going to sound mean," Brady confided in me, "but I just *cannot tolerate* fat people."

I almost choked on my fro-yo.

"I mean it's so obvious," he continued. "Just diet and eat right. Don't come crying to me—if you're fat it's your own fault."

WHAT? I thought. *Why did he have to say that??* And also that word: *tolerate.* A person can not tolerate lactose, but they can tolerate someone who is fat.

I wanted to stand up and yell, but I remembered the advice in *The Fascinating Girl*: "Never try to change a man, gentle prodding is the way."

So I said, "I think it's hard for fat people because their challenge in life is visual. And they can't just ride by on good looks, instead they have to develop personalities. So I think in general, fat people are very nice. Not that I know anything about it."

He looked at me. "Yeah, you're right," he said. "They're either nice or they're just bitter."

I didn't kiss him good night; I didn't even kiss him on the cheek. I left the date early, walked into my apartment, kicked off my shoes, and threw down my purse. As I did this I caught a glimpse of the *sacred dress* in the mirror. I was everything I'd dreamed of but I didn't feel proud. I felt like Amber Cunningham. That's when I realized, what made my grandmother beautiful in that dress wasn't her looks, it was her.

The Man of My Dreams
Is an Atheist

I met Matt shortly after my disastrous date with Brady, in the spring of 2005. I'd been accepted into the page program at the *Late Show with Dave Letterman* and I was working the day that we met.

While my father got to brag about his "daughter who lived in the big city and worked for *the* David Letterman," it wasn't glamorous. I was an adult cheerleader. My job was to mingle with audience members and pep them up before the show. I'd interrupt people and begin, "How's everyone doing today?" If they didn't answer enthusiastically I was supposed to shake my head with disapproval, hold my hand to my ear, and say, "You're about to see David Letterman. *Now* how are you doing?" It was "You and your family want to be left alone, but I'm an actor and I need attention," take two.

And then one day, a totally normal Tuesday, I was scanning the line looking for a person to "pump up," when I saw a man standing by himself reading a book. I say that as if "a man standing by himself reading a book" is intriguing. In and of itself, it's not. If he were a bald man, or a short man, or an elderly man, I would never have noticed him. But this man was handsome: tall, light brown hair, medium build, and when I think about my first impression of him I can honestly use the line I've always wanted to use: "There was just something about him."

For starters, he didn't look up from his book once, nor did he let the pace of the line or the pushy tourists draw him from his focus. And it wasn't just that, as he read he would smile or laugh at different lines. You knew what was happening in the book just by watching him.

I spied on him for at least a minute before I made my approach. I nearly chickened out, too, but I figured if he found me intrusive, I could always pretend it was my job to interrupt people, because it was. I walked over to him. When he didn't notice me, I made a scuffing noise with my shoe. When that didn't work, I cleared my throat, leaned over his shoulder, and said, "I see people reading that book on the subway all the time. Is it good?" This was a lie. I'd never seen the book before in my life.

He looked up, and I guess I knew right then that I loved his eyes, the hazel color of them and the way they looked at me with a certain thoughtfulness. I also knew that I wanted him to look at me much longer than any three-minute "peppy" conversation would ever allow for. But that's all we got. A three-minute conversation about books before we were interrupted.

"Tickets and IDs," a page called out.

I looked up. *Crap,* we were at the front of the line.

"Will I see you inside?" he asked me.

"Probably not," I said.

"Well, it was nice to meet you."

"Nice to meet you, too." I wanted to say something else like, *Meet me after the show so that we can talk more,* or, *I already like you so much that I suspect some day I'll write a book about you.*

Instead, I backed away from the line. "Enjoy the rest of your book," I called out.

"I will." He held it up and waved good-bye.

This would've been the extent of our exchange, were it not for what happened next. As I watched him walk into the lobby, following the back of his coat with my eyes, I heard a voice. *That is who you are going to be with,* it said. Nothing like this had ever happened to me. *Him?* I freaked out. *I don't know anything about him! For all I know he's married and lives in Milwaukee.*

Go after him. Go. Now, the voice insisted.

And so I did. I pushed open the side door and ran into the lobby. Standing on tiptoe, I scanned the crowd. Over three hundred audience members were waiting in a long maze. He was nowhere to be seen. *NO!* I weighed my options. I could climb under the red ropes, push through the crowd, and then say, "Fancy running into you here," after knocking ten people over to get to him.

On the other hand, I could try to find him on Fifty-third Street after the show. But there'd be five hundred plus people leaving at the same time and four exits, so the odds really weren't that great. Before I could come up with even a semblance of a plan, a page brushed by me. "They're calling places." It was time to let the audience in. I walked into the inner lobby of the theater. *It's probably better this way,* I decided. *I mean, he probably isn't Mormon, and like every other guy I've ever dated he'll probably want to have sex.*

I dragged out the "box on a stand" that I use for discarding the audience members' tickets. Before the audience entered the theater it was my job to take their tickets and put them in this box. As I opened the lid, a tiny give-away pencil, the kind they have at libraries, rolled off the top of the box and onto the floor. I looked down at it, the sharp point, the eraserless bottom. *It's not too late,* I thought. *He's still here—he's somewhere in this line.*

As quickly as I could, I found a scrap of paper and wrote the following:

To the guy I met in line,

I have an extra ticket to a Dave Eggers reading on Friday. If you're
interested, give me a call: 917-579-0955.

Elna

I'd barely finished writing when the doors sprang open and the
audience rushed in. I was grabbing people's tickets at my usual speed:
five hundred fifty tickets in less than three minutes. (Only this time
my inner monologue went something like this: *Take ticket, check to
see if it's real, look for the guy in line. Take ticket, check to see if it's
real, look for the guy in line.*)

There was a guy in a gray fleece. *That's him,* I thought. *No, that's
not him; it's a bearded man. That's him. . . . Oh, wait, no, that's a
woman. Wait. What does he even look like? Did I make him up? I
made him up. . . . He was too perfect, and too smart and too. . . .*

All of a sudden I saw him—blue coat, book, and all. He looked
up at me. My heart was beating so loudly I could hardly think.
Don't look at him; if you look at him you'll chicken out. I focused on
the job at hand. *Ticket, ticket, ticket,* I counted, *blue coat.* I glanced
up. *Him.*

In one swift movement I grabbed his ticket, reached into my back
pocket, took out my note, and shoved it into his hand. The crowd
pushed forward. He was gone before I could gauge his reaction. But
it was okay, not all was lost, he had my note, all he had to do was call
me and . . . *shit.* The realization of what I'd just done came crashing
in. *I'd lied.*

When am I going to learn? It's just, things happen so quickly and
I follow through with them so thoroughly that it's only in the after-
math that I realize the error of my ways. You see, I wanted my note
to seem nonchalant, like a casual request, not like I was hitting on

him or like I was a stalker or anything. So I thought, *We talked about books, right? If I invite him to a reading, he'll want to come along.* The only problem is I didn't have tickets to a Dave Eggers reading. In fact there wasn't even a Dave Eggers reading; I'd made the entire thing up.

Now the situation was problematic on two fronts. If he didn't call me, I'd be devastated. If he did, I'd have to talk my way out of my mess. I had written myself into a bad sitcom with a miniature pencil and no erasure.

The guy I met in line called the very next day and said that his parents were in town, and unfortunately he wouldn't be able to make it to the reading.

"That's okay," I reassured him. "I mean, *you're really missing out*, but—"

"Elna . . . ," he interrupted me.

"Yes . . ."

"Matt."

"Yes, Matt?"

"Do you want to know what I'm thinking . . . ?"

"What're you thinking?"

"That you should see a movie with me next Tuesday?"

"Yes!"

I must've sounded pretty eager because he laughed at me. "I like what I hear," he said.

"Me, too."

We agreed to meet on Tuesday in front of the statue of George Washington at Union Square. When I got there, I saw him before he saw me. He was standing directly underneath George, reading a book. I was worried he'd look up as I approached and that we'd have to spend thirty awkward feet smiling and fake looking away. Only, he didn't see me until I was practically in front of him.

"Hi." He glanced up from his book. I'd forgotten how cute he was.

"Hi," I stammered. *Leave it to me to stammer on one word.*

"Thanks for meeting me."

"Of course."

We stood there for a few minutes. I'm sure we spoke. I probably told him what I did that day, he probably told me what he'd done. I don't remember a thing. I do, however, remember looking at his shoes, his jeans, his hands, and his face. *Did you ever think you'd be this lucky?* NO. The answer was no.

"I checked the movie times," Matt said. "We have an hour to kill before anything good starts. Wanna get a drink?"

"I don't drink—" I said automatically. *Crap.* I bit my tongue and waited for him to ask the usual question—*Why?*—so that I could deliver the fatal *I'm a Mormon* blow.

Instead, he shrugged his shoulders and said, "Smoothies?"

"Sure." I let out an unintentional sigh of relief. "I love smoothies!"

"There's a great café around the corner." He stuck his hand out. "Shall we?"

"Yes." I took his hand in mine and just like that, two strangers who'd met at the Letterman show were walking down Fourth Avenue, together.

"Shit," Matt said as we approached the café. "The street's closed."

We both looked down the block. It wasn't just closed. Thirteenth Street was blocked with blue police barricades. There were trailers, lighting equipment, cameras, and a film crew.

"What do you think they're filming?" I said.

"I don't know. Wanna find out?" he said, like it was a dare.

"Yes." I smiled mischievously.

"I like what I hear." He squeezed my hand, and pulled me around the blue barricade and down the forbidden block.

"Hey, you two . . . ," someone shouted.

We stopped, dead in our tracks. A man with a walkie-talkie was glaring at us.

"Us?" I pointed to myself.

"Yeah, you." He sounded annoyed. "Extras are supposed to stay in Area C."

"Sorry," Matt answered. "We'll get back to our places."

That's right, the guy grunted.

On the other side of the street there was a fluorescent orange sign that read AREA C. "Over there," I whispered.

"Good eye," Matt whispered back.

Just then, a woman stopped us. "We need street extras to go to places," she instructed. We just looked at her.

"*Karl!*" she yelled impatiently. A frazzled production intern came running.

"You're street extras?" he asked us.

"YES," we both answered.

"Great, go over there." He pointed to a tree a few yards away and that was it, no direction, no further explanation, just "street extras" and "tree." It was enough. We walked over to the tree and waited for the next step.

"You're good at this," I told Matt. "Other people usually hold me back."

"I have the same problem," he agreed.

A camera on wheels sped by us. "Action," the director yelled. Everyone stopped what they were doing and froze. The silence was uncanny.

What do we do? I mouthed.

"Just act natural," Matt instructed, "and whatever you do"—he leaned in to my ear—"don't fuck this up." I almost started laughing, but stopped when I saw the two police officers. They were heading directly toward us. *Oh, no.* My heart stopped for like half a second, until I recognized one of them from the movie *Clueless. Actors,* I thought, *not cops—actors.* The actors walked down the block, passing us along the way. A few yards later, a "gangsta" in a puffy jacket cut them off. They started harassing him.

I looked at Matt. It was exciting being in the middle of everything, but more than that it was exciting because I was sharing it with him.

"Cut," the director yelled.

The whole street came back to life. People ran from camera to boom, to set, to lighting, to wardrobe.

"Should we head back to Area C?" Matt suggested.

"I don't know." I pointed to a fluorescent green sign. "What about Area D?"

"Now we're talking." He smiled.

There was too much going on for anyone to notice us, and so we snuck behind the Craft Services food tent and over to Area D—which turned out to be a big trailer with three doors: Lucy, Desi, and Makeup. Matt pushed me toward the third door; I shot him a *don't you dare* look. Just then an attractive woman with curly black hair poked her head out from behind the door. She had a makeup kit tied around her waist, and a foundation brush in her hand.

"Did the director send you here to see me?" she asked.

"Yes," I answered.

"What for?"

"Black eyes," Matt and I said simultaneously. It wasn't preplanned, either; my jaw dropped and I can only imagine the face I must've made.

The woman waved us in. "Take a seat," she instructed. We sat down in front of a mirror that was surrounded by at least fifty light-bulbs and she went to work on the two of us. My shiner was a big crater-looking thing, black, blue, then yellow. Matt's looked more like a country. When she finished, she took a step back and surveyed our wounds. "You're all set," she said proudly. "You can head back to Area C."

We were halfway back to the set when I felt Matt pull me in the opposite direction.

"We're not going back, are we?" I said.

"No," he answered.

"We're making a run for it, aren't we?"

"Yep."

We snuck out the same way we came in, Thirteenth Street and Fourth Avenue.

At this point, we were too wound up to sit through a movie. And so we spent the rest of the night running around the city with our shiners.

"Two smoothies," Matt placed an order at Jamba Juice. "And can we get a side of ice?" He pointed to my face.

We walked into Whole Foods next. As we passed the busy check-out line, we noticed people staring. I released my hand from Matt's, an act. *"Just leave me alone,"* I yelled. *"I need a spelt cookie!"*

"Baby, baby, I'm so sorry," Matt pleaded, right on cue.

Two hours later we were standing in front of my apartment.

"This is you?" Matt said.

"Yep," I said. "My apartment's tiny, but it's a good location, unless you count the fact that we live across from the Cock, not that I've ever gone there but—"

"Elna?" He cut me off.

"Yes?"

"Can I take you out again?"

"Yes."

"Good." He took a step forward. "Can I kiss you?"

Before I could even answer, he wrapped his arms around my waist, pulled me into him, and kissed me. It was a different kind of beginning—he didn't want anything from me, he wasn't trying to feel me up or grope me—he just held me, like I mattered to him. *Why is he being so nice to me?* I thought. *What did I ever do to deserve this?*

With my hands on the back of his neck, his hair filling the space between my fingers, I felt happier than I think I've ever been. *Thank you, God! Thank you for taking every little wish I've ever made and putting them into one person.*

Matt took a step back and looked at me. "Your black eye is smeared," he said.

I reached my hand up and touched it.

"And all this time I thought it was real." He shook his head. *"Poser."*

We were dating after that. I tried to play it cool, but I was crazy about him. And whatever, I'm not just a sucker for a cute boy—Matt was a catch: a Yale grad, a doctor, and a seasonal river guide. When he told me about a project he'd done for Habitat for Humanity in which he created an outreach program for homeless meth addicts—I was done for, completely hopelessly smitten.

And the best part was, the feeling was mutual. Or at least I felt like it was. He loved listening to me tell stories, and after every date, he'd set another date up. And more than that, we made each other laugh. I laughed more with him than any guy I'd ever dated. It was the perfect relationship . . . except for one teeny tiny problem. Matt didn't know I was Mormon, probably because I didn't tell him. I totally rationalized this, too. *In addition to being Mormon,* I thought, *I'm many other things, so why should I let my religion define me?*

But the truth is, I wanted to be able to date him for more than two weeks and I was afraid he might just see my religion as a cockblock, so I didn't tell him. I figured if I could get Matt to fall in love with me, the Mormon thing wouldn't be that big of a deal. In a *Cruelty thy name is Mormon* sort of a way. There was a major catch to this: Usually my reason for not sleeping with someone was obvious. Now I had to find a way around it without saying something lame like, *I'm on my period . . . for eternity.* I'd never watched porn, so I was rusty on the old art of sexual seduction, but I owned a Carmen Electra striptease workout video. According to Carmen, it was all about "keeping him wanting more." *Dip, dip, dip.* She'd bend forward until you could see directly down her sports bra. *Eye-contact,* she'd instruct. *Scoop it up. . . . And walk away, ladies, walk away.*

I applied this philosophy. On our third date, Matt and I made out in the courtyard of my building. When he put his hand up my shirt and onto my breast, I moved it away coyly. "That's more of an eleventh date activity," I said.

"Ah, yes, the arbitrary eleventh-date-boob-touching rule." He laughed.

After that, I decided to play it safe, taking a cue from my time as a freelance babysitter. When parents in Manhattan want their kids to get together with other kids, they organize elaborate playdates. That's basically what I did. I took Matt to the Bronx Zoo, brought a box of animal crackers, and played a game where we had to identify each one and match it to the animal. Matt seemed to enjoyed it, but then again he could've just been on his best behavior because he was trying to get laid. Either way, we had fun. We watched baby gorillas wrestle, and then we fake wrestled, too. And at the end of each adventure, he would walk me to my door and we'd kiss like crazy. Sexy kissing, full of mixed messages. I'd dangle the carrot, so to speak, and then run inside.

And while this plan worked in theory, by our sixth date, I started to feel guilty. While I wasn't lying, I was purposefully misleading Matt. And aside from the sex, I felt like there was this huge part of me, my faith, that I was keeping from him. When Matt asked what I did on any given day, I'd omit the part where I studied my scriptures for an hour, wrote my thoughts in a journal like I was writing them to God, and then prayed. Or if it were Sunday I'd say, "I went to brunch with some old friends," instead of the truth: "I taught a Gospel Essentials class on repentance in church."

He can't love me, I thought, *until he knows the real me.* And so I decided to bring it up, *as casually as possible.* We were eating dinner at a restaurant near Union Square when I did it: "Oh by the way," I said, like it had just occurred to me, "I'm Mormon."

By the look on Matt's face, it was the last thing he'd expected to hear.

"I haven't been keeping it from you," I lied. "I was just hoping it'd come up naturally and it didn't. I'm sorry."

"It's okay." He stopped me. "I already know."

"What?"

"Don't think this is weird," he continued, "but after our first date I Googled you."

"You what?"

"I Googled you. And your show *Mexican Mormon* came up as well as an LDS petition you signed to keep *Touched by an Angel* on the air."

"What?"

"Didn't you do a show about . . ."

"Being a Mexican Mormon? Yes. But I would never sign a petition for *Touched by an Angel* . . . unless . . . oh, no . . ." My face turned red. "I'm going to kill my mother."

Matt looked confused.

"She probably signed it for me," I said. "She does stuff like that all the time. When I was in high school she campaigned in front of my school. *Mothers Against Abercrombie and Fitch*. It was so embarrassing." The only time she's ever come close to being obscene was when she bought my brother an ironic T-shirt that said SAVE A TREE EAT A BEAVER. And that's only because she didn't get the irony.

Matt laughed. Just then it dawned on me. "*Wait a second*. You've known that I was Mormon the entire time we've been dating?"

"Sort of," he said. "I mean, you never talked about it, so I figured you were just raised Mormon. You're not still practicing, are you?"

I bit my lower lip, "Yes."

"Really?" He looked genuinely perplexed by this. "Elna . . . ," he said. "I'm an atheist. Can you be with an atheist?"

I'd been so worried about his response to my religion that I'd never considered the flip side. Dating an atheist meant going against everything I was raised to value: *No temple marriage. No family for eternity. No religion at all on his part.* It didn't seem like the kind of decision a person could make in an instant, but then I looked at him. "Yes," I answered. "Can you be with a Mormon?"

He was quiet for what seemed like forever, but what was probably more like thirty seconds.

"Yes," he said.

"Really? Are you sure?"

"Yeah, I'm sure. . . ." He looked into my eyes. "It's just . . . I like the shit out of you."

"That's the most romantic thing I've ever heard!" I almost started crying.

Then he kissed me. In the middle of the crowded restaurant, Matt pulled my chair into him and he kissed me. In that moment, I remember holding him the way you hold something you've almost dropped seconds after nearly dropping it.

I opened my eyes and smiled. "You're great," I said, like a sticker you get for doing your homework in second grade.

Matt put his hand on my face and lightly pushed my head backward. "Nerd," he said. We both started laughing.

"What should we do now?" he asked me.

"Take me on an adventure," I said.

That night we snuck onto a beach on the Long Island shore and almost got arrested for trespassing. It was exactly what I had in mind. Only, when Matt dropped me off at my door and we kissed in our usual fashion, he called "bullshit."

"So when you said I could touch your boobs on the eleventh date, you meant, eleven times infinity?"

"Smile," I said, like we were on *Candid Camera*, "you've been *Mormoned*."

We managed to go out two more times without mentioning the words *Mormon* or *atheist*. But as much as we tried to ignore them, it was like there were these grander things looming above us and they would not leave us alone. "Did you know there are studies that prove red wine is good for your health?" Matt said one night at dinner.

"Yes, I heard that," I answered. "Did you know there are studies that show the power of prayer?"

"Seems like a hard thing to prove."

"Have you ever tried praying?" I asked him.

"No. Who would I pray to? I don't believe in a higher power."

"Oh, yeah . . ."

We went from making jokes and discussing books, movies, and ideas, to having conversations based only around religion, without being too specific. *Just ignore it and it will go away.* We did our best.

That weekend, we went to a birthday party for one of Matt's close friends. By the time we got there, the birthday boy was already drunk. Matt introduced us.

"Are you his Mormon girlfriend?" his friend asked.

Both Matt and I paused uncomfortably. We hadn't addressed either issue, my religious status or the status of our relationship.

"We've been hanging out," I answered.

"What do Mormons even believe?" he continued. "I mix them up with Jehovah's Witnesses. Do you use zippers?"

"That's the Amish," I answered. "You're stereotyping the wrong religion."

Matt laughed.

"But Mormons are the ones who wear weird underwear, right?" He winked at Matt. "I guess I should be asking you that?"

"Don't be a douche bag," Matt said.

"Mormons wear a thing called the garment," I tried to answer politely. "So is today your actual birthday—"

"I have one more question," he interrupted. "And then, I swear I'll stop. Do Mormons worship golden cutlery?"

"Are you insane?" Matt made a face at him.

I wish for my sake that Matt's friend was insane; only I knew exactly what he was talking about. He was referring to the golden plates Joseph Smith had translated, the ones that produced *The Book of Mormon*. Only he'd mixed up the word *plate* with *cutlery*.

I should've just let it go. Or made a joke like I usually do. Instead, I felt this strange need to explain myself. Not even for the sake of my faith; I just didn't want Matt's friend to think that Matt was dating a lunatic.

"Mormonism is a *Christian* religion," I began. It came out way more defensively than I'd intended it to.

Both boys looked at me with surprise.

"We don't believe we are a new religion or a new church," I continued. "We believe we're the restoration of Jesus's original church." For the next ten minutes I explained my religion to them. It was a difficult task; I was trying to teach them about miracles and still sound like a liberal intellectual. The other problem with Mormonism is that, while the core principles are simple, it's easy to go off on tangents that when taken out of context (or in context for that matter) don't make any sense.

"By patterning our lives after the life of Jesus," I continued my pitch, "we learn to become like God. So that eventually we can create our own worlds and be Gods, too," I finished.

I thought I'd done a good job explaining everything (I covered the basics, and I didn't say anything about Pocahontas being a Jew), until I looked up. Matt and his friend were staring at me blankly. It was the same look you'd give a stranger if they stopped you on the street and screamed, *I just killed an alien with a giant green knife whoobly wooobly wooooo, religion!!!!*

It wasn't their expressions that unnerved me; it was the sudden awareness of everything I'd said. There it was, laid out on the table for Matt to see: I'm an actual Mormon. It isn't something I just arbitrarily happen to be; I understand it and still believe.

Matt's friend was the first to break the silence. "*Golden plates,* not cutlery," he said. "I knew I got that from somewhere."

I took his comment in. "Exactly," I said. "Are you religious?" I tried changing the subject, but Matt stopped me by asking, "Do you believe *The Book of Mormon* and Bible literally?"

"Huh?" While I knew that he was there for the entire explanation, I'd kind of hoped he wasn't listening.

"In the Bible it says the earth was created in seven days. Do you believe that over scientific evidence that proves the earth is billions of years old?"

"I don't know," I said honestly.

"You should know," he told me. "It's a simple question. Either you believe it, or you don't."

"I guess it's one of those things I try not to think about," I answered.

"But you're part of a religion that takes a firm stance on it."

"There are a lot of things my faith takes a firm stance on that I'm not sure about."

"You disagree with your religion?"

"Yes."

He shook his head. "I could never be part of something I didn't entirely agree with."

"It's impossible to *entirely agree* with religion," I countered. "If everyone based their faith on common sense no one would be religious—faith is totally illogical."

"That's why I'm an atheist."

I didn't say anything for a full minute. I didn't know what to say. The air around us felt thick, and the light that was usually there was gone.

"Since when did we get so serious?"

"I don't know," Matt sighed.

"What's your favorite flavor?" I perked up in my chair.

"Flavor of what?"

"Candy."

"Banana, I guess."

"Let's get out of here and buy as many banana flavored things as we can find, and have a banana flavor party."

It was a temporary fix. We went back to his place and ate banana pudding, banana Laffy Taffy, and banana sorbet—playdate number seven. Only it wasn't just a playdate; it was a potential sleepover. By the time we finished our pudding, it was one in the morning.

"Matt?" I said, like I was about to ask a leading question. "I hate taking the subway this late at night."

"Do you want to sleep over?" he asked.

"That'd be great," I said, like it was all his idea.

"You can sleep in my bed," he offered. "I'll take the couch."

"That's okay." I sat on his bed nonchalantly. "We can sleep together."

"Oh." He looked surprised. I'd never spent the night before, but he went along with it. He got me an extra pair of pajamas, we brushed our teeth together, and then we climbed into bed.

"Good night." Matt leaned over me to turn off the lamp.

I immediately started trying to make out with him. He didn't know how to respond. And so instead of doing anything hot or heavy, he patted me on the back like I was his autistic cousin and moved to the far side of the bed.

I could feel my shoulder tingling. *Did he really just pat me?* It was infuriating. What happened to the way we used to kiss? It's as if now that he knows I'm a Mormon, he's teaching himself not to be attracted to me.

I turned onto my side so that I was facing him. "You know I can do some stuff sexually," I said. By "some stuff" I meant he could grope my boob barely and I could pretend not to notice, or maybe we could start to dry hump, but the minute either of us got aroused, I'd have to stop it. "I'm not an asexual being."

"I know." He reached across the bed and placed his arm around me.

"We could do more," I repeated.

"Elna," he said, "if we're not going to sleep together, I sort of find the foreplay thing to be frustrating."

Ouch. Matt moved a little closer to me, shifted his pillow, then closed his eyes. I tried to go to sleep, too. But whatever, I couldn't just let it go.

"Do you want to have sex with me?" I asked.

He didn't respond. But I could tell that he'd heard me because his body got all tense.

"Not now," I quickly corrected, "but in general, is it something you'd want?"

"It's tricky," he finally said.

"Why is it tricky?"

"Well, for a girl her first time is very meaningful, and I wouldn't want you to do something you regretted. So, no, it's not a good idea."

"I see," I said. His answer disappointed me. I wasn't even sure why. I mean, it was a respectable answer, one my parents would applaud. And besides, we were on the same page, I didn't want to have sex, he didn't want to have sex with me. *Great.* But at the same time, I felt like we were entering a relationship catch-22.

"We've been dating for what, six weeks?" I offered. "So even if I wasn't Mormon it's not like we would've had sex already."

Matt laughed.

"Why is that funny?"

"It's not funny. It's just, well, usually people have sex way before six weeks."

"They do?"

"Yeah, I mean, if they like each other."

"How soon do you usually have sex with someone if you like them?"

"I don't know. It depends on the person and the circumstances. But if I know I want to be in a relationship with them, usually within the first two or three weeks."

I nearly choked. "How can you know someone well enough to have sex with them after two weeks?"

"You don't. That's why you have sex."

"Have you had sex with a lot of people?" I asked.

He gave me a *Come on, you're not allowed to ask that question* look, and then said, "Not that many, but I've been having sex since I was a teenager."

"So it's going to be hard for you to not have sex?"

"Elna, I don't necessarily feel like we're at a place in our relationship where we would be having sex. It's just the *never* part that's problematic."

"I can have sex once I'm married," I said optimistically.

"You do realize that's the same thing as saying never," he laughed.

I got quiet again. "You wouldn't wait for marriage to have sex with me?" I asked.

"I don't believe in the institution of marriage," he answered.

Of course he doesn't. I practically threw my arms in the air with defeat. "So where does that leave us?"

"I don't know," he said, like he was saying, *Please go to sleep.*

"Okay, fine. Good night."

"Good night." He rolled over again and closed his eyes.

We were quiet for a few minutes and maybe he was sleeping, or maybe he was thinking like me, either way I couldn't take it . . .

"Is it because I'm ugly?" I blurted out.

"Oh, give me a break." Without even looking Matt put his whole hand over my face and shook it. *"You know you're beautiful,"* he practically yelled. "But maybe this is just too much to take on—"

"No," I cut him off. "There's no such thing as too much. *I promise*, anything is possible."

"I like you because you believe that. *Now go to sleep,*" he said and then he leaned in and kissed me, the way I remembered him kissing me from the beginning, like I mattered.

It didn't work. We both started laughing.

When I woke up the next morning there was a space the size of a person in between us. *Room for the standard works,* I thought. *Room for the Holy Ghost.* Only we cut through the space: We were holding hands.

I can turn anything into a reason for believing things will work out. As I was walking home from the subway that morning, a ladybug landed on my shoulder. *It's a sign,* I thought. And then when I stopped at the corner deli and bought a Diet Coke, I noticed that the bottle said: "One in twelve people win a prize when they look under the lid." *One in twelve.* It seemed like the same odds that we were up against. *If I win something, it means we'll stay together.* I closed my eyes like I was making a wish, opened the bottle, and flipped the lid. "You win a free Coke," it said. *We're gonna make it!* I started jumping up and down like I'd just won the lottery. *Everything is going to be fine!*

We went to the new Star Wars movie the following Tuesday. I was determined to ignore everything we'd been arguing about and just go back to the beginning. *We will not discuss religion. We will not discuss sex. We will only have fun,* I decided. It seemed like it was working, too. I wore a cute outfit with matching heels, and for a minute I felt like a girl again, *the girl on the date*—until our walk to the subway.

"What do you think about cloning?" Matt asked.

"I don't think about it," I said, "unless I happen to see a movie about it. But in general, it doesn't come up."

"But doesn't it make you question your faith?"

"Why?" I made a face. "They haven't figured out how to do it yet."

"They've cloned sheep."

"So? It's a sheep, not a human."

"Yes, but they're very close to successfully cloning humans," he said.

"That's impossible." I looked at him, eyes wide. "They can clone a sheep, and it can move its eyes and walk and act alive, but they will never be able to successfully clone a human being."

"Why not?"

"Scientists can't create that thing that makes us alive," I said earnestly. *"They can't create a person's soul."*

"I don't believe in souls," Matt said dismissively.

"What?" I stopped in the middle of the sidewalk, breaking the flow. Several annoyed pedestrians bumped into me.

"*What?*" I repeated. "You don't believe people have souls?"

"No."

"How is that even possible?" I turned and faced him. "I thought everyone, regardless of religion, believed in souls?"

"I don't." Matt shrugged like it was no big deal.

"So what makes you, *you?*" I asked.

"All the things that have happened to me," he answered.

"But when you die, what'll leave your body?"

"Nothing. My heart will just stop beating."

"Are you being serious?" I said, reevaluating everything I'd come to believe that Matt believed. It was too much. If I tried really, really hard, I could accept the notion that there wasn't a God and that maybe *just maybe* we'd ended up on earth by chance. I could even accept that death was it, the end—but I couldn't possibly believe that there was nothing inside of me.

"Yes," he answered.

I put my hands on Matt's shoulders and held him in place. People were still pushing by us, glaring or grunting passive-aggressively because we were blocking the sidewalk, but I didn't care. I held onto him until it felt like there was no one left on the street but us. I stared deeply into his eyes without speaking; I looked into the hazel, I looked past the yellow specks, and I searched until I found *the him* inside of him.

"What are you doing?" he finally said.

"I am looking at your soul," I said sincerely. "Matt, I can see it. I know that it is there—*it speaks to me.*"

He tried not to laugh. "What does it say?"

"FUCK YOU!" I shouted.

If Matt looked surprised it was nothing compared to my face. It's not a word I use that often, but when making a religious point, it was all that came to mind.

"Fuck you," I repeated, still channeling his soul. "I've been living inside of you for twenty-nine years and you've been ignoring me the entire time!"

"My soul sounds angry." Matt laughed.

"Tell me about it." I sighed. "I think it just feels neglected."

We reached the subway station, and said good night. Matt was halfway down the steps when he stopped and looked back up at me. "Just so you know," he shouted, "they're very close to cloning a human being."

"If they clone a human being," I shouted back, "a fully functional, emoting, thinking human—I will have sex with you that very day."

Several people stopped what they were doing and stared at me; one woman covered her son's ears.

Matt jogged back up the steps. "Deal," he said.

"Deal." We shook on it.

"I'm going to read *Popular Science* every morning now," he said, walking back down the steps.

"I am, too," I called after him. For my own sake, I wanted it to be possible. I wanted scientists to clone a person and announce it on the morning news. Not for genetics, or scientific progress, but because if a soul was something that could be obtained in a petri dish it would nullify my definition of God and I could sleep with Matt guilt-free.

It was only later that night that I realized Matt hadn't set up another time for us to meet. When I called him three days later, he said he was going out of town for a wedding. I waited another week before I called again. But it didn't matter, I already knew what was happening. In spite of everything, Matt was phasing me out. And it's so interesting, because every girl knows when she's being phased out, even if the guy coincidentally doesn't pick up his phone that day. It's like *you know* because you feel it. *How am I supposed to go back to a world without Matt? I can't just make the line at Letterman walk backward and undo my feelings for him.* Unlike Christian or any of my other one-date wonders, my feelings for Matt felt irreplaceable. I wanted to get to keep him. So I started thinking about why he was pulling away. *It's probably because I'm Mormon and it's probably because I won't have sex.*

And for the first time in my life, I started to really question these things. Not the way I had in Sunday school, as a fun way of riling up the teacher or to annoy my parents. I questioned them as truth, as necessity, as the only way of living. *It's not fair,* I thought. *How can religion take away love? But how can love take away religion?* Followed by, *God is supposed to be love, right? So if that's the case, is love God? Is choosing to follow my feelings for Matt a religious act, or is choosing my religion over a relationship religious?*

Matt called a week later. He didn't apologize for disappearing or even mention that it was weird. He just invited me out on a playdate. He was going to an outdoor exhibit at the pier and he wanted me to join him.

We met at Union Square. Matt was waiting in our usual spot, standing underneath George Washington. He looked up from his book and waved. And the thing is, you can never know what another person is thinking, but the minute I looked at him my fears were confirmed: *He's moving on.*

"Hey, dude," he greeted me like an old friend.

"Hey." *Did he just call me "dude"?*

"How stoked are you about seeing some art?"

"Pretty stoked," I said.

We went to the exhibit, or we got to the exhibit, and just as we approached the first sculpture it started to rain. Not drops. Buckets. A downpour. We ran under the awning of a public bathroom, which wasn't exactly the most romantic place to kill time, but it was the nearest place to hide. Sandwiched in between a group of German tourists and a businessman on a conference call, we tried catching up.

"How was the wedding?" I asked him.

"It was nice," he answered. "How's Letterman?"

"Fine. Pamela Anderson was on yesterday and her boobs are as big in person as they're on TV."

"Good to know." He nodded.

Apparently this was all the information I'd stored up in two weeks. *Really impressive*, I thought. *Stop the presses . . . Pamela Anderson's boobs are big. I hate myself.*

Matt peered up at the thick gray clouds. "Doesn't look like this rain is going to let up anytime soon," he said.

"We can just skip the exhibit," I offered. "Wanna go to a movie?"

"I think it's too early—" he said.

I looked at my cell phone; it was twelve-forty. "Yeah, you're right. We could watch a DVD at my place?"

"I like what I hear," he said.

In the seconds it took to hail a cab, our clothes were soaked all the way through. Matt opened the taxi door for me. "Tenth Street and Avenue A," I said, shivering.

The driver stepped on the gas and we headed across the bumpy cobblestone streets of the West Village. It was a chaotic trip, rain rattled on the roof of the car, the windshield wipers blasted at full speed, and the driver leaned forward in his seat and cursed the entire way. But it didn't bother me—I managed to block everything else out except Matt. As long as we were together, we still had a chance. I turned in my seat to face him. The window behind his head was fogged up; it felt like we were in a cloud. *I want to kiss you,* I thought, but then I hesitated. It was hard to know where to begin. *Do we start from where we left off? Or do we go back to the tentative holding of a hand?*

I slid my fingers across the gray leather seat, and linked them through his. "Hi," I said.

He turned toward me. "Hi," he answered.

And suddenly there it was, the same look he'd first won me over with and my heart beating so loud I was worried he'd hear. *Hi.* I imagined him coming home from work with groceries. *Hi.* I imagined waking up next to him, a down comforter folded under my arms. *Hi.* I imagined an entire middle for our beginning. *Hi. Hi. Hi. Hi.* How was work? Is your headache gone? Did you need me to pick up the dry-cleaning? Can you get the kids while I put gas in the car? *Hi.*

The cab came to a rolling stop in front of my apartment.

"I got it." Matt pulled out his wallet.

"Are you sure?"

"Yeah, you get the next one," he said.

"Okay!" It was all the affirmation I needed: *He said, "the next one."*

We walked into my apartment and took off our wet shoes.

"Can I make you lunch?" I asked.

"Sure." Matt set his coat on a chair. "Do you need help?"

"Here." I tossed him a kitchen towel. He looked confused, like I was asking him to clean my house or something.

"It's for you to dry off with." I laughed.

"Oh, thanks dude." *DUDE!* He put the towel over his head and started looking through my rather limited collection of DVDs. I cringed when he got to my sister's section, which included such classics as: *The Lamb of God, Passage to Zarahemla, Baptists at Our Barbeque, God's Army,* and a bootleg copy of *The Passion of the Christ.* When Matt picked up the wacky comedy *Mobsters and*

Mormons and started reading the plot synopsis— "Mafia hitman Carmine 'The Beans' is placed in the witness relocation program and sent to an all-Mormon community in Utah"—I walked into the kitchen to spare myself the shame.

Taking out some of Tina's bread, I made us grilled cheese sandwiches. I don't eat things like grilled cheese, or bread, but I decided, *Whatever, I'm just going to act like a normal person for one day and then forget about it.*

We put on *The Usual Suspects.* I sat down on the couch next to him. We ate lunch together; it felt really normal.

It didn't make sense that I'd be there—I mean these guys were hard-core hijackers, Kevin Spacey was saying. *But there I was.*

We watched the movie for another fifteen minutes. Or Matt watched the movie and I debated the best position in which to sit. *Do I lounge with my legs on top of him? Do I shift so he's pushed into the corner, or does he really just want to pay attention and should I sit calmly by his side?* I tried to read his face for clues. Unfortunately, he caught me staring at him.

"Are you cold?" he asked.

"Huh?"

"You're shivering."

"Oh . . ." I hadn't noticed it, but yes, I was. My shirt wasn't completely dry and now that we were inside with the AC on, I was freezing.

"Yeah." I shrugged my shoulders. "I should probably change." I stood up, accidentally blocking the screen. Matt moved his head so that he could see around me. I walked into my bedroom and shut the door.

Alone, I felt a particular kind of freedom; I could make any face and ask any question that I wanted to. So I did. I flung my hands from side to side, stretched my facial muscles into an expression that most closely resembled a sad clown, and quietly sighed. *Why is he changing his mind?*

Relax, you're overanalyzing everything. I pulled off my T-shirt and tossed it onto the bed. It landed on top of the nineteen other shirts I'd tried on earlier. *No you're not; he's clearly over you.* I opened my dresser drawer and rifled through my clothes. *How do you get a person to stay when they know all the reasons they should leave?* I wondered. My hand touched something smooth, silky; it felt cold against my fingers. I looked down—the blue slip.

What if wear that?

You can't wear that! It's like the middle of the afternoon on a Tuesday . . . I laughed nervously and took my hand off the slip. When I did this, the fabric slinked forward, as though it were moving of its own accord. *But Elna,* I reconsidered, *you own that, and you've never worn it.*

I stepped on one sock and then the other, yanking them off. I unbuttoned my jeans and slid them down. I unclasped my bra and tossed it onto to the floor—a race against my conscience.

It caught up quickly. *What are you doing?* It asked me in a panic. *Are you going to have sex?*

I pulled the slip over my head and turned to see my reflection in the mirror. Avoiding my eyes, I looked at my body. It still fit, I was still sexy. *I'm a woman,* I thought. *A woman with long arms, pale skin, pronounced collarbones, a waist, hips, and toes.* I stood tall, defiant, *and I'm capable of choosing my own life.* I dangled my right arm behind my head, the sexiest move I could conjure. "Yes."

And then I thought about this word and why I love it so: *When you say yes everything can change—I want to change.*

I walked over to the bedroom door, took a deep breath, and pushed it forward. It swung open with a loud *whoosh,* and smacked into the wall. It was unnecessarily dramatic. I cringed.

I could hear Matt moving in the other room. *You can do this.* I took a step forward and poked my head out from behind the door. By flinging it open, and then hesitating, I'd effectively gotten his attention. The movie was on pause, and he was sitting up in his seat, waiting for my entrance. I figured it'd be best to ease him into the idea that I was suddenly wearing lingerie. I rotated slightly—one shoulder visible—and watched him process the thin strap on my bare arm.

"What are you doing?"

I stepped out from behind the door into the empty, open space.

Matt just stared at me.

All of a sudden, I felt naked. *I'm completely visible—the lights are on, there's nothing to hide behind—it's just me, my body, me.* It's terrifying to let someone else look at you. But the look on Matt's face, it was good. I stood up tall. *I am what I am.*

"Why are you trying to torture me?" Matt said.

I pressed one finger against my lips. "Shhhh. . . ." I walked over to the couch and slid the light switch down until it was so dim it was practically off. And then I knelt in front of Matt and put my hands on his knees.

He didn't move. He just sat there, looking out of place. Like a giant in a child's chair, or a boy in a giant's chair, I couldn't tell which. *I will never meet anyone like you again.* I leaned forward and kissed him—for a moment it felt like he was thinking, *Don't touch the stripper; they throw you out if you touch the stripper.*

I ran my fingers through his hair. "It's okay."

I felt him relax. *"God, I missed you."* He sighed.

"I missed you, too."

"I'm sorry," he said. "I know that I've been an asshole, but it was just so hard to . . ."

"Shhhh," I stopped him.

He put his hand on my cheek. I turned my head and rested it in his palm.

"I really like your face," he said. I almost started to cry.

From there he kissed my neck, my collarbones; it tickled. I lifted up his shirt and kissed his stomach, his chest, his left shoulder. There were so many places on him I'd never gotten to show how much I liked. I went from one to another, but there was just more skin, more ground to cover. Kissing him, I felt a familiar pull; the momentum was even stronger this time. *What is this?* It felt like the light was shifting, or the air had changed. And then Matt was on top of me, kissing me back, and I was holding him as close as I could. And then it happened . . . With my arms around his back, I leaned into his ear and I heard myself say . . .

"You need to pray and find out if God exists."

Matt froze. *"What?"* he said.

What did I just say? "Nothing," I reassured him. "I didn't say anything."

This explanation didn't help. While Matt was still on top of me, I felt like he was somewhere else. I waited a moment and then I tried to kiss him again. *Pretend that didn't happen.* I pressed my lips to his. He felt reluctant. *Just pretend it didn't happen.* I kissed his neck. *Please?* I kissed his ear. I kissed him and kissed him and kissed him. *Go after me,* I wished. And then, all of a sudden, just like that, he did. He picked my body up, and pressed me down on the couch, and for a few seconds he was on top of me. And it was incredible. I had no idea that he was so much stronger than me—that he'd been exercising so much restraint. In the heat of the moment, I leaned forward for a second time, and pressed my lips against his ear. "How can you know that God doesn't exist unless you at least ask?" I whispered.

"What?" he said.

I clamped my hands over my mouth. *What is wrong with me?* I almost yelled, *I just want to have sex right now, and instead I have God Tourette's syndrome?*

Matt moved me off of him abruptly and sat up straight. I reached my arms out but he blocked them.

"Elna what are you trying to say?" he asked.

What am I trying to say? I sat there for a moment with such a mixture of feelings.

When I finally spoke, my voice was so clear, I didn't think I was the one speaking. "The only reason I believe in God," I said, "is because I prayed and I asked. And how can you know for sure that something isn't true unless you at least ask?"

He was quiet for a moment.

"Do you want me to pray?" he said.

I took a deep breath. "Yes," my voice cracked.

He looked directly into my eyes. "Okay," he said, "I can do that. I can pray."

"Really?" I said in disbelief.

"Yes."

I wasn't sure if I was supposed to hold my breath, make a wish, or say a prayer of thanks.

Matt stood up and reached for his coat. "I should probably get going," he said.

"Okay," I said.

The minute he was gone, I rushed over to the couch and knelt down. Folding my arms, I began:

Dear Heavenly Father,

I know that I pray all the time but please let this prayer count more than all of the other ones. In fact, if you answer this prayer, you never have to answer another prayer of mine ever again.

I cleared my throat.

If Matt prays and asks if you exist, will you please answer him?

I love you, God, I know that you are up there. I know that you know who I am, and that you love me. Please show Matt that you love him, too. Answer his prayer.

I say these things in the name of Jesus Christ, Amen.

* * *

After I finished this prayer, I sort of made a mistake: I called Tina. I couldn't help it; I have to tell Tina everything. I didn't tell her the whole *I'm ready to have sex, oh, wait, no* part. I just told her about Matt agreeing to pray and how big of a deal it was because he was twenty-nine and he'd never prayed before. I also mentioned that I was praying for his prayer.

"I'll pray for him, too," Tina said earnestly.

A minute later I got a call from my parents. Apparently they'd just talked to Tina, and they wanted to let me know they were praying, too, and that they called my grandparents, and my grandparents were praying. Pretty soon a family tree across America would be praying for Matt to get an answer—it was Atheist Intervention Day.

How effective is prayer really? Can one person pray and find God? And if thirty people are praying for that one person, do we have the power to influence that person's answer? And ultimately is there one truth up there, high in the sky, and can Matt reach for it? Can he hold it in his hands? And if so, is it the same truth as mine?

I didn't hear from him for another two weeks. When I did, we set up a meeting in Union Square, at our statue.

"Hi," I said when I got there.

"Hi," he answered.

When we set up the date over the phone, he asked me what I wanted to do. *See a movie, get dinner, or go to a museum?* I suggested we play it by ear. Now that I was there, in front him, I didn't want to move.

"Movie?" he asked, "Or food?"

I sat down on a bench. "Let's just talk for a minute," I said.

"Okay." He sat next to me.

We talked about the previous two weeks. About his job search, about the guests who'd come to Letterman, and about the books we'd been reading. I'd been reading classics. Not even because I wanted to, but on the off-chance that Matt might ask, and I might get to impress him.

And yet, it didn't matter how much I'd read, or whether he found me to be smart—what mattered was that I was a Mormon, and he wasn't. The more we talked, the more I avoided the question I most wanted to ask.

Finally I decided, *It's not something that just comes up tangentially, you actually have to bring it up.*

"Matt," I interrupted him. "Can I ask you something?"

"Sure," he said.

"Did you pray?" My voice sounded intense, filled with imperative.

He looked at me. It was as though he'd been expecting the question the entire time.

"Yes," he said.

"You did!" I tried not to sound shocked, but a big part of me thought he wouldn't do it. It was huge.

"And," I stammered, "and what *happened?*"

"Well"—he choose his words with care—"I went into my room, shut the door, and I knelt down and I prayed and I asked God if he existed."

"And . . ." I leaned forward.

"I listened, like you told me to. I sat in silence, for a long time, Elna and I listened."

"And then what happened?"

"I listened and then I realized, even if I did get an answer, it would just be me telling myself I got an answer because I wanted to be with you, Elna." He looked at me earnestly. "It wouldn't be real."

"And . . ." I said. *Please be more, please, God, cue the angel.*

"And that was it," he finished.

That was it?

I was quiet for a minute.

"That was your answer," I finally said, a sadness weighing my voice down.

"Yes," he nodded.

There was another silence.

"But you're not going to be with me, are you?"

"No."

"Doesn't that make you sad?" my voice cracked.

"Yes." He looked at me. "Yes," he repeated, "it does."

"Didn't you feel *this*?" I waved my hand back and forth, from his chest to mine, "Didn't you feel like . . ." I wanted to say, *like we were meant to find each other, like it was all part of something? Like you were my soul mate, except you didn't believe in souls . . . but I don't need you to . . . and more than anything didn't you feel like you could love me?* But I didn't actually say anything at all. I just kept moving my hand back and forth, from him to me, and from me to him.

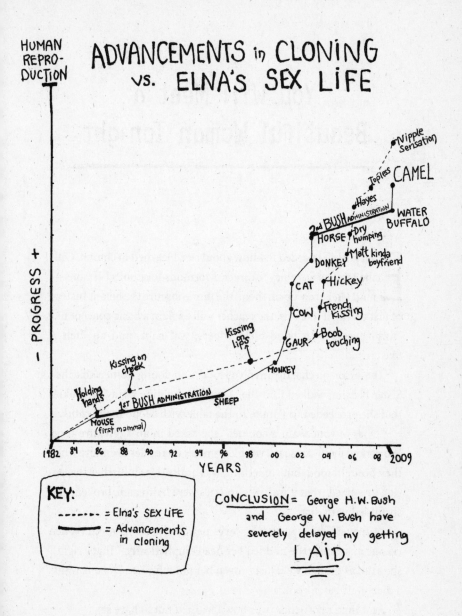

You Will Meet a Beautiful Woman Tonight

Everything I needed to know about sex, I learned in church. Only the lessons were never direct. Mormons love object lessons—I mean it, I grew up on them, the more obscure the better. Instead of just telling it like it is, the teacher will explain a basic concept like "forgiveness" with windshield wipers, wet naps, and an Etch A Sketch pad.

The lesson on chastity involved food. Our young women's teacher, Sister Nelson, walked into the classroom holding a tray of cookies that she proceeded to slam onto the table with a loud metal *clank*.

"Does anyone want a cookie?" she asked in an aggressive tone. We perked up in our seats; young women's was easier to endure when they brought food, but something was amiss. Upon further inspection I realized what it was: The cookies were half-eaten, broken, and sprinkled with dirt.

"*Anyone?*" she repeated, her eyes panning across a room. When no one answered, she nodded her head emphatically. "That's right," she said, as though we'd just proven her point for her. "*No one* wants a dirty half-eaten cookie."

And that, my friends, was how I learned not to have sex.

I was taught a similar lesson in regards to dating and "nonmembers." When I was twelve I attended a church youth conference called "The Dangers of Dating Outside of Our Faith." We learned about Esau who sold his birthright for a mess of pottage, and Sampson who lost it all for the whore Delilah. But the most valuable lesson was saved for the closing remarks when the speaker, a middle-aged football coach, stood in front of a hall of Mormon youth and held up a small branch.

"Does anyone think that they can break this twig?" he asked.

A kid in the front row raised his hand.

"Well, let's see you do it."

The kid walked up to the podium and took the twig in his hands, *snap*.

"Good work." The speaker smiled. The boy was about to head back to his seat, when the speaker stopped him. "Wait . . . ," he said. From behind the podium he pulled out a pile of twigs tied tightly with twine. "Do you think you can break this bundle of twigs?"

The boy flashed the audience a cocky smile. Taking the bundle with both hands, he began to twist and pull. Nothing happened. He shifted his arms for leverage, his face flushing red with frustration—and still nothing happened.

"That'll do." The speaker took the bundle out of the boy's shaking hands and held it up triumphantly. Not a single twig was broken.

"So it is with us," he concluded. "If we stick together, all the forces of the adversary combined will not be able to break us."

Sitting there, in white tights and Sunday shoes, I thought about everything I'd learned about love. From *Pocahontas* to *Cinderella*, to the copy of *One Hundred Years of Solitude* that I was trying to decipher. *What does this have to do with love?* I wondered. *Because I am not a twig. I'm a human being with complex emotions and when I fall in love I fall in love.*

It was with this attitude that I left home, moved to New York City, and tried dating everyone from Jeff to Christian to Matt. It was a noble cause, the pursuit of love, but it got me into a lot of trouble. And more than that, it made me feel torn. Like every date I went on that wasn't with a Mormon was an act of defiance against God.

And so, after Matt and I broke up I decided to just give in. *Okay, fine, God*, I said, in a state of post-breakup despair, *I will do what you want me to do. I will date only Mormons. But you need to bring in a Mormon man of my dreams and you need to do it right now.*

Never make a deal with God where you set the terms. Trust me, it's a bad idea.

On my way out of church the following Sunday someone handed me a flyer. *The New York Regional Mormon Singles Halloween Dance.*

I couldn't stop what happened next: *Hope.* I started making connections no one had asked me to make . . . *You don't receive a witness until after the trial of your faith*, I paraphrased a scripture.

I flipped the flyer around to look at the back. "Join Us for Jolly Jack-O'-Lanterns This Spooky Saturday, October Twenty-ninth." *This can't just be a coincidence? I've ended up at the dance every year for a reason. It's all been leading up to this year: the year I meet the Mormon man of my dreams. God, you owe me at least that.*

If only I'd stopped there. But, no, my inner overachiever kicked in. *I'm going to go to that dance,* I decided, *and I'm going to meet the one . . . but in order to do that I have to have the best costume ever.*

I started to brainstorm: *a Barbie doll*, no, too cliché; *a bearded woman*, yeah, right. *Marie Osmond . . .* only the gay Mormon men would appreciate this. Just then it hit me, in a flash of light. *I'll be a fortune cookie, and when guys pull out the fortune it'll say, "You will meet a beautiful woman tonight,"* at which point I can wink and say, "Look no further." Brilliant.

I spent all week building my fortune cookie costume. I bought a beige mattress pad, wire, and a whole bag of cotton stuffing. Once I had all the ingredients, I drew a giant circle in the center of the mattress pad and cut it out. I used the wire to shape the fabric, and I pulled the ends of the folded cookie together just above my head, making a crease that spanned from my stomach to my chin. Finally, I added the cotton to give it a nice fortune cookie puff. But by far the most complicated part of the costume was the fortune. I decided to make it retractable, that way every guy could have his own experience with it. In order to do this I took apart one of the stanchions from my job at Letterman and I "borrowed" the mechanical part at the top. It was ingenious. I detached the red rope and replaced it with a roll of thick receipt paper. On this paper I wrote "You will meet a beautiful woman tonight" in black Sharpie. I must've written it at least fifty times. That way a guy could pull the fortune out, let it go, and it'd retract. Or if he wanted to, he could rip the fortune off and keep it, and I'd still have forty-nine more chances.

The night of the dance arrived. I put on beige leggings, a nude tank top, and a pair of white flats. Then I slid the finished cookie over my head. I looked in the mirror and marveled at my own creative talents. YOU WILL MEET A BEAUTIFUL WOMAN TONIGHT. I pulled the fortune out and let it roll back inside. *This is the best costume ever.*

I walked from my apartment to the subway wearing the fortune cookie. On the way there, I noticed people staring. A lot of people thought it was really funny, which made me smile. And so, with a spring in my step, I got on the N/R train, took it to Forty-second Street, and then switched to the 1 train heading uptown. That's when things got weird.

The minute I entered the car I heard a shrill voice. "*Oh, noooooooo!*" it said.

My costume wasn't exactly the easiest thing to maneuver in, but I managed to crane my neck and find the source of the noise (like everyone else on the semicrowded train). A black woman was sitting with two small boys, looking furious.

"*Oh,* noooooooo! No, no, no, no, noooooooooooooo!"

I was trying to figure out what was wrong, when the woman looked directly at me. "I got my children with me," she screamed. "*I got my children with me!*"

Is she talking to me? My peripheral vision was limited so I turned to my right and left. No one else was there. The woman moved on to making eye contact with the other passengers, trying to get their affirmation. "Can you believe—?" She pointed at me. Now there was no mistaking it, all of her aggression was directed at me.

"You should be ashamed." She shook her head slowly. "I got my children with me!"

Just then, the subway doors sprang open, Sixty-sixth Street, Lincoln Center. I ran out of the car, still totally confused. Walking up the steps, I tried to get back into my previous groove, but her anger was disconcerting. *I guess she had a bad experience with Chinese food,* I decided.

I crossed the street and walked through the front door of the Mormon temple. DANCE-GYM, THIRD FLOOR, a sign read. I walked over to the elevators and pushed the UP button. *Bing,* the doors opened. I was about to get in, when I just so happened to glance to my right—and into the full-length mirror.

"*Oh,* noooooooooooo." My jaw dropped open in horror. "No. No. No. No. No."

Something had happened to my costume. As I was walking, the center had folded in on itself—creating flesh-toned flaps. I did not look like a fortune cookie, I looked like a giant vagina. And you can't go to a *Mormon* dance dressed like a giant vagina.

I held my arms up at my chest in an attempt to cover up my indecency. *What do I do?* I had a moment of crisis. *Do I run? Do I stay? But "The One," he's supposed to be up there.*

And so, in one last desperate attempt to win that Mormon Man of My Dreams, I took my vagina off and hid it in the broom closet (which I guess is what you do every time you go to church). In just beige leggings and a nude tank top, I took the elevator up to the dance.

When the doors opened, I ran out and ducked behind the floral print couch. "Psst." I recognized a girl farther down the hall. "Pssst."

She turned around.

"Hey." I poked my head out. "Can you go find my sister, Tina, Tina Baker?"

The girl nodded her head and walked into the gym. A few minutes later Tina emerged dressed as a black cat. While we hadn't planned it, we'd both chosen to go as pussy.

"Tina," I whispered. She didn't hear me. "Tina!" This time I practically shouted. "Down here!"

"Elna?" She walked over to me, her face looking more and more alarmed the closer she got. "What happened to your fortune cookie costume?"

"I looked like a"—I could hardly finish the sentence—"a giant vagina."

"What?"

"My costume started to"—I made little gestures with my hands that demonstrated inward folding—"fold in on itself." My voice cracked. "I looked like a GIANT VAGINA!"

Tina started laughing. "Wait right here."

She came back a minute later with a poncho she'd stolen off of a friend. "Here, Brigham said you could borrow this."

"Thank you." I pulled it over my head and stood up. It came down just above my knees.

"Come on," Tina said. "You're missing the dance—it's fun this year."

We walked through the gym doors, moving long dangly orange streamers out of the way with our hands. And then there it was, the dance, preserved as if in a time capsule, the one consistent thing in this inconsistent world. "I Will Always Love You" by Whitney Houston was playing over the loudspeakers. A guy dressed as a bean stalk, or a green crayon, I wasn't sure which, immediately ran up to Tina and asked her to dance. She looked at me as if to ask for my permission.

Go ahead. I nodded.

I wasn't surprised when no one asked me to dance. The evening was far beyond "going according to plan." Instead of wallowing, I walked to the side of the room and leaned against the stage. From where I was standing I could see the entire room. A disco ball was hanging from the basketball hoop. It sent little dots of light across the congregation as it spun.

A thirty-eight-year-old man—still a virgin, still dressed in a duck costume—was busy doing the electric slide. It was an all-time low. Also, the irony was not lost on me: *I am a dirty cookie.* After all of my restraint, my vagina had finally made its public debut, but wrong crowd. *Wroooooong crowd.*

There's a trick to knowing when to leave the party and I wish I knew it. Walking back through the dangly orange streamers and out into the street, I didn't really know where I was headed but I figured, *You always have to go somewhere.*

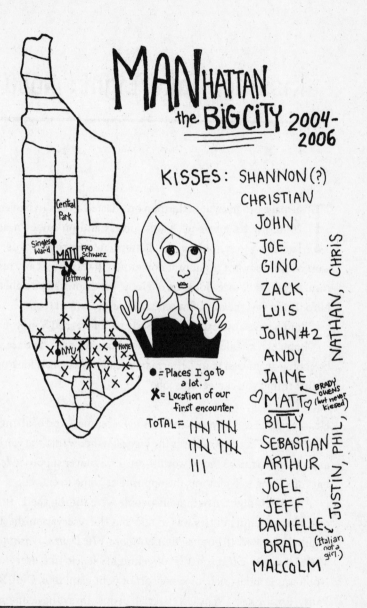

MAN HATTAN
the BIG CITY 2004-2006

KISSES: SHANNON (?)
CHRISTIAN
JOHN
JOE
GINO
ZACK
LUIS
JOHN #2
ANDY
JAIME
♡MATT← BRADY OWENS (but never kissed)
BILLY
SEBASTIAN
ARTHUR
JOEL
JEFF
DANIELLE
BRAD (Italian not a girl)
MALCOLM

NATHAN, CHRIS

JUSTIN, PHIL,

● = Places I go to a lot.
✗ = Location of our first encounter
TOTAL = ⌶⌶⌶⌶ ⌶⌶⌶⌶ ⌶⌶⌶⌶ ⌶⌶⌶⌶ |||

Central Park
Singles Ward
MATT
FAO Schwarz
Letterman
NYU
Home

Kissing, Take Eight: Nobu

The page program at Letterman only lasted a year. In November 2006, my time was up. I was jobless and on my own again. Luckily Vinny, one of the Letterman security guards, also worked the door at a restaurant downtown. It wasn't just any restaurant. It was the Tribeca location of Nobu, partly owned by Robert De Niro. Nobu was the most famous sushi restaurant in town.

"I don't have any restaurant experience," I warned Vinny.

"Bubbles," he said (this was his nickname for me), "I've seen you bouncing around in your Letterman sweater. If you can look pretty in that thing, you can get this job."

He was right. I was hired as a hostess in December. And of all my jobs in New York City, this one was the biggest window into the world, or at least a particular kind of world—one I was never supposed to be a part of. Going to Nobu was the opposite of going to church.

Any given night, five famous people were dining there. In fact, one of my opening duties was to take out the reservation sheet and highlight all the VIP guests. *Mandy Moore-VIP, Denzel Washington-VIP, Leonardo DiCaprio-VIP.* Weeknights it felt like everyone at Nobu was famous, rich, or some sort of politician. Bibi, Didi, Bobo, Pansy, Rock, Shack. Why is it that rich people always have inanimate object or baby names?

Weekends at Nobu were reserved for the tourists who'd heard the restaurant was the place to be and swarmed the entrance.

"Is there anyone famous here tonight?" they'd ask, leaning over the hostess table in hopes of getting a glimpse of a celebrity's name.

"Just you," we were instructed to say, before flashing a fake smile. In reality, by very virtue of asking the question, "Is anyone famous here tonight?" the asker had proved to us that they didn't deserve to know.

My time at Nobu taught me a lot about celebrities. For starters, there were several different kinds: the young people who asked for booths in the front so that everyone would have to pass by them, the old pros who'd lounge in corner booths, and the reluctant celebrities who'd ask to be hidden in the back room. No matter what they wanted, business stopped for them. And for the most part, they expected this. I used to think there was a system in the world. Like if things didn't work, it was because they were broken. But broken things were being fixed for celebrities all of the time. "Babe, could you be a doll and get us a table for ten in five minutes?" It was as if they needed to be treated like they were famous in order to believe it.

The remaining celebrities I mention will be assigned fake names. One incident in particular stands out. It involved a senator, a comedian, and a drug dealer; let's call them Harry S. Truman, Lenny Bruce, and Al Capone.

Al Capone was a Nobu regular. His ruse was that he managed a hedge fund, but really he was a major drug dealer who was constantly hooking up celebrities with coke, heroin, or ecstasy. Whenever he came into the restaurant (always without a reservation), we had to scramble to give him the best table. Helping him always made me feel uncomfortable. Like I was assisting the devil in some contractual way.

One night I was working the late shift. We had a large table at the front of the restaurant where Harry S. Truman was dining with his friends. The senator—young, handsome, and charming—was sitting next to his date, a Martha's Vineyard wealthy blonde. They were having a jolly time, making jokes and passing around saké, when Al Capone and Lenny Bruce walked in.

My first thought was, *What's someone cool like Lenny Bruce doing with slime like Al Capone?*

Just then the senator stood up. "Al, Lenny." He raised his arms to greet them.

"Harry," both Al and Lenny said. The senator walked over and the three hugged, fist-bumped, and buddy hand-slapped. They then proceeded to have a private conversation in front of the hostess podium and effectively in front of me.

"Meet my girlfriend," the senator said, calling the blonde over.

She twittered over to them in her tiny heels, short skirt, and designer top.

"Hi, I'm Valerie."

After she performed her duty, the guys continued catching up. Lenny Bruce and Al Capone were facing me. Valerie and the senator were facing them, which is how I noticed something they couldn't see. As he talked, calmly, politely, Harry S. Truman stuck his right hand up the blonde's skirt until he was fingering—practically fisting—her publicly. All the while, she smiled and nodded, like a petite puppet being controlled from underneath.

As I watched this—the senator, the blonde, Lenny, and Al—I was filled with a terrible feeling. Not just concerning me, but for the entire state of the world.

If the celebrities, politicians, and drug dealers are hanging together, I thought, *then the rest of us, well, the rest of us are properly screwed. We're being fingered in public and we're smiling like it's a normal, everyday thing.*

I swore I'd never go out with a customer. When you get to see behind the scenes, the VIP life gradually loses any appeal. But one night, a slow night, I think it was a Monday, I was working at Nobu Next Door when the private phone line rang.

"Thank you for calling Nobu Next Door, how may I help you?"

"I'd like to place an order to be picked up."

I took out the to-go form. "First name?"

"Warren."

"Phone number?" I continued.

"310-897-3993."

"Great, Warren, what would you like?"

"Shishito peppers."

"Uh huh."

"A vegetable roll."

"Uh huh."

"An order of the miso eggplant."

I waited for him to continue. When he didn't speak I was worried I'd lost the connection.

"Hello?" I said.

"I was waiting for you to say 'Uh huh.'" He used his higher register for the *Uh huh* so that it was clear he was mocking me.

"Uh huh," I repeated.

"And one eggplant special."

"Great. Your order will be ready in twenty minutes." As soon as I hung up the phone I realized I'd made a major mistake. We were out of eggplant. He'd ordered two different eggplant dishes, and neither could be made. I hesitated before calling back. Three-one-zero, his number; it meant only one thing: The caller was from L.A., the area code of entitlement.

"Hi Warren, it's Nobu Next Door calling. Unfortunately, we're all out of eggplant, so we're going to have to change your order."

"You're out of eggplant?"

"Uh huh," I said.

"I don't think so," he shot back. "How about this, *little lady*, I know there's a deli nearby, how about you run outside, get me some eggplant, and make my order as planned."

I knew not to talk back to customers and I knew how to handle myself in situations like this, but something about Warren made me act before thinking.

"How about this, *little mister*," I said. "How about you roll with the punches and we make a new order. How's that for a plan?"

There was a silence. If there'd been a boundary, I'd clearly just overstepped it.

"Do you know who you're talking to?"

"No," I calmly said.

"I'm friends with Nobu," he said.

"Nobu's very friendly," I answered.

Warren let out a laugh. And like that, with that line, he was suddenly my friend.

"What's your name?" he asked. "I like you."

"Elna," I said. "And your order minus the two eggplant dishes will be ready in twenty minutes."

"I'm coming down there now. I want to meet you."

"Take your time," I shot back. "Dillydally along the way." And with that I hung up the phone.

When the door to the restaurant swung open a few minutes later, I looked up and nearly died. Standing in front of me was an older actor I've loved my entire life, Warren Beatty. *What is Warren Beatty doing here?* My mouth dropped open.

I say Warren Beatty, but it wasn't really Warren Beatty. Again, I can't use the real actor's name because I'd get sued, plus I found out later that he was married and way older than I thought—sixty-seven. What I will tell you is that the person who walked in wasn't just an actor, he's a writer, too, and he's up there with Robert Redford, Paul

Newman, and Jack Nicholson in terms of classic sex appeal, age, and fame. Also, my all-time favorite screen kiss, one that I've watched over and over again, belongs to him.

"I'm here to pick up my order," he said.

Suddenly I made the connection, the to-go food, the asshole—it was Warren Beatty.

"Oh, great, yes, it'll be up in a moment—" I sounded flustered.

"You're beautiful," he interrupted.

"Excuse me?"

"I said to myself as I drove down here, no matter how ugly this hostess is I'm taking her out."

"Shoot for the moon," I offered.

"What time do you get off work?"

"Eleven."

"Meet me at B's at midnight, it's on West Twelfth Street."

I already knew the location. The bar is small and so exclusive that three men guard the entrance. It doesn't have a name either; people call it *B's*, short for bar. Of all the bars in New York City, it's probably the hardest to get into. If they say, "We're having a private party tonight," they really mean, *You're not hot enough.*

The busboy walked up with a bag of to-go food. I passed it to Warren. "See you at midnight," I whispered.

I wasn't sure what I was doing but I had to follow this one through. There were so many things I wanted to ask Warren Beatty. And so, the minute work ended I took a cab home and reenacted the makeover scene from every ugly duckling teen movie. Bye-bye work shirt, hello short skirt and heels. *Adios* bushy eyebrows, hello foundation and lip gloss.

By the time I got to B's it was already twelve thirty. As I approached the hidden entrance, I noticed that two blondes who fit all the right measurements were trying to talk their way in.

"It's closed for a private party," one of the doormen said. Getting in was going to be harder than I thought.

The girls tried anything from "Pretty pleeeease" to "It's my birthday" to "We came in from out of town and it's our one night in the city!" (followed by the pee-pee dance). I waited a few feet down the block for them to finish their appeal. My legs were shivering but I figured if I approached too soon, I'd get the same "We're closed" response for the sheer sake of consistency.

Just as I was about to turn around, one of the doormen looked up and noticed me standing there. "Good to see you again." He nodded in my direction. "They're waiting downstairs."

"Thanks." I walked past the two girls and three men, down the five steps, and into the bar. I'd never seen the doorman before in my life. But I know the game—by watching the Nobu clientele I'd learned how to mimic the small nuances of exclusivity. There's only one problem: If you can make it all the way inside, you're in a room full of people who've mastered the same skill—which doesn't exactly make for depth or good conversation. Which is why I only go to places like this for Warren Beatty.

When I walked inside I noticed him immediately. He was sitting with his elbows on the bar and his head was bent down over a drink. He reminded me of a cowboy.

I walked up to him. "Hi," I said.

"You made it."

So began our conversation. And by conversation I mean a real, legitimate, smart-people conversation. I didn't act like a fan or a hostess. We talked about books, book-binding, pamphlets, brochures, paper. And it was great. He took me seriously, and as the conversation led from one interesting topic to the next, I looked around me at the hipsters and celebrity kids. It felt great to be in a room I typically classified as shallow and to swim deep.

"I used to want to be an actor, now I think I want to write," I began. "But I can't seem to do it. Was your first book a challenge?"

This is where the conversation turned. Warren Beatty didn't answer; instead he put both of his hands on my hips and pulled me into his crotch so that he had his legs pressed against my sides. My eyes grew big. The oldest man I'd been out with prior to this was thirty-five. And while I didn't know Warren's real age, he looked to be at least fifty-five, older than my father.

"Let me buy you a drink," Warren said.

I thought about it for a second. In the six years I'd lived in New York City I hadn't touched alcohol once.

"I don't drink."

"Oh, come on," Warren Beatty said. "I'm getting one."

"No, thank you."

"Are you sure?" He looked at me as though not getting a drink would personally offend him.

Before I realized it I was saying, "Oh, why not?" and shrugging my shoulders with a smile.

"What would you like?" he stroked my hand.

I don't know the first thing about drink names. *Sex on the Rocks? Jack Frost? Pink-Eye?*

"You pick," I squeaked.

"I'll have a whiskey," he ordered from the bartender, "and a sweet wine."

The sweet wine was for me. The bartender uncorked a bottle and set an empty long-stemmed glass in front of me. I picked up the glass. Both the bartender and Warren Beatty looked at me.

"I thought you wanted a drink?" Warren said.

Whoops. I set the glass back down. *Drinking 101: Let the bartender fill your drink first.*

Take two, I waited for the bartender to finish pouring, held the glass up to my mouth, sniffed it, because I'd seen people do that at Nobu, and took a sip. *Hmmm, not bad,* I thought, trying to hold back all the novice reactions my face wanted to make, including a slight choke when I got to the strong aftertaste.

"You like Yeats?" Warren resumed our conversation.

"Yes."

"Have you been to Ireland?"

"No."

"I could take you there sometime."

"If I could count the number of guys at bars who have promised me that . . ." I stopped short. His hand was moving in little circles on the small of my back. *Oh, my gosh,* my legs went weak . . . *Warren Beatty knows how to touch a woman.* I mean it. It was the perfect amount of pressure, any softer would've been too soft, any harder would've hurt.

I relaxed into him. Just as I did this, I felt something else . . . his other hand going up my skirt. *Whoa there.* I put my free hand over his, and moved it down to my knee. *Should I tell him I'm Mormon?* I looked at my glass of wine. *Too late for that,* I decided. Besides I knew what would happen if I did. I've only been on one date with a celebrity before. It was with an eccentric French director that I met at an art opening. When I told him I was Mormon the first thing he said was, "Can you have ze sex?"

"No," I answered.

"No sex?" He looked at me in disbelief. "Well if you can't have ze sex, what can you do?"

For the sake of simplicity I took my left arm and lined it up just under my collarbones. "Nothing below here," I said. I took my right arm and lined it up to my knees. "Nothing above here."

"What about your armpit?" he asked. "Can your boyfriend do anything he wants to your armpit?"

I thought about it. Armpits seemed pretty harmless. "Yeah," I said optimistically. "My boyfriend can do anything he wants to my armpit."

"This is good," the Frenchman said. "He can stick his penis in and out of your armpit, and if you grow hair there it is almost like *vagine.*"

Is it too late to change my answer? I wondered, pulling a cardigan over my bare shoulders and covering any hint of an invitation.

I wasn't about to make the same mistake with Warren Beatty, not if I wanted him to keep paying attention to me. So I kept my mouth shut. But a moment later Warren's hand was going up my skirt again and no amount of pushing it down seemed to work. I had to think of another reason that this was not okay.

"Look," I faced him. "A year ago a big shot senator came into Nobu with this young blonde. He didn't think anyone could see, but I accidentally caught him publicly fingering her. I swore I would never be that girl. Okay?" I nodded my head at him, to emphasize I meant what I was saying. A simple *no* should've been enough. Instead, it was as though I were saying, *Look, there's this thing about me, I know it's "crazy" but it's just this issue of mine, I don't let men finger me in public, please love me anyway?*

"I understand." Warren took his hand off my thigh and moved his attention to my face, kissing my neck and then my ear. He was about to kiss my mouth when I looked around the crowded bar and tensed up.

"What's the matter?" he asked.

"There are a lot of people here," I answered.

He shifted in his stool and surveyed the bar. "These people?" he asked. "You think these people can see us?"

"Yes," I answered.

"These are the most self-absorbed people in the world. They can only see themselves."

This was the perfect thing to say, mostly because it was true. Several people appeared to be looking in our direction, but if you really tried to pinpoint it, they weren't looking at anyone, or anything.

"You're right." I laughed. And with that, the "hump" that I like to refer to as "my propriety" went right out the window. I started full-on making out with Warren Beatty, right there, in front of everyone. And the line I said earlier about the pressure on the back and the any softer any harder thing, it applied to his tongue, too. I could hardly process it. I was, right smack in the center of the movie kiss, waving my wineglass like a prop. It was perfect, until . . . his hand started to inch its way back up my skirt.

A voice in my head spoke up. *Is this the way things are supposed to be?* We can call it a conscience, or perhaps it's just fear, but either way, it was pretty loud. *Is this what your life is going to be now? Do you gradually put a check mark next to all the things you said you'd never do? And what about the glass of wine?* I felt the thin stem of it with my fingers. *Does this man get to redefine you just because he's famous?*

I stopped kissing him. "Sorry." I set down my wine and moved his hand to my butt, a consolation prize, then I picked up where we'd left off. Because whatever, I'm not a saint, latter-day or otherwise. I'm a woman. And when things feel good, they feel really good. Besides, I already knew what I was going to do: leave. But I figured, *You might as well binge before you purge.* I spent the next fifteen minutes kissing him and trying to get away with as much as I could. When we came up for air for a fourth time, I broke away. "I have to go now," I said.

"Come home with me," he said.

"That's okay," I answered. "I don't go home with *men*." My excuse sounded slightly off. *Monkeys, yes,* I almost added, *but men, no.*

"How do you know this situation will ever present itself again?" Warren asked me.

I took it in. Just like I get the subtle nuances of exclusivity, I understand the subtle nuances of star power. *How often do you get to sleep with Warren Beatty?* was his real question.

"I don't," I said. "In fact, the situation probably won't present itself again. But ultimately when I wake up in the morning I wake up with myself, and I have to be happy with the decisions I've made."

He made a face at me. *That's crazy talk,* his eyes said.

"It was nice to meet you." I stood up to leave.

"Let me walk you out."

It seemed harmless enough. Except, while walking across the cobblestone street outside, "Let me walk you out" turned into "Let's at least share a cab."

While my intuition told me that if I got in the cab he'd try something more, I wasn't ready to close the door on Warren Beatty. Because I knew once I did, he'd go home and I'd go home and we'd never see each other again. *It'll be fine. I can call the shots,* I decided as Warren opened the door to the cab, *plus it's environmentally conscious to carpool.*

I hate my own ability to rationalize. Being alone in a taxi with Warren Beatty was like being in a cage. His hands were all over me. And I liked it, and I didn't, and I did. And I didn't. And just before it escalated to a point of any real major religious mistakes, we reached my apartment.

"Good night." I kissed his cheek, jumped out of the cab, and shut the door behind me. I was almost to my apartment when it occurred to me, *I didn't hear the cab door slam.* I stopped. A second later, the door shut softly and the cab drove away. I turned around slowly. Standing on my curb directly across from me was Warren Beatty.

For a second it seemed totally unreal. *I can't shake Warren Beatty?*

"Can I come in with you?" he asked.

"No," I answered. "I don't bring guys home with me."

"Oh, come on." He gestured toward my street, Avenue A at three A.M. on a Saturday. Several drunk people were stumbling by. "These aren't exactly the Elizabethan times."

"You're not going to lure me in with Shakespearean peer pressure," I shot back. I expected him to at least laugh. Instead, he paused, his forehead wrinkled, and it looked like he was trying to remember something.

"Please?"

I couldn't help it. I started laughing out loud. It wasn't the word *please,* it was the way he said it, like he was trying to remember it. *What's the magic word again? Oh, yeah: please.*

"Did you hear how you just said that?" I stopped him. "It was too good. You do not need to come home with me," I stressed. "You need to go back to your place and write that down, so that some day a character of yours says please and when he says it, he says it just like that."

"Just let me come inside." He laughed.

"Sorry." I shifted my weight from hip to hip and made an apologetic face.

"You must realize how cute you are?"

Hearing those words come from him, it was like being hit by a spotlight. *That's it,* I thought. *That's the reason I raced to the bar from Nobu. It's why I drank a glass of wine, and why I did one too many things. I wanted to know that I was pretty and hearing a famous man say it was more meaningful.*

"Good night," I said, this time for real.

"Oh, come on." He blocked the door. "I just want to see you in your underwear."

"Sorry." I turned my key in the lock.

Warren leaned in, his face almost touching mine. "Just show me your tits," he whispered.

"No, thank you." I pushed the door open and ran into the vestibule of my building.

"Good night." I waved as I opened the second glass door. My apartment is the first door, just after the entrance. I took a single step and turned to open it. While I fumbled through my keys, I could still see Warren through the glass. I smiled as cute as could be, waved a final good-bye, and opened my door. In the privacy of my own apartment, I flipped on the lights and started doing the icky dance, shaking my fingers and gagging. It was then that it occurred to me, *My window faces the street, the lights are on, the curtain is open.* I turned. Warren Beatty was standing outside my window, looking genuinely concerned. Robotically, I put my hands at my sides, stomped across the room to the bathroom, and closed the door.

I'm Not the Kind
of Girl Who . . .

Everyone gains weight back, at least a little of it. I knew this. I'd watched it happen to other people. But that wasn't going to be me. I was a success story.

Only, when I started working at Nobu I was around food for the first time in four years. Not just customers' food, they served the staff a family meal at midnight. It didn't consist of high-end sushi. They'd set out troughs of pasta or stew, cheap food that fed dozens of employees. Oprah says, "Don't eat after nine." Pork roast at one A.M. was hardly on my maintenance diet. Within two months, I gained back fifteen pounds.

After I lost weight, Dr. Levin told me, "If you gain back five pounds, don't stress about it, but if you ever gain more than ten come see me and we'll put you back on the program."

Only, I didn't want to go to back on the program. Dr. Levin had also told me I was his favorite patient, a true success story, and I thought it'd be embarrassing to return. And so, determined to undo the Nobu fifteen, I decided to do something stupid: I looked on the Internet for the medication I'd taken during my diet (I couldn't get these pills from Dr. Levin anymore because he only prescribed them to the obese). To my surprise, I found a Web site where, if I lied about my weight, I could purchase it. I wrote two hundred fifty pounds, ordered two bottles of phentermine, and clicked on express delivery.

When the pills arrived I knelt down and thanked them for their very existence. I took three a day and just like that, my appetite was gone. I didn't need family meal. Hell, I didn't need any meals. I was back on my diet, full force. And it was so nice to have some momentum again that I followed it all the way through. I woke up early and went running, I gulped down a gallon of water each morning, and I ate only steamed vegetables. Only this time there was one major difference: I didn't need to lose eighty pounds. One hundred sixty pounds was technically already in the weight range for my height, only I'd gotten down to one forty-five and I preferred being there.

I love to apply myself. Within two weeks I lost fifteen pounds. As I shed this weight I noticed that I was getting more compliments and more attention. *Why not lose another five?* This way, when I went off the medication, I'd have a safety net.

A week later, I was getting ready to go to my friend Ptolemy's birthday when, at the last minute, I decided to make him a card. What was initially supposed to be a simple birthday card became a cupcake card with thirty-one hot glue–gunned candles and a pop-out sign. Only the more I worked on it, the more I felt the need to perfect it. I colored each candle in obsessively. By the time the card was finished, it was 1 A.M. I ran out the door, but got to the party just as everyone was leaving.

"I'm so sorry," I tried to explain, "I was making your card and lost track of time."

"How long did this take you?" Ptolemy asked, opening my masterpiece.

I counted it out in my head. "Six hours . . ." I said.

When I woke up the follow morning I felt extremely tired, and a little bit dizzy. I walked into the bathroom, peed, stood up, and blacked out. When I came to a few minutes later, I was lying on the tile floor. The towel rack had mysteriously been ripped off the wall and I was surrounded by dusty bits of plaster.

What happened? I stood up cautiously and looked at the place where I'd landed. In my cramped New York bathroom it was a wonder I hadn't hit my head on anything. I took a few steps, nothing was broken. I was just a little sore.

Why is Tina always out of town when I actually need her? I thought, opening the bathroom door. I took three steps into our living room when suddenly it happened again, only this time I did hit my head, on the small side table next to our couch. When I woke up I was lying on the living room floor, my head throbbing. I reviewed my symptoms: I was passing out, and I was exhausted.

Oh, no. I immediately knew what was wrong with me: I'd been kissing a lot of boys lately. *I have mono!*

I called Alison, a former Letterman page and one of my closest girlfriends. I explained what was happening and asked her if she'd take me to the hospital. I also called my bishop's counselor, Brother Wagner, who's the president of Saint Vincent's Hospital. When we got to the hospital, he was waiting out front with a wheelchair. (This is one of the things I love most about Mormons. I make fun of my church, I roll my eyes at the culture, but whenever I'm in a crisis my Mormon friends are the first people on the scene.)

Brother Wagner took my blood pressure and immediately put me on an IV.

"I'm pretty sure it's just mono," I confessed to him awkwardly, like it was an STD.

"Does your throat hurt?"

"No."

He touched my neck. "And your glands don't feel swollen?"

"No. But I've kissed a lot of people this month, and last month. Well, and the month before that, too."

"I'm going to take your blood and run some tests," he said, unfazed.

A nurse wheeled me into a private room and Alison, who had to go back to work, said good-bye. I was alone when Brother Wagner returned with the prognosis a few hours later.

"Other than exhaustion you don't have any of the symptoms of mono," he began. "But we want to keep you here overnight because your blood pressure is extremely low. In fact, if it were any lower, you'd be dead."

"*Why?* What's wrong with me?"

He opened my chart. "Who prescribed phentermine to you?"

I bit my lip. I'd almost left the "Are you taking any medication?" question blank for fear it'd incriminate me.

"I got it off the Internet," I answered.

"Do you have any of these pills on you?"

"Yes." I pointed to my purse. Brother Wagner handed it to me. I opened it and took out a bottle.

"You shouldn't be taking this," he said, reading the label.

"But I took it before and this didn't happen."

"When?"

"Three years ago when I went on a diet."

"Do you know what phentermine is?"

"No."

"It's an amphetamine."

"*Ampheta* what?"

"An amphetamine," he explained. "It's half of the drug fen-phen, which got pulled from the market when a number of people using it went into cardiac arrest. It's basically a derivative of speed."

"*What?*" My voice trailed off as my diet, start to finish, flashed before my eyes. To me it was an out of body experience—Christ was dwelling inside me. I was waking up early, jogging incessantly, my appetite was gone, and I had an obsessive need to clean: All because of God. Only this change in my behavior hadn't started the night I got back from Wookey and prayed for His grace. These symptoms began two weeks later when I first took phentermine. *My BIG miracle,* I realized, *the closest thing I had to evidence of God's existence, was actually just me—ON SPEED!*

I slept for the rest of the day. At 6 P.M., just before visiting hours were over, my best friend Kevin came for a surprise visit. Kevin is my other half. He's eccentric, he has wild blond hair that sits in a poof on the top of his head and a very distinct way of dressing inspired by Diane Keaton that involves color and layering.

He tiptoed into my hospital room, looking like an evil villain in dark sunglasses, a teal tuxedo shirt, checkered suit coat, tight black pants, and pointy shoes. I'd never been happier to see anyone in my entire life.

"Kevin!"

He took one look at me. "Are you insane?" he said.

"It's nice to see you, too."

"You look like you've just been exorcised."

"I feel like shit."

Kevin sat in a plastic folding chair and took out a cigarette.

"You can't smoke in here," I told him. "And besides, it'll kill you."

He put the cigarette back in his pocket and glared at me. *You're one to talk.* Kevin's the only person who knew about the diet pills. I took them before each meal and every time I did he lunged at the pill bottle, screaming, "*Intervention!*"

"I know what you're thinking," I began. "But it was an honest mistake. I just went too far too fast. I'm not the kind of girl who diets her way into a hospital."

"Where exactly do you think you are right now?" Kevin asked.

Touché. I didn't say anything. I didn't have to. Kevin's the type of person you can be completely honest with, no judgment. Which is why he is so central to my life. I tell him all the things I can't tell my family.

"I come bearing gifts." He opened his bag and took out a Kingsley Amis book, a Hello Kitty drawing pad, and a pack of markers.

"I love you," I said.

A nurse came in a few minutes later to tell us that visiting hours were up. Kevin made a face, and said farewell. I felt his absence immediately. The room was devoid of all color. And so, even though I don't like it, I turned on the television to pass the time. I only got two stations, ESPN and VH1. I chose the latter; *Plastic Surgery Obsession* was playing, a "documentary" with sassy comments and clips of the *craziest* plastic surgery moments of all time. I watched the entire show.

As the countdown got closer to the *Number One Craziest Moment*, I felt sick. Not because I was in a hospital, but because of all of it: the obsession with beauty, the desire to look young, to cheat death, and to weigh nothing. Coupled with the belief that self-worth, character, and individuality are qualities that we can buy; an obsession that I, in spite of everything, still feed into. I lifted my head off my pillow and looked down at myself.

My hospital gown had tiny sheep on it, and there was a thick IV coming out of my arm. *I can't believe I did this to myself.*

Just then, Jocelyn Wildenstein's face flashed onto the television screen—half-woman, half-pussycat meets bottom of tractor. *At the very least,* I consoled myself, *I'll never get plastic surgery.*

AGE 25

What I believe:

- There are no atheists in my fox-hole. (bad joke)
- The less you say you know—the better.

On the fence:

- The church is true.

- God and Jesus live!

- I am here to be tested.

- Sex before marriage is the second worst sin.

- I am supposed to be a missionary.

- Joseph Smith was a prophet.

- The Book of Mormon is true.

- There is a man out there specifically for me.
- I should strive to live a life free of sin.

What I used to believe:

- My diet was a miracle!

- No drugs for me.

- That I have my own best interests at heart.

- God answers our prayers.

- If a man really loves you he'll wait.

- If you do what's right, God will bless you.

- Masturbation is EVIL.
(but I don't want to talk about it) OKAY.

- I hope I can find him.

Point of No Return

No man can serve two masters for either he will love the one or hate the other, or so the Bible says. I've always tried to love the world and church equally. But it was like riding two horses. I had one foot on the back of each. As long as these horses were close together, I could continue with my journey. But the more that time passed, the farther apart these horses got. I wasn't riding either one well, and since my legs were in the splits and my eyes were bulging—the journey wasn't all that enjoyable.

It wasn't moving to New York, losing weight, meeting Matt, or working at Nobu that put me into contact with the "things of this world," it was everything. One of the positive aspects of the breakup was that I started going after my creative dreams again. I did this partly because I'd given up performing after FAO Schwarz and I missed it. And I did it partly for Matt. He loved hearing me tell him stories, and I secretly wanted him to see a flyer for one of my shows on the street, and I wanted him to come and fall in love all over again. And so, after a two-year hiatus from writing and performing, I got back onstage and started trying to do stand-up. As a result, my life became even more disjointed. I'd go from hearing dick jokes to hearing church sermons, and then back to dick jokes again.

One Sunday, when the bishop walked up to the podium to begin our sacrament meeting, I accidentally clapped my hands and made a loud *Woo!* Everyone turned around to glare at me. I slunk down in my seat. I wasn't trying to make a commotion, I'd just forgotten which world I was in.

If I wasn't performing comedy, I was kissing men I didn't really like to prove that I still had it. Which I did, down to an art. I'd begin with an audacious intro, followed by a funny anecdote. We'd dance, and then make out until it got to a nipple, or an unzip. *STOP!* I'd cut things short, and run off feeling validated but empty.

My hospitalization for accidental drug abuse was the final straw. The drug abuse part wasn't what upset me. It was the revelation that my diet was aided by speed. It caused me to lose the remainder of my faith. For years the idea that my diet was a miracle had sustained me. In fact, it was the main reason I couldn't have sex with Matt. I thought, *He only wants to see me naked because I lost weight and I look more attractive now. And this only happened because I prayed and asked God for a miracle. Misusing my new body would be like taking a gift from God and defiling it.*

And they say religion makes people crazy?

I was a wreck. I would sit in church every Sunday and think *I gave up an incredible person for stale bread and an uncomfortable pew.*

I'd wanted Matt to get an answer from God for himself, but I also needed him to get one *for me.* An atheist believing in God was like scientific evidence of His existence. And if God was real, my religion was worth practicing.

It wasn't just a breakup. It was an existential crisis.

In spite of Matt's prayer, I still believed that God would answer me if only I'd ask. That's how Joseph Smith founded the Mormon religion. He was trying to decide which church to join when he read a passage in the Bible that said, "If any of ye lack wisdom, let him ask of God, who giveth to all men liberally and upbraideth not." He followed this advice, prayed, and started a faith.

I needed wisdom. I needed to know what to do once and for all. And so I decided to follow the example of my father and do what he did when he was nineteen, driving through the desert on his way to serve a mission. I would ask God for a point of no return. If I got one, I'd be Mormon. If I didn't, my religion and I could go our separate ways and I wouldn't feel guilty. I've been seeking this my entire life— an out that didn't go against my conscience.

Not everyone needs this. In fact, most of my friends who were raised religious walked away from their churches without difficulty. "It just wasn't for me," they decided. If you're wondering why it's so impossible for me to leave, it's because of something Jesus said: "If you do my will you will know it is of me or of Him who sent me." Which basically means, if you follow my teachings you will gain faith that they are true. In spite of my doubt, I practiced my religion and up until this point every choice that I made proved to be the right decision. Doing what I was supposed to do and then feeling good about it is what helped me to sustain my faith. It was my anchor, my ballast. Now I wasn't so sure. I'd let go of Matt, and instead of a pay-off, I got misery.

Is it right to suppress my sexuality? Or do religious choices just make me happy because I was trained to feel this way? I wondered. *Is there a God up there that's trying to remind me that I am like him, a spiritual being living in a physical moment? Or am I merely a physical being that's going to live, die, and then cease to exist? Will my choices on earth really help me progress in heaven? Or is heaven a made-up place, and am I just making sacrifices for an imaginary reason?*

And so, on a cold afternoon in October, after wrestling with my thoughts for the millionth time, I locked myself in a classroom on the third floor of the chapel. With the intention of making up my mind once and for all, I knelt down, folded my arms, and said the following:

Dear Heavenly Father,

Hi. I'm kneeling on an ugly beige carpet, next to some cheap metal folding chairs in this church classroom. I wish I were on top of a mountain, or in the middle of the desert or on the high seas, so that I could ask you this question and get an answer in a more scenic location. But I live in New York City, and there is nowhere else that I can think to go where it's this quiet. So I'm here, in this dumpy room, asking for my point of no return.

God, I want to know what to do with my life and I need you to answer me. Please give me a spiritual experience that'll anchor me. Give me something that for the rest of my life I can look back on and say, "When I was twenty-three I had a moment—and I've never looked back since." I will walk in any direction you tell me, but please God I need a direction. . . .

I say these things in the name of Jesus Christ, Amen.

That was it; my prayer. I said *Amen*, kept my eyes shut as tightly as possible, and waited. At first all I could hear was my own voice in my head: *What if I don't hear anything? Or what if I do—how can I be sure it isn't just me?* I'm not sure how long it was that I sat there wondering if I'd get an answer. But after a few minutes something happened. I felt a warm feeling in the center of my chest and I was overcome by a certain familiar stillness, a peace I'd almost forgotten.

"And after the wind an earthquake; but the Lord was not in the earthquake. And after the earthquake a fire; *but* the Lord *was* not in the fire: and after the fire a still small voice."

Tell me what to do, I asked the voice to direct me. What followed was a series of questions.

"Is everything you want in life available to you at Nobu?"

No, I almost laughed.

"Is everything you want in life available to you when you're on stage performing?"

I thought about it. *No,* I answered.

"Is everything you want in life available to you within your family?"

Yes.

"Is everything you want in life available to you within you?"

Yes.

"Is everything you want in life available to you within this church?"

I hesitated—there it was the mother of all questions.

Yes, I answered.

The minute I said this, I knew that it was true. Maybe not for the rest of the world, but for me, my church is true for me. *Then why do I keep fighting it? God, I want to give in.* As I said these words I felt the sensation of letting something go, a physical release, a surrender. This was followed by a tremendously good feeling. I tried to place it: It was like being in love, only bigger, more secure. It was this feeling that'd lead me to have faith in the first place. And I realized I hadn't just felt this way when I was on speed or during pivotal spiritual moments. It was something I'd been experiencing all along—as long as I had faith and acted on it, God was with me.

And I guess it isn't something you notice, until it's gone and it comes back—but I felt at peace with God and myself once more. And this feeling, it trumps all the other feelings—nothing I've ever tried has been able to replace it: not a trip to the spa, not cynicism, not becoming pretty, not celebrities, not attention from men, not even love.

It wasn't a big answer. God didn't appear to me in a vision but it was enough to keep me going, at least for another year.

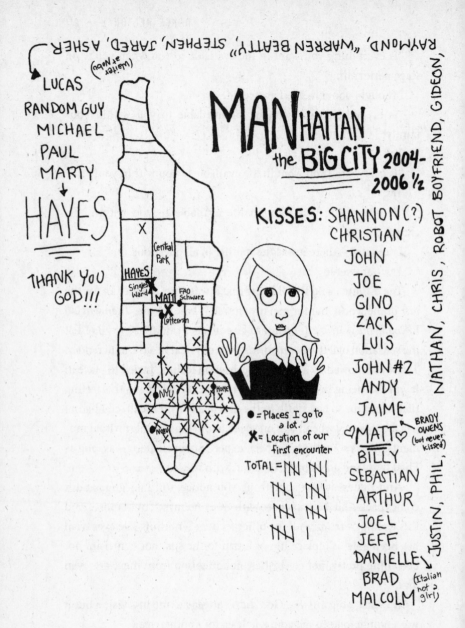

I Like Your Orange Notebook

A week after my prayer, I was sitting in church when I noticed an attractive guy sitting across from me in the center pew. *He's hot,* I thought, *for a Mormon,* and by this I mean he wasn't wearing pleated chinos, and his hair was longer than the standard Mormon missionary cut. He was nondenominationally cute. He looked like the guy from the film *Never Been Kissed,* only shorter.

I spent the rest of the service figuring out how to introduce myself to him without being too obvious. Only my subtle approach was thrown off kilter when the service ended and he stood up and walked out of the chapel.

Oh, no. This had happened once before. *The attractive guy in church incident of 2004.* I'd noticed an equally cute guy in sacrament meeting two years earlier. I'd spent the entire hour planning out our future together. The speaker gave the closing prayer, I opened my eyes and he was gone, never to be seen again, possibly a figment of my imagination.

I couldn't let this happen again—I jumped out of my seat and bolted for the door.

Hot guy . . . hot guy . . . hot guy? I scanned the lobby for any sign of him. It was too late, he was gone.

No! Why, God? Why? I was about to break into a desperate fit of single virgin rage, when the attractive guy stepped out of the bathroom. He looked at me. I looked at him. We really had no reason to talk to each other. But since when does that stop me? I took a step forward, and gestured to the notebook in his hand. "I like your orange notebook," I said, the semiretarded schoolgirl all over again.

And that was it, the start of Hayes and Elna. It was literally the beginning I'd joked about not wanting. *I want to meet the love of my life in a magical way,* I told a crowd of people at a comedy club. *I'm walking across the Brooklyn Bridge, he's coming from the other direction, we run into each other in the middle. "Oh, it's you!" we'll both say.* I don't want to meet him at church! *To tell my kids a love story that begins, "We met in the lobby. I was drinking from the tall water fountain, he bent down to use the shorter one, and when he turned the knob, my water decreased!"*

Regardless of how we met, Hayes was the first Mormon I ever dated, a fact that surprised him, since he'd only dated within the church.

"You've honestly never dated another Mormon?" he asked me.

"Nope."

"Why not?"

"There aren't that many Mormons in New York," I said. "Plus, my mom says every time I meet a guy at church I subconsciously sabotage it. I'll probably try and do that with you." I added, "Don't let me."

Hayes told me later that this was how he knew that I liked him. By our fifth date we were already "going together." We saw each other almost every day. It was my first real relationship. And by "real" I mean consistent, mutual. Within a week we had a routine. I'd call him at midnight as I was leaving work. He'd talk to me during my cab ride home, I'd talk to him as I was getting ready for bed, we'd tuck each other in.

We'd been dating for a month when Hayes was asked to give a

talk in church for Mother's Day. He stood in front of the entire congregation and said that he loved his mother, and that the role of the men in the church was to find women to honor as much as they honored their mothers. His goodness charmed me. *Who knew someone talking Mormon could turn me on?*

Perhaps it was the fact that every woman in church was watching, but when Hayes finished speaking and sat down next to me, I rested my head on his shoulder—the church equivalent of peeing on your territory. Sitting there, our fingers interlaced, I felt different than I'd ever felt before. The only word to describe it is docile. For the first time in my life I felt legitimately docile. The kind of happy where you can't tell if a woman is actually happy or on prescription drugs. Either way, I was high.

My first round of sabotage started the very next night at work. Hayes stopped by Nobu to surprise me. My boss thought it was so sweet that he let me take a break. Instead of going outside, I paraded Hayes around the restaurant. *I have a boyfriend!* I introduced him to all the waiters and hostesses and then walked him outside and kissed him good-bye.

When I got back inside everyone was waiting at the podium for me. "What do you think of him?" I asked excitedly.

No one answered. Instead, they all looked at me like I had something in my teeth but no one wanted to tell me about it.

"He's sweet," one girl finally said.

"He's cute, too," another hostess interjected.

"What did you think?" I asked Neil, a waiter.

He shifted his weight from one foot to the other. "I should go check on my table. . . ."

"What's wrong?" I persisted.

"It's nothing," he said.

"No, what is it?"

"I hate to be the one to say this . . . ," he began, "but I think your boyfriend is gay."

"What makes you think that?"

"I don't know, I have really good gaydar. . . . Plus, he's a total fag."

"He can't be gay." I looked at the group earnestly. "He's Mormon."

All five people standing at the podium avoided eye contact by looking up or to the side.

"*Max.*" I stopped a waiter passing by. "You didn't think my boyfriend was gay did you?"

"I already made a joke to the entire kitchen about it." He shrugged.

The thing with restaurant talk is you're not supposed to take it to heart. Put thirty overly qualified people in a room and make them do work that's beneath their real talents, and they'll find ways to cope with it. The way we coped with it was by "taking the piss." It was our routine. A customer would walk in wearing a pair of Tommy Hilfiger khaki shorts with lobsters embroidered all over them. While this customer checked in, the hostesses would give one another disapproving looks. *Wait for it, wait for it,* I could practically count it out in my head. Once the customer was five steps out of earshot a hostess would begin, "Were those crabs? What should I wear to Nobu tonight? Oh, yeah, my STD shorts."

I tried not to take part, but sometimes you'd see something too good to resist. I called this bad habit "Did you see . . ." because that's usually how the sentence began. "*Did you see* the she-man?" or "*Did you see* the hair plugs on table five?" "*Did you see* Elna's homo boyfriend?" was most likely spread around the restaurant before I even began our tour. Karma's a bitch.

If I were smart, I would've dropped it. Only, I'm not smart. Plus the observation wasn't unfounded. *Hayes does have a certain way of walking,* I thought. *His voice is a little higher than most guys'. He takes care in how he dresses, and his best friend is a guy named Marcus and they like to surf and afterward they massage each other.* My face went pale. *Oh, my gosh, I'm dating a homosexual.* I downward spiraled from there. *Of course, the only Mormon guy I've ever clicked with, of course he has to be gay.*

Even though we had a routine, I didn't call Hayes during my cab ride home. "Too tired to talk," I texted him. "I'll call you tomorrow."

"K. Want 2 meet 4 lunch tmrw?!?" he texted back.

Even his texts seemed gay.

I couldn't sleep that night. *So what if he's gay?* I overanalyzed. *I have nothing against that. But if he's gay he should just accept it and be who he is. I don't want to be the wife and eventually produce the kids that make him straight out of duty and obligation. I deserve to be with someone who is genuinely attracted to me.* Around three in the morning I stopped overthinking, got down on my knees, and said a prayer.

"Heavenly Father," I began, "is Hayes gay? It's okay if he is, but I can't be with him. Please, just tell me if he's gay?"

A calmness came over me and I felt an answer to my prayer. "Just drop it."

You see, I thought as I crawled back into bed. *Everything is perfectly fine. You're finally dating a Mormon, he likes you, quit trying to ruin it.*

I tried to preserve this sense of calm, but the next morning, I was a mess all over again. Late for lunch, I pulled a shirt over my head and accidentally hit my hand against the closet door. It left a small scratch. *Damnit.* I ran out the door.

It was the first thing Hayes noticed. We were waiting in line for our to-go food when he took my hand in his and said, "That wasn't there yesterday."

"I just did it."

"I'm sorry." He kissed it better. As he did this, I leaned my head against his back. *Why?* I made a pained expression. *Why can't I just be happy with someone this good, why do I have to doubt everything? Surrender.*

We found an open table overlooking the park. It was sunny outside, the fountain was on, and happy couples were lounging in the grass. I wanted to be like them, happy, merry, *gay*, but it was like everything had been turned on its head. I looked at Hayes; he was sitting forward in his seat, his legs were crossed, and his wrists looked loose, dangly.

"How's your finger?" he began. The way he emphasized the *s* on "How's" immediately caught my ear. *Does Hayes have a lisp?*

"It's fine."

"How'd you hurt it?"

"In the closet . . ." I stopped midway, my face frozen with terror. "*I mean, on the closet.*"

"Are you okay?" Hayes asked me.

Don't do it, don't do it. I tried to stop myself.

"Are you gay?"

"What?" he looked hurt, startled, like I'd thrown water in his face while simultaneously punching him.

I wanted to backtrack, to undo what I'd just said, but also, I wanted to know.

"It's okay if you are." I cleared my throat. "I just can't be the woman you use to avoid it."

He was silent for a full minute.

"First off," he began, speaking slowly and clearly. "I don't mean to sound cocky, but I'm used to the women I date being really into me, and not, well, not thinking I'm gay. And second, in case you actually need to know this, no, I'm not gay. I've never been attracted to a man, I've never had a dream about a man." He shuddered as he said this, like it was hard for him to even entertain the idea. *"I'm not gay."*

"Okay," I said. "I didn't think you were."

"Then why did you ask me?"

He had a point. "One of the waiters at the restaurant said maybe you were," I said. Hayes looked hurt by this, too. "But I said you weren't, and no one *else* thought you were gay," I lied unnecessarily. "Just him."

"Elna," he interrupted me, "I want you to know that this is a choice that you're making. No one is making you do this—you're choosing to be with me. And if at any point you decide that you don't want to be in this relationship, just tell me. No matter how far along we are, even if we're walking down the hall of the temple on our way to get married, spare my feelings and tell me the truth."

Perhaps he was right. Perhaps it was just about being afraid. "I'm sorry," I said. "I want to be with you. I shouldn't have brought it up. Forgive me."

That night we saw a movie. Afterward we went to my apartment and had the best make-out of our relationship. It was passionate, tender, and a little angry, like I can only image make-up sex might be. Out of breath, I lay in Hayes's arms and held him as close to me as I could. We were still for a minute or two before he broke the spell: *"Now* do you think I'm gay?"

My second act of sabotage happened about a month later. We'd barely recovered from round one when I got restless. Having a boyfriend had been my ultimate goal for years, but now that I'd accomplished it, I realized: Being in a relationship is sort of boring. It wasn't Hayes's fault. He was wonderful; paying the phone bill, picking up my dry-cleaning, and when I was performing, he'd photocopy flyers and send out Evites. He did all the things an attentive partner does. But when you're in a relationship without the possibility of sex it feels more like you're flirting with your personal assistant.

And then there was all of our church drama. On the one hand it was nice to finally get to share my religion with someone; on the other, it was a real pain in the ass (or *rear*, if Hayes were writing this). It was hard enough dealing with my own insecurities, thick legs, or habit of chewing an entire pack of gum in one sitting. Now my faith was under the microscope, and boy did Hayes have his opinions.

Our first real fight happened because I skipped the last hour of church. That night, after Sunday dinner, Hayes told me that he was worried I wasn't religious enough for him.

"I'm afraid I'll always be pulling the weight," he explained.

Maybe it's the fact that I'm sensitive to the word *weight*, but this really rubbed me the wrong way. I explained that there were many ways of being religious, and that my faith was personal and not his to judge. He apologized, but after that I was paranoid. I stopped making jokes that were off-color and if I read my scriptures or did anything remotely kind, I'd immediately tell Hayes, to help prove my piety.

This all came to a head one fateful fast Sunday. In the Mormon-faith, the first Sunday of every month is fast Sunday, which means you don't drink or eat for twenty-four hours. I'm really bad at fasting because I'm always on a diet, so if I give up food completely, my body thinks it's the end and freaks out. I tried to explain this to Hayes. Instead of letting me off the hook, he suggested we fast together—and I quote: "There is no *I* in TEAM." Unfortunately there's one in THIRSTY. By lunchtime, I was dehydrated. So I snuck into the bathroom, tilted my head under the faucet, and started chugging water. It was only after I finished, water dripping down my face, that I realized I was literally drinking behind closed doors and hiding it from him. I stormed back into the living room.

"Do you see this?" I pointed to the wet mark on my shirt. "I drank water!" Hayes looked confused.

"And that's just me, I drink water, so why should I have to hide it from you?"

If I were head over heels for Hayes I could've put up with our religious misunderstandings—but that was the other big problem. Seeing Hayes for the first time, amid a room full of Mormons, was a delightful surprise, but it was never magic. I didn't feel overwhelmed, lost in dreams, propelled to action, incapable of loving anyone else.

"You don't need that feeling," my mother consoled me. "It goes away over time. Every lasting relationship ends up being about the day-to-day routine." She said this like it was a good thing, like love was a game of Chutes and Ladders, and Hayes and I had managed to leap all the way to the top: stability.

I wasn't sold.

"Do you feel like our relationship is lacking passion?" I asked Hayes one night.

"I don't believe in passion," he answered.

"*What?* How can you not *believe* in passion?" I gestured wildly. "Whether or not you experience it, passion exists, *it's real!*"

"Fine, passion exists," he said, "but I'm not looking for that. I think it's a hype. To me love is about inspiring another person to do good. Elna, the more good that you do, in service to God, to your family and to our friends, the more I feel you love me."

Ughhhhh. Don't bring God into an argument about passion. It reminded me of "The Christian Relationship." In the church's "Marriage Preparation Guide" (yes, I own one) the secular relationship is represented by a picture of a man and a woman staring into each other's eyes. Next to this, there was another picture of a man and a woman holding hands and looking skyward; a dotted line goes from the woman to the man, to the sky, and then back to the woman, making a triangle, with God at the apex: That's "The Christian Relationship." And while I understood the appeal of being a part of something "bigger than yourself," after Matt I wanted God and romantic love to be separate experiences.

"Passion isn't all it's cracked up to be," Hayes finished his speech. I thought this was the end of it, but the next morning he sent me an e-mail entitled "Passion." It was the least passionate document I'd ever read: a well thought-out argument about the merits of service as love, with scriptures backing up his ideas.

At work that night I had a conversation with Vinny, the Nobu and Letterman security guard. Vinny's an Italian Catholic from the Bronx who grew up around the mob; he's also a retired cop, NYPD. After two jobs together he knows me pretty well. In fact he was at Letterman the day that Matt and I first met.

"Vinny," I began. "Do you believe in soul mates?"

He thought about my question. "Nah," he shook his head. "Take my wife—she grew up five blocks from me, only we didn't meet till we were thirty-five. I'd been in the army, I'd traveled the world, and still I married a girl from Astoria, Queens. What are the odds that my soul mate grew up five blocks away? Is it fate? No. In the end, people just marry other people who are like them."

I was disappointed by his answer, but nodded my head.

"You know what your problem is?" he continued.

"What?"

"You believe a buncha different things, you've lived in a buncha different places, and now, nobody's like you."

"Thanks, Vinny. No one tells you what being unique actually means: that you'll die alone."

"I thought you found your Mormon man."

"It's complicated."

"You know what I think about it?"

"What?"

"I was a big kid and growing up in the Bronx, the mafia was always trying to recruit me. I coulda made a shitload of money, too. But you wanna know why I didn't join?"

"Why?"

"Because I'm too smart and I ask too many questions. And when the big boss says to put cement boots on some poor schmuck and throw him in the river, and you ask him, '*Why?*' you get thrown in the river, too."

"I see ..."

"It'll always be hard for you to be a Mormon 'cause you're too smart and you ask too many questions."

"You're right, Vinny. Being a Mormon is a lot like joining the mob."

When I got home from work that night, I opened up an old shoebox and pulled out the only picture I had of Matt. Tina took it. In the picture we're sitting on my bed, Matt's looking down at a book, and I'm looking at the camera, smiling. I missed him.

It's stupid what a few weeks with someone can do to you, namely prevent you from ever moving on. But I'd been thinking about him more and more each week. I couldn't get over the feeling I'd had when I was with him. Maybe I'd imagined it, maybe it was inflated by a faulty memory; either way, I didn't feel the same way about Hayes. *If only I could see Matt again*, I thought, *then I'd know if I was still capable of feeling passion. I'd understand if it was important to me or not.* It'd been a year since our breakup. I'd deleted his number after two unreturned phone calls, and then regretted it because I had no way of reaching him.

Facebook was invented for moments like these. I joined and looked up Matt's name. Sure enough, he was there. I closed Hayes's letter on passion and wrote one of my own, only mine was to Matt.

The letter was long, but basically it said three things: *I hope you're doing well, I'm finally dating a Mormon, I miss the shit outta you.*

I knew that pressing send would open up a can of worms, but I did it anyway.

He called me the very next day. I was walking though Central Park and picked up not knowing it was him.

"Elna?" he said.

Oh, my gosh—hearing his voice was so momentous that I had to sit down.

"Hi," I said.

"Hi," he answered. "I just got your message."

"Good old Facebook," I offered.

"I'm really glad you contacted me," he said. "I've been thinking about you lately."

"You have?"

"Yeah, I got that job in Zambia."

"You did? Congratulations!" While we were dating Matt told me he wanted to work at a hospital in Lusaka. He'd written the president a letter, but hadn't heard anything.

"Yeah, I'm actually moving in three days."

"How long will you be gone?"

"I'm not sure—it's a permanent position."

"Oh . . ."

"But I want to see you before I go—"

I said yes before he finished asking.

We met for lunch two days later. Ever since our breakup I'd been experiencing anxiety. The moment Matt turned the corner I realized why. I missed him.

Lunch was uneventful; we spent the majority of the meal catching up. The conversation fluctuated between feeling both natural and totally forced. If someone were to look at us, they'd immediately know the occasion. *We're just friends now! Can't you tell?*

Kevin has a term that perfectly describes it: "The nice lady at the conference." Let's say you run into an old lover or ex–best friend at a business conference, both of you are wearing name badges. You say hello politely, and ask each other surface questions like *How's your sister doing?* But all along there is this mountain of knowledge and history that's passed between you, only neither of you acknowledge it because now things are different—now they're just "the nice lady at the conference" to you. Like the Elliot Smith lyric, "You're just somebody that I used to know."

I thought we would leave it at that, but as we were walking out of the restaurant, Matt slipped up. It happened because I made a stupid joke, I don't even remember what I said, but he laughed and caught my hand in his.

"God I wish you weren't Mormon," he said.

"You do?" I looked at him in shock.

"Yeah."

"*I knew it!* I knew you liked me!"

"Of course I liked you. What makes you think I didn't?"

"You moved on so easily. You never called. . . ."

"It wasn't easy," he interrupted. "And I didn't call because, what was the point? We tried to have fun, but it always came back to the same discussion."

"Yes, but the way we left things, it was hard for me to move on," I argued. "We had the perfect beginning and an ending. No middle. So whatever, who knows? Maybe if we'd kept on dating we would've broken up a month later because you would've asked me to pick up bread on the way home and I would've forgotten and you'd yell, 'You never listen to me, it's over!'"

He laughed.

"It's not fair," I continued. "I never got the chance to see if you were the guy who could sit through a bunch of horrible comedians to see me do a routine you'd heard a hundred times before, and still say I was great. And you never got to see if I was the girl you wanted to come home to after a really long day of doctory things."

"Yes, that's what we call it . . ." he laughed again.

"Paying the phone bill, picking up our dry cleaning, making flyers, we never got to experience the normal everyday things. So who's to say we would've been good at them . . ."

"I have a feeling we would've been great at them."

We walked in silence for a moment. When we got to the crosswalk, I stopped and faced him.

"Do you still think about me?"

"How could I not? You've read more books than any other girl I dated."

"That's funny. I used to lie about reading just to impress you." I laughed.

He looked me in the eye and I realized throughout the entire lunch we'd avoided making eye contact.

"I really like your face," he said.

It totally caught me off guard. A tear slid down my cheek.

"But hey," he stopped me. "You met a Mormon guy, and that's what you wanted all along."

"No . . ." I wiped my face with my both of my hands. And then I took a breath. *This is that moment*, I thought, *when you only get one chance to say what you really want to say, please help me say it.*

"I know it is possible to feel this way about other people," I began, pointing to my heart, "I know that there are a lot of ways to love and that each person I date will bring out a different part of me and I will love them all differently. But I will always like how I liked you the best."

"Oh, God."

Matt pulled me into him and held me there. *Fuck, I like you so much,* I thought. And for a second, in the circle of his arms and mine, it was possible to change all of it, to be together. I wanted to live in that second, freeze time, freeze consequences, live. That's when Matt leaned in to kiss me. I was about to go through with it, too, an inch from his mouth, when I stopped myself.

"I can't do this," I said. "I have a boyfriend."

"Sorry." He let go of me. "I just got nostalgic."

"For what?"

"For you."

"But I'm still here," I said.

"No," he said, shaking his head. "No."

"How'd it go with your friend today?" Hayes asked me later that evening.

"Huh?" I'd been staring into space.

"The guy you saw today, the guy you briefly dated, how did it go?"

"Fine."

I'd gotten Hayes's permission to see Matt. I hadn't explained all the details, but I told him I was seeing an ex-boyfriend who was moving to Africa. He didn't seem to mind. Until after. Whether I'd intended to do it or not, it shifted my way of seeing him, and he could tell. It was like I had an invisible scale, Hayes or a fantasy.

We spent the next week arguing over really stupid things. And then it was Friday. Hayes worked in the Mormon temple every Friday night. I met him in the lobby after his shift. I wanted to have "the talk." But I wasn't sure what to do, break up with Hayes for a guy I'd never see again, or stay and make it work. Either way, I wasn't expecting what happened next. He walked out of the temple, still in his church clothes, and sat down in the seat next to me.

"Hi, sweetie," he said.

"I have to tell you something . . ." I stopped, unable to finish it. *I'm breaking up with you,* didn't feel right.

Hayes waited for me to continue.

"I—I love you," I said.

We both started crying. No more kinks, no more wrenches. We were a couple.

A Body of Work

My family and friends thought I was crazy when I told them that on December 22, 2006, I was going in for major plastic surgery. I was twenty-four, a healthy woman with no visible flaws, and plastic surgery went against both my character—I am confident, I accept myself—as well as my religion. But I had a good reason. When I lost weight, I lost it fast. This left me with a layer of excess skin that hung off my body like a sweatshirt. I'd used skin-firming lotions, I'd exercised, but no matter what I did I still looked like a melting candle. Surgery—a doubleheader: tummy tuck plus breast implants—was my only option, and even though it seemed like a get-rich-quick method to becoming attractive, and even though I once swore, in a hospital bed, never to fall into such a trap, I decided to go for it. And to be completely honest, while my friends and family were frightened, I spent hours scrolling down the "Before and After" results page, daydreaming.

It was only on the day before the procedures, when my teenage sister Jill asked, "So, what time do you go under the knife?" that it occurred to me: I am about to be cut in half. Suddenly I found myself in a total panic, calling the number in the back of a self-help book *Prepare for Surgery, Heal Faster*, and paying $150 to talk to the author.

Miraculously, Peggy Huddleston, Harvard professor, expert in mind-body medicine, actually answered the phone. Her book was written for people with cancer, not someone getting a tummy tuck and implants, but I convinced myself that Huddleston was the only person who could help me. I explained my situation and she asked if she could walk me through a meditation to prepare me. She began to count backward from ten. Since I was paying by the minute, I thought about suggesting, *Can't we just start from five?* Peggy's voice was calm and breathy, it sounded just like it did on the meditation tape that came with the book. *Three, two, one.* Lo and behold I was in a meditative state.

"I want you to interview your body," Huddleston began.

"Okay," I said, willing to try anything.

"Ask your body how it feels."

"Body," I said, "how do you feel?" I waited for an answer. "It says it feels scared."

"What emotion can you send your body to make it feel better?"

I listened to my body. I would have picked courage, superhuman strength, but my body chose something else altogether.

"Gratitude."

"When does your body want gratitude?" Peggy asked.

"Every time I see or touch the scar across my stomach, I need to send my body gratitude, and then it will be willing to go through this surgery."

"Can you agree to do that?"

It seemed like a fair enough trade. I give my body gratitude, it will accede to my cutting it in half. "Yes," I replied.

"Alright, now say good-bye to the skin that will be leaving you."

I thought about everything my skin and I had been through. "Good-bye," I said.

My skin replaced my insecurity about my weight. I didn't get to just feel complete. I transferred the feeling of imperfection onto the loose skin. With a weight loss of one hundred pounds or more, the average person is left with ten to fifteen pounds of sagging skin, draping from stomach and breasts, legs and arms, back and buttocks. On some people the skin retracts. Other people, like me, aren't so lucky. It had been three and half years since I had become thin. There was no getting around it, the skin wasn't going away. I took comfort in the modesty of Mormonism.

Only, after a few months of dating, Hayes started to bring up the topic of marriage, and that's when it struck me: *I might be naked in front of someone else!* It wasn't until the reality of marriage, and therefore sex, arose that I realized someone else besides me will see my skin. My body is not just mine.

I decided to confide in my close friend Alison. (At this point I had shown only my mother the suit of skin I carried under the tight girdle I wore every day.) Alison looked at my skin and simply said, "Go get plastic surgery. You've worked too hard, you don't deserve this." She showed me a picture on the Internet of a tummy tuck. Until that moment, I'd had no idea I could be fixed.

As a Mormon I had always thought that the first man to see me naked would be my husband. As it turns out, that man was a plastic surgeon. I remember nervously taking off the medical gown for him during my first consultation. He looked at my body, took a step back, looked at it from different angles, lifted my breasts and dropped them. He then proceeded to tell me all the things I could do to change my appearance.

After I put my clothes back on, the doctor talked me through the fine print.

"I should warn you," he began, "one of the side effects of getting breast implants is that you may lose your nipple sensation."

"*What—*"

"Not all women experience this . . ."

"—your nipples have sensation?"

Aside from death, the potential hazards weren't too detrimental: My boobs would feel fake. Hayes had never touched a woman's breasts before, so it didn't matter. I was ready and willing to go for it.

All I needed was ten thousand dollars. Yikes. I called my parents, explained how much it meant to me, and asked if I could use the money they'd set aside for my wedding to pay for surgery. At first my mother was opposed to it. She said that if Hayes were a good man, which she believed he was, he'd love me no matter what my body looked like. I told her that that was all well and good but that if she ever wanted a grandchild I'd have to get naked and as long as I looked like Lumiere from *Beauty and the Beast*, I wasn't taking my clothes off.

She considered this. "Perhaps your extra skin was a gift from God," she said, "a suit of armor given to you to protect you from premarital sex."

"Wow," I said, "you nailed it."

My father agreed to support me, but he wanted to make sure it was safe first. And so I found a doctor near their home in Seattle that came highly recommended and was half the cost of a New York surgeon. In September 2006, I flew home to meet with him. My mother, still hesitant, came to the appointment with me. When they brought out a Tupperware full of fake breasts and I caught her feeling one, and then fondling her own boob for comparison, I knew she was on my side.

We scheduled my surgery for December 22, four months away.

Now that the surgery was set, I had to tell Hayes about what I was going to do. There was no way of getting around it. He knew I had lost a lot of weight, but he didn't know about the skin. First I brought up the fact that I had to get implants to fill in the skin on my chest. He was surprised and said, "Boobs or no boobs it doesn't matter to me. I look at it like an ice cream sundae. Boobs are the cherry on top. If I don't have the cherry, who cares? I have a whole sundae." Then he asked if he could see my stomach. In the six months we had been dating, I'd managed to avoid this. At first I said no. But one night, as we were lounging on my bed, I hesitantly lifted up my shirt, thinking how gross my torso must look to Hayes. His eyes lit up in what could only be described as sheer wonderment. He cupped the soft skin in his hands, stretched it out inches away from my body, and played with it like a kid would a new toy. When it became clear to me he could have gone on like this for hours, I pulled my shirt back down.

"Elna, everyone is self-conscious about their bodies," Hayes said, and proceeded to take my feet in his hands—I was wearing red Mary Janes—kissed the top of each foot, and told me I was beautiful. A few days later I flew to Seattle.

I had thought I was ready, until the night before when my sister brought up "knives." There was still one missing piece from the puzzle: gratitude.

I got off the phone with Peggy and spent the rest of the day preparing bedside activities for my future immobile self. But no amount of distraction could take away my anxiety. As I tried to fall asleep that night, I touched the soft, loose skin on my stomach and realized this would be the last night my stomach wouldn't have a giant scar. The following morning the plastic surgeon would cut along my bikini line an incision that began two inches behind my left hip bone and ended two inches behind my right hip bone. The excess skin from my stomach would be chopped off, my stomach muscles would be tightened, the doctor would literally fashion me a new belly button, and the excess skin on my chest would be filled in with saline implants. I would be unconscious for over four hours and during this time my heart could stop beating. It's funny, but there's nothing quite like the prospect of death to put things into perspective. All the time I'd spent hating my body, I'd failed to realize one important thing: *At least I'm alive*. And while the odds were incredibly low, I was terrified of dying during my procedure. So I did what most people would do in this situation: I turned it around and blamed the God I'd prayed to for help losing weight in the first place. "WHY ARE YOU MAKING ME DO THIS?" That's when I realized, *No one is making you do anything. This is a choice that you are making, so when you wake up tomorrow, you had better act like this is your decision.*

When I woke up the next morning I was a different person. I felt confident and prepared: I was in the zone. We drove to the surgeon's office. Outside he had placed a statue of a golden swan. I turned to my mother and thought of every other woman who must've seen this swan before her surgery and rolled her eyes. "Your ugly duckling is finally becoming a swan," I joked. We went in and I signed a bunch of legal papers—"in case of death" I won't hold anyone responsible. Then my parents left and I was escorted to a room in the back where I would disrobe and the doctor could draw on me. As I stood completely naked in the center of the room, watching in a mirror as the doctor, using a purple marker, covered my stomach, lower abdomen, armpits, and breasts in dotted and straight lines, I realized that over the months of preparing for surgery I had completely redefined my relationship to being naked. I had taken my clothes off so many times—for sizings, doctor's opinions, and my "Before" pictures—that I was no longer nervous or embarrassed by my skin. I was what I was.

I entered the operating room and stood under a bright light while a nurse took a cold sponge and covered my body in Betadine, a sanitizing solution. It turned my skin a brown-orange color; I remember thinking that I looked like a sweet potato. She walked me over to the operating table and I lay down. Another nurse connected the IV. I looked down at my body. "Thank you," I said, just as the IV kicked in and I passed out.

I was under for four and a half hours. The doctor removed roughly two pounds of flesh from my stomach, and added two pounds of saline to my breasts. I woke up in severe pain. My entire torso was tightly bound with thick bandages that pushed my shoulder blades together, preventing me from taking a full breath. Two drainage pumps inserted in my stomach drained blood, pus, and guts from me, and it would be my father's job to empty the pumps every few hours and record the amounts.

A nurse leaned over me. "Everything has gone very well. You're doing great sweetie; now we just need you to stand up and walk to your car." I knew I was an outpatient, but how could anyone send me home like this? They lifted me up—I was not myself, I hurt so badly. Someone called me by my name, "Elna," and I thought, *I'm not Elna.*

A few hours later, in my bed at home, I regained consciousness. I asked to speak to Hayes on the phone. One side effect of the drugs was that they made me act like a five-year-old. In this state I explained to Hayes: "I feel like the bad guys got me and tied me up real tight to the railroad tracks, and you were supposed to save me but the train came, and instead of running over me I was too big and it hit me but it couldn't get past, and now the train is on top of me." Which in the simplest terms is exactly how I felt. I went in and out of consciousness for the next few hours. At about 3 A.M. I hit the lowest of my lows, waking up in so much pain that the thought occurred to me, *I don't want to exist anymore.* But the smarter me, behind all the pain and drugs, replied, *Are you saying you want to die? You are not going to die over a boob job. I won't let you.*

The next day they removed the bandages. I secretly hoped it would be like the blind woman receiving sight. It wasn't. My stomach was bruised and severely swollen. The incision, with stitches poking out, was bloodred and stretched across my entire midsection. My boobs were swollen and it felt like two aliens were trying to escape from under my skin. I closed my eyes and they bandaged me back up.

I realized then that surgery wasn't the quick-fix method I had presumed it to be. It doesn't break any of the laws of the universe. It's not cutting any corners. You pay for what you get. And all I could think was, it didn't have to be this way. I was born healthy. I brought this on myself.

As I dealt with this unexpected remorse and physical pain I became very aware of my body. I thought about what I learned when I was five: that having a body would be the foundation for my character and would be the means by which I achieved good in the world. I started mulling that idea over in my head. And you know when you stare at something for too long and it loses its shape? *Why,* I wondered through a scrim of pain and remorse, *is it only through a body that I experience life?*

I asked my parents. My mother simply said: "That's a very good question, but there are some things we just don't have the answer to."

I started to accuse her of having blind faith, but my father interrupted me. "Elna," he said gently, "I don't know why I have to have a body or why you have to have a body. But I do know that when you were born I saw your pink slimy little body and I fell in love with it. And the minute you entered that hospital room I felt your presence. I knew who you were. And I knew that that body was the only way I could have you. And that's not blind faith, that's intuition."

I thought a lot about my father's advice during my recovery. And about the things my body has asked for over the years: "When are you going to realize, this is your only chance?" And for gratitude. I can finally say I am grateful for my body. Not because I got plastic surgery and look better, but because it's pointless not to be: This is the only body I'll ever have.

Heartbreak, Mormon Style

Deciding to get married is a really big deal. For the record, I never thought that Hayes and I were ready. We'd been dating for four months when he moved back to Utah to finish his senior year at BYU. I stayed in New York. The rest of our yearlong relationship was long distance. We'd visit each other every few weeks, and talk every night, but still, we never got to know the ins and outs of a daily relationship. It was more like treading water. He'd call to tell me what he did. I'd call to tell him what I did. But we never did anything together because we were so far apart.

In October, Hayes called to tell me that his friend was getting married to the heiress of the Marriott fortune. A nice catch, even if the sex was bad he'd have free continental breakfast for eternity.

In November, Hayes flew me to Washington, D.C., so that we could attend the wedding and spend a week together.

We met at the Marriot Hotel in downtown D.C. It was always a relief seeing him—the comfort of knowing you at least have a boyfriend. He kissed me on the cheek and picked up my luggage.

"We have an hour to kill before the reception," he said.

"Let's check out our room." I smiled.

We took the elevator up to the top floor only to find that we'd been upgraded to a honeymoon suite, and gifted a basket of goodies—compliments of the bride. And so we did what any young couple is prone to do while staying in a hotel. . . . We built a giant igloo out of all the objects in the room and hid inside of it.

We were lying in the igloo, kissing, when Hayes looked at me and said, "I'm most likely going to ask you to marry me, and I'm most likely going to do it soon, how do you feel about that?"

"Most likely, if you ask me to marry you," I cleared my throat, "I'll most likely say yes, most likely?" When I finished he was grinning ear to ear.

Later that night, we danced together at the wedding reception. For the first time in my adult life, I imagined what it would be like to actually marry someone. I'd been cautious not to dream about marriage, in case it never happened. (But on the off-chance that it did, I was prepared. I'm the only girl I know who actually has a hope chest, compliments of my mother. Marry me and you get a handmade quilt, some china, and crystal from Poland—I'm just saying, I come with some perks.) Dancing in Hayes's arms I let myself believe: Like the Marriott wedding, my wedding was huge, lavish, my family gave their blessing, it was the way love was supposed to be.

We stopped dancing for the bride to throw her bouquet. I tried to catch it. Naturally, it went to some fifteen-year-old Mormon girl. And if the bouquet is supposed to symbolize who gets married next, fine, I couldn't argue that.

The next day Hayes left for Utah and I flew to New York, basking in the afterglow, until my feet touched the ground. MARRIAGE? I completely panicked.

It wasn't abnormal. Every other time Hayes had mentioned marriage I'd gotten extremely nervous, ill.

My friend Jim was the first person I told. Jim had founded a popular storytelling series in New York. I performed at his show in 2006 and afterward he introduced himself to me. Since this fateful meeting, we rendezvous every few months for artist dates where we talk about spirituality and sex. Jim is a New York icon and a bit of an eccentric. He's also one of the few intellectuals I know who has thoroughly researched Mormonism. In addition to our "church talks" I go to him for love advice because he's dated *many* women in New York City, including Candace Bushnell, the writer of the original "Sex in the City" column, so Jim knows his stuff. Today's topic: marriage.

"I think my boyfriend and I are going to get engaged." I tried introducing it like it was totally normal. Except I'd been kind of embarrassed of the relationship so most people didn't even know I was dating Hayes.

"You don't sound too thrilled about it." Jim picked up on it immediately.

"No, it's *exciting.*"

He smiled, waiting for more.

"Okay, fine," I cracked. "To be completely honest, I want to get married, but every time I think about actually going through with it—I get sick to my stomach."

Jim does this thing where he listens intensely, and when he likes what you're saying, his eyes light up, which makes you not only want to tell him your story, but also perform it.

Next thing I knew I was delivering a monologue. "When I think about marriage," I said, "I get a weird pounding in my head, and I feel like I'm experiencing a phobia. It feels familiar, only I can't place it. Which drives me insane. Like when you have a recurring bad dream, where there's something scary around the corner, and you know if you just turn the corner, you'll understand what it is, but you always wake up too soon—"

"Does it remind you of anything in particular?" Jim interrupted.

I closed my eyes.

"Biology," I said. "We dissected rats in biology, it reminds me of the smell."

"Formaldehyde?"

"I guess so."

"Death," Jim said rather loudly.

"Come again?"

"The feeling you're describing is death, it's a memory of something you're familiar with but you've never actually experienced. You associate marriage with death."

"I do?"

"And marriage is death—the death of self."

"It is?"

"It's also rebirth into another you, so it's not necessarily a bad thing. Still, artists think it's the death of their individuality."

I spent the next few days brooding over Jim's analysis. Soon every red flag I'd ignored was back, front and center: There was the time Hayes said, "When I'm at work and you're at home with the kids will you resent me?"

"*No,*" I answered him in a dumbfounded voice, "because I'll be working, too."

Then there was his special way of patronizing. I called it the "Oh, Elna." I'd say something bold in Sunday school and he'd pat me on the knee. "*Oh, Elna.*" I'd knock over a glass. "Oh, Elna." I'd try to and get him to break into an abandoned building. "*Oh, Elna.*" When I told Kevin about this he said, "How can you be with someone who loves you in spite of the very best things about you?"

And finally, there was his complete lack of spontaneity. One evening, while visiting Hayes in Utah, I spotted a giant haystack along the side of the road and I made him pull over. "Let's climb to the top." I opened the car door and took off running across a field. I remember watching him from atop the thirty-foot haystack ten minutes later. He was still yards away, maneuvering his way across the field like he way trying to avoid a land mine. It was only then that I realized that the field I'd raced through was covered in manure.

But my patriarchal blessing specifically said I would marry a Mormon man who loved me dearly. Hayes fit this criterion. In my mind he was the Good Choice that I needed to make. I knew what I had to do: I had to go to the Mormon temple and ask God if marrying Hayes was the right thing to do, and if God said yes then I would do it.

This wasn't an original idea; it's what Mormons do. There's a big emphasis in my religion on receiving a spiritual confirmation of what you're about to do. That way when the marriage gets rocky you don't question it because: It was something God told you to do. And aside from that, it's how my dad knew to marry my mother. My dad went to a Mormon temple and prayed, *Is this the right decision?* and he said he heard voices, and he recognized those voices to be the grown-up voices of his future kids and we told him, *Go, get married—do it now.*

I fasted for two days, no water, no food, and I went to the Mormon temple, and I said, "God, I've decided to marry Hayes. Is this the right thing to do?"

At first it was silent, too silent. And then it happened. I heard something. *Yes, Yes, Yes,* all through me, *YES, do, do, do.*

With Hayes by my side, I went home for Christmas and got plastic surgery. A month and a half later I moved to Utah. It was the equivalent of swallowing all my pride. Plus I lost the ability to say, "I've never lived in Utah." But Hayes still had four months of college, and I figured if we were serious about a wedding in July, we needed to live in the same place. I rented an apartment down the street from Hayes, I bought a gym membership, I bought groceries—canned foods, and all kinds of things you can't return.

My second night in Provo, the shit hit the fan. We were invited to a costume party for someone's thirty-first birthday. Hayes wanted to go dressed as ghosts. So we bought two white sheets and cut holes in the eyes. But then we realized we looked like Klan members, so we stopped at the drugstore and I bought ribbon and made a blue bow tie for him, and a red bow for me. Girl ghost, boy ghost.

Hayes was holding my hand, leading me around the room and introducing me to all of his friends. I tried to enjoy myself, but I was having a costume malfunction: My bow was too heavy and it kept pulling the sheet down so that the ghost eyeholes were at my chin. No matter how many times I pushed it up, it fell right back down. Eventually I just gave up and let Hayes lead me. He started talking to an old friend. Standing there, with nothing to look at but a white sheet, I was struck by the irony of the situation.

All this time I've associated marriage with death, and here I am, being led around a party under a white sheet, like a corpse at a morgue.

I laughed. But at the same time, it wasn't funny. *Am I only capable of being in this relationship if I'm a muted version of myself? Me underneath a sheet?*

The danger of ascribing meaning to unrelated things is that you're not necessarily right. I wasn't in a morgue, I was at a costume party with my soon to be fiancé. But still, the thought was paralyzing. I let go of Hayes's hand, hoping it'd make him notice me. More than anything, I wanted him to lift up the sheet and assure me it was all okay.

But he didn't notice me. Instead, I stood there overthinking. *God knows what's best for me*, I tried to tell myself. *He wouldn't tell me to marry Hayes if it weren't the right thing to do. Be humble. Trust Him. You don't need to kick and scream and fight every good thing.* At the same time, I felt a pounding in my head, and the same queasy feeling, nerves. Only this time I was closer to turning the corner than I'd ever been.

Hayes found me twenty minutes later. He lifted up the white sheet and slid underneath. It felt like we were in the igloo again. *He has the most beautiful eyes,* I thought. *I've never met anyone with more beautiful eyes.*

"What's wrong?"

Don't do it. "Nothing."

"What's wrong?"

"Jim told me that I associate marriage with death. And I didn't believe him at first, but here I am about to marry you—being dragged around like a body in a morgue. What if he's right? If I marry you, will I stop being me?"

"When are you going to stop?" Hayes looked completely deflated. "When are you going to want me, too?"

The next morning, I woke with a start, that *oh, no what did I do, what did I say* feeling, and it's funny, but after all we'd been through I did not think words were enough to separate us, but the right words were. I tried to make it up to Hayes the only way I knew how: by being a better Mormon. I had his roommate sneak me into his apartment and, while he was sleeping, I cleaned the entire thing top to bottom. Then I made him an omelet, and served breakfast in bed.

But it was too late, he was already retreating. Every night he came up with a new excuse for us not hanging out. "I'm watching a movie with Marcus," he explained, "and afterward we're going to start a band."

I'd moved across the country for him and suddenly he was too busy for me. But the moment I knew things had really gone sour happened a few days later. We were at his second cousin's wedding when Hayes's aunt ran up to him to give him a hug.

"Who's this young lady?" She smiled at us.

Hayes looked totally flustered, "This is . . . uhhh . . . *my friend* Elna."

He broke up with me a week later. I begged him to rethink it. In retrospect I'd been pushing him to break up with me the entire relationship, but when he actually did, I felt like I'd messed up fate—I'd destroyed God's plan for me.

"Go to the temple," I cried. "Pray about it, please?"

"I'm not in the right state of mind for that," Hayes said.

"Please," I begged him. In my mind, if God had answered me yes, then he would answer Hayes the same way, so really it was all we needed.

The following morning Hayes went to the Provo temple to ask God if he should marry me.

It was the longest day of my life. I was lying in bed when Katherine, my roommate of two weeks, knocked on my door. "I'm taking you somewhere," she said.

"Why?" My face was puffy and the room was littered with used Kleenex.

"Because I've been where you are right now, and I wish someone could've done this for me."

She drove me up the canyon to Park City and paid for a day at the spa. I was too out of it to really enjoy myself, but I will always be grateful for the gesture of kindness. As we drove back down the canyon I stared out the window at the rocks, and the melting snow, and thought, *I am at a crossroads right now, and rarely does one get to be at a crossroads and realize it.* I focused on what it felt like. *Ha,* I laughed, it was the same feeling I'd once loved, the state of being between unlimited possibility and reality. *In an hour I will go to Hayes's house, knock on his door, and find out if I'm going to get married in a Mormon temple. Or in an hour Hayes will break up with me and I'll be right back in the middle of the unknown.* As scary as it was, I wanted the unknown. To me, not knowing was living.

Hayes broke up with me an hour later. In spite of my realization that this was what I wanted, I took it very badly. I cried for two days and then, in an attempt to win him back, I sat on his doorstep and waited for him to come home from school.

Only he was late—two hours late. *I should've brought a book,* I thought. *Oh, no, now I have to pee.* To keep myself distracted, I started collecting these giant dried peapods that'd fallen from a nearby tree. Soon I had a whole pile of them. Which is how the idea came to me. Crawling on all fours I arranged the peapods into giant letters: I LOVE YOU HAYES, I wrote for everyone, even people flying overhead, to see.

I sat down on the steps to admire my handiwork. Only as I stared at those giant words, a crippling feeling came over me. *Is that even true?*

Just then, Hayes's car pulled into the driveway. For a split second I thought about diving onto the ground and scattering the letters. As it turned out, I didn't need to. Hayes thanked me for the gesture, told me our relationship was definitely over, and said that I should go back to New York. I tried to wrap my arms around him, to hug him one more time. But he jerked away. It was unintentional. Still, it startled me, the idea that this person who had once so certainly loved me could change almost overnight.

I packed my bags and left the following morning.

"Breakups are good practice for dying," Jim consoled me in an e-mail. "Since that's what they are anyway."

Great, I thought. *Now everything reminds Jim of death.*

I spent the next two months living in New York and behaving like a heartbroken zombie. Luckily, I had something to look forward to: I'd been accepted to Yaddo, an artist's colony.

I left for Yaddo in July. The month I thought I was going to be married ended up being the month I began this book. It brought me back to life. I met other artists, I lived in a mansion, I worked harder than I'd ever worked. Suddenly, I felt happy again. Right on cue,

Hayes e-mailed me. He wanted to know what I thought about starting again. He wasn't convinced himself, but thought we should revisit things. His e-mail sent me into an emotional fit. I didn't know what to do. *Is Hayes really my destiny?* I went on a walk to think it over.

I was wandering through the Yaddo forest, overthinking, when I stumbled upon a small lake with a huge broken tree slumped over it. It looked like a rainbow, something straight out of a fairy tale. I decided to climb it. I wrapped my arms and legs around the trunk and shimmied up to the highest point twenty-five feet off the ground and overlooking the forest.

The answer to my dilemma came in an unexpected form: a bird. It was perched on a branch next to me. As I sat there, I watched it dive into the water, and then return to the same branch and shake its feathers off. A second later, it dove back in, shook itself off, and dove back in. The bird repeated this action so many times that I started to wonder if there was something wrong with it. That's when it occurred me. *It's just having fun.* My eyes welled up with tears. I'd spent so much time thinking that God had created me to "do what was right" that I'd forgotten, *I was also created to be happy.* Hayes did not make me happy, a document from a patriarch could not tell me how to be happy, I was in charge of my own happiness.

In spite of the fact that I have terrible balance, I set my hands on the tree trunk and pushed myself up into a standing position. Looking out at the lake, the forest, the blue sky, I raised my arms above my head and let out an exhilarating scream. For a second, it felt like I was flying.

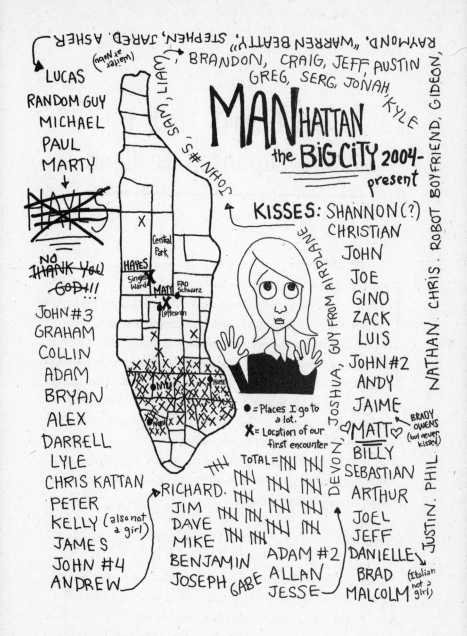

Another Tunnel

The E-mail That I
Wasn't Supposed to Send

I bet you thought that was the end of the book. I did, too, or at least when I proposed writing a book, that's where I thought the story would end. But then something seemingly impossible happened: I sold the idea for my manuscript, and for the first time in my life I wasn't just a struggling artist, freelance dog-walking and hostessing at Nobu. I was a girl with a book deal and a cash advance. I looked at my check and tried to wrap my head around the number of zeros. It would've taken me another forty years of picking up pieces of shit, or seating them, to earn the same amount.

While I planned on saving most of the money, I decided to treat myself to one thing: *If I could buy anything I want, what would it be?* I knew the answer immediately.

Hey, Matt.

I opened up my laptop and wrote the following e-mail. For the record: I was never really going to send it. It was more like a dare. One I had given myself, but still one I had to take. The dare, as I imagined it, was to rewrite history by facilitating a second chance.

I don't know if you're still in Zambia, but my girlfriends and I are going to South Africa in the spring to visit some family friends of mine. I'm not sure how far Zambia is from South Africa, but if it's close, I'd love to come up and say hi. Obviously if you have a wife, a girlfriend, or a live-in maid/lover this could be weird, but if not, it'd be fun to see you. It's been a while. I hope you're well. X Elna

I read the e-mail over. It was pretty good except for a few points: 1. I didn't have a trip to South Africa on the horizon, and 2. There were no family friends. Okay fine, my e-mail was ridiculous—*Is Zambia close to South Africa?* As if I didn't own a map. If I was going to be this indirect, why even bother with an e-mail? I might as well just show up at his local food market with a fruit basket balanced on my head and say, "Oh, hey, fancy running into *you* here!"

At the same time, when Hayes and I broke up the bottom had dropped out: A Mormon man wasn't going to solve everything. When we were together, I'd still questioned my faith.

As a result, I spent the six months following our breakup living in limbo. I wasn't sure I wanted to be Mormon anymore. Only I hadn't acted on it—instead, I felt like I was standing on one side of a stone wall, looking over it. The other side was intriguing. So intriguing that I'd built an entire imaginary life there: In that world, I smoked, hung out with artists, took lovers, had tattooed sleeves, and frequently wore dresses without any underwear.

In reality, my life was the same as always: After Yaddo I returned to Manhattan and continued going to the singles ward. In September the bishop gave me an assignment, probably to keep me on the straight and narrow. Every Sunday I was supposed to teach a "Marriage Preparation" course. As I stood in front of the class and told them about the benefits of temple marriage, I felt like I was treading water, speaking in hopes that I'd believe again. When what I really wanted was to be on the other side. Only, crossing over the wall and living out my fantasies meant letting go of everything that I already knew. And I wasn't ready to walk out into the unknown, to let go of my convictions, to live without God.

And yet for all of the "factual discrepancies" in my e-mail, it was the most honest thing I'd ever written. I was actually going after what I wanted in life, no apologies. I reread it.

P.S. I added in my head, *I miss the shit outta you.*

And just like that, I pressed SEND. In fact, I was so determined I accidentally sent it twice.

When I woke up the following morning, I felt immediate regret. Sending my e-mail was the equivalent of drunk dialing Matt only without the excuse because I'd done it stone-cold sober. I opened my laptop to assess the damage when I saw his reply in my inbox. It was brief and to the point:

Re: How's it going?

Elna, so good to hear from you. South Africa is just a quick flight away. I'd love to see you, I can even take your girlfriends and you on safari if you'd like. X Matt

I reread the last sentence. *My girlfriends and me? Shit.* I'd forgotten this lie altogether. Why had I been so specific? The good news was: Matt wanted to see me. The bad news: I had to find not one, not two, but several female friends and convince them to go to Africa on a whim.

I called every girl I'd ever met. "Want to go to Zambia in a few weeks? It'd be fun!"

"Doesn't your ex-boyfriend live there?"

"Oh, that old fling? I'm just going for the cultural experience."

No one took the bait. It was too expensive, too hard to get off work, there were visas, shots, and a coup had just broken out in Kenya, a neighboring country. Big deal.

"No" means nothing to me.

God bless Alison and Pri, I dedicate this book in part to both of them. We'd worked together as pages at the Letterman show. In fact, they were both there the day I met Matt. Alison had moved to Oregon and Pri was living in both New York and Pakistan. We'd been meaning to get together, and they both had the travel bug, so when I begged them to go to Africa, they actually agreed.

Two girls equals "girlfriends," I thought. *YES!* And so I began the complicated process of organizing everything—not exactly a strength of mine. I was happy to blow my entire advance but Alison and Pri were on a tight budget. And after talking to several travel agents I realized going to South Africa and Zambia was twice as expensive. While I'd love to visit South Africa some day, I was really only doing it for the sake of my bluff. And so, to cut down on costs, I sent another e-mail to Matt.

> So it turns out that my family friends won't be in South Africa during the month of March. Would it be okay if we just based our trip out of Zambia? Going to both countries seems like a lot to do in two weeks, and I'd rather get the most bang for my buck.

Technically I gave him two excuses for one lie. Could I be any more transparent? Matt wrote me back and said he was happy to host us the entire time. He also recommended we fly into Tanzania and spend a few days in Zanzibar since it was en route and the most beautiful country he'd ever visited. The following day I bought a ticket from New York to Tanzania to Zanzibar to Zambia and return.

"Whom are you traveling with?" The travel agent made small talk while she waited for my ticket to print.

"My two girlfriends," I answered.

"Well"—she handed me the ticket and smiled—"enjoy your *ladies' vacation*."

It was either the gayest thing I'd ever heard, or this is an actual term reserved for trips where girls take girlfriends to visit ex-boyfriends in faraway lands. Still, holding that ticket in my hand was unbelievable. Going to Africa was no longer just a crazy idea in my head, *it was actually happening*.

I wasn't going to tell my parents about my trip. Tina (their spy) had moved to Boston a few months earlier and they, along with my youngest sister Jill, had moved to Siberia. They really did. I'm not kidding. They relocated for my dad's job. Boeing started a joint venture with a Russian company to make titanium parts for the new Boeing 787s. My father is currently the CEO of a titanium factory near the Ural Mountains. Which makes him sound like an evil villain. While they're isolated in the freezing cold, I think it's the perfect addition to my bit: I'm a Mexican Mormon with a home in Siberia now.

I actually haven't been to visit them yet, but when I do, my goal is to run down the halls of the factory and knock things over while chanting, "It's Daddy's factory!" in a pretentious British accent.

But back to my Africa trip. With an ocean and a vast land mass in between my parents and me, I felt like I could do whatever I wanted without getting caught.

Only at the last minute I was worried that something bad might happen to me, so I called to tell them about the trip. They were unfazed. I expected my mother at the very least to disapprove. A year earlier, when things weren't going well with Hayes, she warned me not to "blow my one and only chance at love." After I did, it was as if she'd given up hope that I'd ever want the life she wanted for me.

A week after our breakup she called to tell me about a dream she'd had. "It was so strange," she began. "You were a famous person who'd fallen from grace and to make money you were giving tours of your hometown. Only it was a fake hometown, not a place we ever actually lived. *Oh, Elna*, it was awful. You were heavy again, you had grown facial hair, and you were incredibly bitter. In fact, you reminded me of Rosie O'Donnell. 'Step right up and see the home of the famous Elna Baker,' you kept saying. It really worried me Elna, please don't let this happen."

It doesn't take Carl Jung to analyze this dream. It's pretty clear that my mom is still deathly afraid that I'll become a lesbian. Perhaps all I needed to me make this switch was a nice *ladies' vacation*.

I will never forget landing in Dar es Salaam. We were incredibly unprepared. Only, we didn't realize it until we were making our final descent and I asked Alison, "What language do they speak here?"

"I don't know," she said. We both turned to Pri.

"Don't look at me!" she answered, her eyes wide.

"I thought for sure you'd know."

"What does the travel guide say?" she asked.

"I didn't bring one. . . ."

"I don't have one either," Alison said. We turned to Pri for a second time.

"Don't look at me!"

"This should be an adventure," Alison managed to say optimistically.

"Yes"—I flashed an unconvincing smile—"it's all possibility."

The minute we stepped off the plane, thirty cab drivers swarmed us. It was a feeling I haven't experienced since childhood, the thrill and panic of being completely and utterly out of your element.

"Where are you going? *American?* Let me show you how you spend your money?" they shouted in broken English.

Before I could get my bearings, someone pulled my suitcase out of my hand. I turned to see a little man waddling off with all our luggage.

"What's happening?"

"He's stealing our bags," Pri said.

"Thank you." I rolled my eyes at her and ran after him.

Luckily, it wasn't theft. It was his business strategy. By locking our bags in his trunk he was guaranteeing that we choose him. But, as a matter of principle, we refused his services. "You can't just take our bags," I said.

He pretended not to understand me. I started miming, *bag, me, give back, now.* Another cab driver yelled at him in . . . well, in whatever language they speak in Tanzania. The man yelled back. Soon they were fighting, pushing each other against the chest and threatening to do more. Meanwhile, another cab driver was picking the first cab driver's lock. The other twenty-seven men had gravitated over to us, still yelling.

In the midst of this chaos, a teenage boy tugged on my sleeve. I looked down at him.

"You dropped something—" he said.

What? I frantically searched for my wallet and passport.

"—my heart," the boy finished with a smile.

I cringed, not because I was mad, but because I couldn't believe I'd fallen for it.

"You give me money?" he added.

"No money," I said.

Just then, the trunk popped open. Without hesitation, the lock-picker took our bags and threw them into his car. While he'd just proven his criminal-like skills, I was too overwhelmed to care.

"Take us to the ferry," I said. We got in his cab and sped off.

Matt had instructed us to take a ferry from Dar es Salaam to Zanzibar. This was our only real plan. After that it was up to serendipity, which isn't exactly the safest way to travel, especially not in a foreign country, but it's my default answer. Unfortunately, I hadn't bothered to check what time the last ferry left. We arrived fifteen minutes too late. And so, with no other option, we he headed back to the airport, through the crowd of angry cab drivers, and over to a small office where I paid a lot more than I expected to for a private plane.

Based on the way things were going—a taxicab mob, no guidebook, and missing luggage—you probably think I was murdered and that someone else is ghostwriting this right now. Fortunately Zanzibar is a magical tiny island where everything goes your way. We arrived as the sun was setting and checked into a hotel with an amazing view of the entire city. And as luck would have it, a friend of a friend knew a girl from Zanzibar named Aailyah. I sent her an e-mail a week before our departure. She called the hotel an hour after we got in and invited us out for drinks. It turned out Aailyah's godfather was the president of Zanzibar. Knowing her was like being given the key to the island. We swam with dolphins, went on a private spice tour, and visited a beach with the finest white sand I've ever seen.

Only it didn't feel like a leisurely trip to Hawaii. The stark difference between rich and poor was overwhelming and it felt wrong to sunbathe on a beach when starving people were yards away.

One night we were having dinner on the beach and admiring the sunset when a large ship pulled into the harbor directly in front of us. We watched a dozen African men wearing only loincloths pile heavy bags of rice onto their backs and load them onto a truck farther down the beach. They walked back and forth and back and forth, clearly exhausted, for the next two hours. It was hard to watch. I felt like a child again, unable to grasp it, sad. When you grow up learning that God loves his children, that he watches out for each and every one of us, and that we all were put here with a purpose, it makes sense, but only from the comfort of your suburban home.

* * *

On our fourth night in Zanzibar we were sightseeing with Aailyah when Pri brought up wedding ceremonies and how fascinating each culture's particular traditions are. Aailyah told us, on the eve of a Zanzibari wedding, the new bride would go through what was called an Unyago ceremony where she'd spend a day with an old woman named Bi kidude and her Taarab tribal drummers. Only married women who had witnessed the ceremony before could also be present. Through music, dancing, movement, and a stick, Bi kidude would initiate the bride into the world of sex.

"What does she do with the stick?" I asked.

"We don't really know," Aailyah answered. All that mattered was that by the end of the day the bride, presumably a virgin, would be a sex expert, too.

"I have to meet Bi kidude."

Because Aailyah's godfather was friends with Bi kidude she was able to arrange a meeting. The following night, Aailyah drove us to Bi kidude's village. Aailyah warned us that Bi kidude was a bit of a live wire, usually either drunk or stoned. And she suggested that we bring a gift. Not just any gift either, Bi kidude was fond of a type of alcohol that was illegal in Zanzibar because it's so strong. On the way there, Aailyah stopped at a bar that sold the illegal drink under the table, in what looked like IV bags. We bought three IV bags and brought them to Bi kidude's hut with us.

A young woman opened the door and let us inside. She spoke to Aailyah. "Bi kidude will be out in a moment," Aailyah translated. "We can wait here." Several straw mats lay on the floor. We sat down.

I could hardly hide my excitement. I was going to ask Bi kidude all of my secret questions, the ones I didn't want anyone to know I thought about like, *Is there a certain way I should move my hips when I'm letting in the penis?* Or, *How do you give a good blow job?*

I'd like to take credit for my moral fortitude, but part of the reason I never had sex, aside from weight, subsequent loose skin, and Mormonism, was because I had no idea how to. And it wasn't just sex, it was all the little things leading up to sex. There were a few occasions in the months post-Hayes where I thought about going for it, but you can't exactly hide the novice expressions your face will make while giving a blow job for the first time, so I always chickened out. I told Kevin about this and he recommended I watch porn for tips.

"Where would I get porn?"

"Just download it off the Internet."

"They have porn on the Internet?" I genuinely didn't know this. But apparently the Internet is full of porn. I was too scared to download it though—I feel like the government keeps tabs on those sorts of things. So instead, Kevin, who's gay, just opened his laptop and showed me a short movie of a man giving another man a blow job. I'd never seen one before, so it was informative, to say the least. But now every time I'm making out with someone and it starts to go in that direction, I flash back to the instructional video and think, I could give him a blow job, but it's kinda gay.

Gay or straight, porn was too crass for my liking. What I needed was a resource like Bi kidude, a wise old soul who could guide me through the landscape of sex—from the taint all the way to the balls, unless, wait, are those close to each other?

I wasn't going to hold back, I was going to ask her anything and everything.

Just then a door opened and a tiny African woman walked in the room. I stood up to greet her. I'd never seen a 113-year-old before, but trust me when I say Bi kidude looked her age. She had a prehistoric quality, her skin was wrinkled and thick as leather. She reminded me of a tiny dinosaur.

I handed her the IV bags and smiled nervously. Aailyah started speaking in Swahili. Bi kidude looked at me and nodded her head knowingly. Then she gestured for us to sit down.

"What did you tell her?" I asked Aailyah.

"That you're a virgin and you want to know about sex."

"Sweet."

We sat in a circle, cross-legged. I put my elbows on my knees, and my head on my hands, preparing to embark on one of the most basic forms of female communication: the slumber party—girls talking to girls about boys.

Bi kidude began by speaking to me in a low voice. I nodded my head and smiled when she smiled.

"What's she saying?" I whispered to Aailyah.

"She says that girls used to always wait, but a lot of women come to her now and she knows they have been popped. She can always tell. It's good if you can wait, she says, but if not, so are the times."

"Ask her if she chose to wait," I said.

Aailyah laughed. She said something to Bi kidude; Bi kidude laughed, too.

I took it this meant *no*. And then I realized it was a stupid question, at least the "choice" part. In the car Aailyah had told us that Bi kidude was forced into marriage at thirteen. She fled from this marriage and walked across the country of Tanzania barefoot. Being barefoot became one of her signature traits. Later in her career Bi kidude was taken to England to perform for the queen. Even in the presence of royalty, Bi kidude refused to wear shoes. This was partly how she'd earned her near mythic status in Zanzibar. It was either that, or her extensive wisdom about intercourse. Bi kidude had learned about sex by being promiscuous. She was proud of it, too. When the women in the village would look at her with scorn she'd yell at them, "At least your husband enjoyed the blow job I gave him last night."

We listened as Bi kidude explained the ritual. The new bride would be bathed three times, her vagina thoroughly cleansed, and then she would learn the rhythms of sex.

"Bi kidude says if you'd like, when you get married, she can perform your ritual," Aailyah translated.

"Thank you," I said. Only this wasn't what I wanted, I needed to know what to do as soon as possible. I was seeing Matt the very next day, and it's not like I went to Africa to get laid or that I think Africa is the smartest place to lose one's virginity. But if things went well, what would I do?

"Do you want to ask her anything else?" Aailyah looked at me.

Yes. I looked at Bi kidude, sweet, small, fragile. *I want to ask you so many things.* Like, *How do you know if it's the right time?* And, *If you give something away that you can't take back, will you lose it forever? And does that even matter?* And, *What does it even feel like? Is it worth the feeling alone? Do you think sex is just a human need, or is it a sin? And am I putting too much pressure on it? Should I just pretend I've had sex and sleep with a stranger who doesn't mean anything to me? Bi kidude help me!* Also, *What's a dirty Sanchez?*

I thought all of these things simultaneously, but when I spoke, all I said was, "I only want to get married once. How do I know I've found the right man?"

Aailyah translated my question for Bi kidude.

Aha. Bi kidude nodded her head, and then she looked into my eyes and started speaking.

"He may not be able to give you clothes," Aailyah translated, "or a roof over your head. And some nights, when you go to bed, you may go to bed hungry. But if you can do this together, with a smile on your face—then he's a good man."

In my world, I was used to analyzing my ideal mate's top three traits: *Does he have a sense of humor? Is he sensitive to my needs? Do we both enjoy* The New Yorker? That sort of thing. Whereas this African woman's priorities were a little bit different than mine: *Can he feed me? Will we have a place to sleep?* Or, *Will he protect me from the rebel soldiers who keep burning down my village?*

I thought about this answer the entire ride home. I'd wanted a golden nugget of wisdom to guide me on my quest for Mr. Right. Instead, I realized, *I'm an asshole.*

When I woke up the following morning I had a pit in my stomach. I was about to see Matt for the first time in two years. With this knowledge came a heightened awareness of everything that was wrong with me as a person. *I had so much time. . . . Why didn't I diet more? Why didn't I become better? Why didn't I volunteer at Amnesty International?*

Both Alison and Pri could tell I was getting nervous. So they took me on a walk, suggesting we explore the city one last time. With only an hour to go, we ended up in a jewelry store full of engagement rings. It was an awkward déjà vu. A year earlier, I'd picked out a ring for Hayes to buy me. Other than the hotel igloo, he'd never actually proposed, but he asked me to shop around and find the ring I wanted. I hated the whole process. Manhattan's diamond district overwhelmed me. I felt like I was being asked to put a price on love, and everything seemed to be saying: the bigger the diamond, the more he loves me.

Only that all changed when I found *my ring*. It was vintage and it had a thin band. When I put it on my finger something unexpected happened to me. It lit up my entire hand and I transformed. I was invincible, I was priceless, I was worthy of being loved. I'd expected Hayes to buy me that ring and I thought it'd be grafted on my finger forever, like a permanent part of my hand. Instead, I was in Zanzibar, and my finger was empty.

I have a confession to make: Hayes was part of the reason I came to Africa in the first place. I lied when I said it was just me giving myself a dare. I wrote the e-mail to Matt after running into Hayes at the Halloween dance. It happened in October 2007. I wasn't planning on going to the church dance that year since the previous dance had ended with my dirty cookie. But I was writing this book, and I figured I had to go, you know, for the sake of research.

Since I was going as a spy, I decided to dress like a celebrity incognito: an American Apparel hoodie, jeans, a fancy handbag, and dark glasses, the perfect outfit for a fly on the wall. Only the day before the dance I tried on the outfit and forgot all about my original intention. *There's nothing spectacular about a celebrity incognito,* I thought. *I want to make a splash.*

I closed my eyes and imagined the costume I truly wanted. That's when I remembered, I'd once purchased a white-and-baby-blue vintage ball gown at a thrift store. I dug it out of my closet and tried it on. Looking into the mirror at the puffy skirt and white sequins embroidered on my chest I knew exactly who I wanted to be: Cinderella.

I spent the next day running around the city in search of the rest of the missing elements. I found a blond wig, a black ribbon choker, long satin gloves, and, at a drag queen shop in the West Village, I actually found glass slippers. When I put all of the ingredients together I was amazed by my ingenuity. Running out the door, I caught a glimpse of myself in the mirror. In spite of everything, there was a hopeful sparkle in my eyes.

I arrived at the dance a little after ten. Not two minutes later, Hayes and his new girlfriend walked in. It was the last thing I expected. In the months since our breakup Hayes had graduated from BYU and accepted a finance job in New York (one he'd originally applied to so that he could be closer to me). Now he was dating a Mormon ballet dancer from Idaho who I'd never met, but whom Kevin, a frequent Facebook user, referred to as *the ugly version of me.*

This was my first time seeing both of them. Hayes was wearing a Spider-Man costume and on his arm was his new girlfriend (who did look a lot like me, only she was dressed like a slutty leprechaun). Standing there dressed as Cinderella, waiting for my Prince Charming, I realized how terribly wrong my fairy tale had gone.

It felt like I was being hit by everything I couldn't handle at once. Really it was more like I was deciding to let one thing represent everything—but either way I took it poorly. Before Hayes could spot me, I ran out the side door and escaped through the emergency exit.

In my haste to get away, I forgot one major logistical concern: the parade. Every year the Halloween Parade blocks all of Sixth Avenue. I got out of the subway and walked up the steps. The West Village had transformed. Police were everywhere, blue barricades blocked the sidewalks, and the crowd was so dense I could hardly breathe.

Determined to make it home, I walked directly into the chaos. Only I was going in the opposite direction of everyone else, which made it even worse. I bumped into zombies and goblins. An S and M guy with a decapitated bleeding head accidentally stepped on my skirt, causing it to rip all the way up to my knee. "Hey Cinderella," a drunk man yelled at me. When I ignored him, he reached over and grabbed my butt.

The action itself wasn't all that violating, but once again, I let one thing represent everything. And in a crowd of demons (that's not a judgment call, literally most of the people were dressed as demons), I thought about my eight-year struggle to be a Mormon in New York. Suddenly it was more overwhelming than ever. Like it all felt pointless because I'd never really win. And a little part of me, the part that believed I was fighting for something worth fighting for, was swallowed up in the crowd. I accepted reality. *This isn't working.*

Later that night, with my costume dissembled and a comforter over my head, I decided to take my first serious non-Mormon action, one that I hoped would guarantee my break. I got out of bed and wrote my e-mail:

Hey, Matt.

Five months later I was at a jewelry store in Zanzibar, looking at engagement rings. *I'm tired of waiting for someone to love me,* I decided. *If I'm going to have a ring on my finger, it's because I bought one for myself.*

I looked down at the display case of rings. There was one that immediately stood out. It was simple, a thin silver band and a small baby-blue stone.

"May I see that ring?" I asked the woman behind the counter.

As I slid it over my finger, the saleswoman explained that the stone was tanzanite, mined in Zanzibar, and it was supposed to bring luck.

Over the course of our three-hour flight into Lusaka to see Matt, I twisted it around and around my finger nervously. *No matter what happens, I still have me. No matter what happens, I still have me.*

As we were landing I wrote the following entry in my journal:

I don't know what to expect. Excited. Nervous. I watched an American couple kiss at the Dar airport and wondered if that'd be Matt and me in a few days. The plane is heading down the runway going straight—if we crash right now I'll die happy. I love this feeling. It's one-hundred-percent concentrated possibility. I'm living a dream.

Matt was waiting for us outside the airport. I only have that one picture of him from when we were dating. And so seeing him, standing there, it was strange. Suddenly he was real, no more or less attractive than anyone I'd dated, but still the person I wanted most in the whole wide world.

"Hi," he said.

"Hi," I answered, suddenly shy.

He gave me a hug. When he let go, I caught Alison and Pri watching us intently.

"Matt," I said, "meet my girlfriends."

Matt's friend was having a birthday dinner at a bar not far from the airport. So we spent the next two hours sampling food and mingling with expats. The entire time, I wanted to talk to Matt. To ask him all about his life in Zambia and see if he was at all like I'd remembered him. Instead, I played it cool and purposefully avoided him. This continued during the drive back to Matt's apartment. Alison and Pri struggled to make conversation, while I said a total of two things: "That's a pretty building" and "Wow, they have a Subway sandwiches here."

What's wrong with me? I cringed. *Why go out of your way? Travel halfway across the world so you can put your heart on the line, only to arrive and act like a deaf mute?*

Matt carried our bags into his studio apartment. It was dire—the walls, ceiling, and floor were made of cement, the roof was crumbling, and to flush the toilet you had to use a bucket of water.

After changing into our pajamas and brushing our teeth, Alison and Pri crawled into Matt's double bed, I took the single mattress, and Matt spread out on the floor.

We needed a good night's sleep. In the morning Matt was going to drop us off at a bus station and we were going to take a ten-hour journey to Livingston to see one of the Seven Wonders of the World: Victoria Falls. I couldn't sleep. The lights were out and I could hear Pri snoring, which somehow Alison seemed able to sleep through. I wanted to talk to Matt. I couldn't have made the trip to Africa without my friends, but now all I wanted was a moment alone. With our trip to Livingston it'd be another three days before I saw Matt again. I couldn't wait that long, I was already losing my nerve. I needed to know before it was too late: *Do you still like me?*

And so, ever the puppet of impulse, I got out of bed and crawled across the floor.

"Are you awake?" I whispered.

He wasn't.

"Matt?"

"Huh?"

"Sorry, I didn't mean to wake you. I just feel like we haven't talked yet and I wanted to say hi before I left again."

"Hi," he said. "It's good to see you."

"I know. I'm sorry if I was acting weird all night," I continued, "I guess I'm just nervous."

"Yeah, how long has it been?"

"Almost two years."

"Wow." he turned his head and looked at me. It wasn't much, but it was enough of a go-ahead. I scooted closer to him and rested my head on his shoulder. "How have you been?" I asked him.

"I've been good," he said, "how about you?"

"Good. I'm not Mormon anymore."

What? I hadn't expected to say this. I'd been trying to decide what I wanted for several months, but all of a sudden there it was, a decision.

"Since when?" He sounded surprised.

"Since . . . uh . . ." I couldn't exactly say *since five seconds ago* so instead I choose a much more legitimate figure. "Three months."

"What does that mean?"

"It just means I'm taking a break."

"Can you do that?"

"I can do whatever I want to do."

There was a silence.

"Do you drink now?" Matt asked me.

"No." I shook my head.

"Have you smoked pot?"

"No."

"What about sex?" he finished. "Have you had sex?"

The answer rested on the tip of my tongue. I'd been honest with my previous answers but now I was tempted to lie. And why not? I lied about going to South Africa with my imaginary girlfriends, and I lied about a three-month religious hiatus, why couldn't I just do it again?

"No," I said. "Not yet."

This was met with more silence.

"But I've tried *some* things," I quickly added. It was the opposite of convincing. I sounded like a middle-school boy bragging in the locker room. *Yeah, I did "it,"* I was saying, praying no one asked me, *What?*

"Matt"—I turned to face him—"I know part of the reason we didn't work out was because I was Mormon, and not that that factored into my decision, but I thought I should let you know."

He didn't say anything at first.

"We don't have to talk about it if you—"

"I'm sorry," he interrupted. "It's just kind of a big adjustment."

"I know," I said.

"And I don't mean to sound presumptuous, but three months isn't a very long time and I kind of feel like you're still a Mormon."

He was right. Completely and utterly right. But *this was* me trying not to be Mormon. *I have to do something drastic, I thought. I can't let him call my bluff.*

And so I did. Quickly, before I could chicken out, I slid my hand down Matt's pants and wrapped my fingers around his penis. It was the only thing I could think of to prove my point. As though I were saying, *You think I'm still Mormon, eh? Would a Mormon be holding . . . a penis?*

And then I kissed him. He kissed me back, tentatively at first, and then with more passion. Meanwhile, my hand just sat there, not moving, like I was using his penis as an armrest. *Fuck.* I considered my options. *Where do I go from here?* And look, it's not like I have to tell you any of this, but I'm trying to be honest. So to be completely honest, touching a penis for the first time, it was thrilling, but it was also really weird. It's not like it felt illegal, which is what I'd previously believed, instead it just felt like it wasn't really mine to be holding, like maybe I was being disrespectful of Matt.

He must've sensed this internal debate, because he stopped kissing me, and said, "Elna, is this okay?"

Silence.

"Honestly? . . . *I have no idea what I'm doing.*"

I always know when I've made the wrong decision. I can feel it in the air.

"I can't do this," he said.

"No," I insisted. "It's fine."

"No, it isn't." Matt took my hand off of his penis and moved it out of his pants. "This isn't the exact analogy," he began, "but it's the only one I can think of: A sixteen-year-old girl may say that she's ready to have sex, but you don't want to be the one to show her how."

"But I'm not sixteen," I said. "I'm twenty-six."

"I know, but that doesn't mean we're not at very different places in our lives. And look, usually I'm very cavalier about these sorts of things, but I can't do this. I know you well enough to know that it'd mean something to you. And I don't want to be that guy."

"Which guy?"

"The one that hurts your feelings."

What do you think this is? I wanted to say. But I was tired of trying to find the right angle to make the feeling I had in my heart for him fit. "Okay," I said. "Just promise me one thing?"

"What?"

"That when we wake up in the morning things won't be weird."

"Of course," he said.

"Good night."

I crawled over him and got back into bed. Lying there on my back, I recapped the situation. The more I thought about it, the more I felt like a twelve-year-old girl, a twelve-year-old girl with a crush on her older brother's college friend. *You're really cute,* the college boy had just said, *and some day some boy will really like you. But right now you're wearing Rainbow Bright pajamas and you have a training bra and braces. So please, go back to bed.*

I tried to shake it off, but it hurt—actually it stung. And more than anything, I wanted to cry about it, but I knew the only thing I could do to embarrass myself worse was to start audibly sobbing. I looked up at Matt's ghetto ceiling instead, and tried to think of something else, anything.

How did I get here? I asked myself. I wanted a reason, something that'd create a narrative, ascribe meaning to meaninglessness, and help me make sense of my life. Instead, it just was. And this was the best answer I could come up with.

Some day, I suppose I will be very grateful for the way that Matt acted. I felt for the ring on my finger and twisted it back and forth. *Except right now, it's my first night in Zambia, he wants nothing to do with me, and I'll be here for another eight days.* I hate myself.

If you think about it, I was always up against a lot. A Mormon in New York, and an uninterested atheist in Lusaka—ours was the most impossible of all impossible love stories. Most people would've given up here, but not me. *"No" Means Nothing to Me.* That's not a joke either. It's actually the title of the only award I've ever received. I got it in fifth grade. They were holding auditions for the middle-school play so I mustered up all the courage I could and tried out. After I finished my reading, the director asked me what grade I was in. When I answered fifth grade, he laughed and said, "You're in elementary school, get out of here."

I came home crying. After hearing the entire saga, my dad gave me the following advice: "Go back tomorrow and offer to help with the show, sweep the stage, whatever they need. If you do did this I promise you that by the end of the year you'll have a part in that play."

He was right. I spent the next six months doing child labor. To thank me for my work the director gave me a cameo in the final show. I was supposed to play a mom picking up her daughter from school. Unfortunately, I didn't understand the concept of walk-on role. I made an elaborate costume, complete with saggy mom boobs. When it was my turn to enter, I walked onstage, tossed one sagging boob over my shoulder, grabbed my daughter, and left.

Later that night, while celebrating over banana splits, my parents told me it was embarrassing how much I'd upstaged the other actors. Apparently for the rest of the play they, along with the rest of the audience, kept wondering, *When does the mom come back in?*

I thought this was the end of it; only, a few weeks later, at the all school awards ceremony, the middle-school principal stood up. "We have a special award to give out today," he said. "It's not going to a middle schooler either, it's actually for a fifth grader." The crowd murmured over the controversy.

"We call this the *"No" Means Nothing to Me* award and we're presenting it to Elna Baker, because 'no' really means nothing to her."

It was the proudest moment of my eleven-year-old life. But as an adult this quality has come back to bite me in the ass several times over. Because guess what? *Sometimes "no" actually means "no."* Unfortunately, I have a very hard time accepting this. I'm the puppy you have to kick for it to go away. And no matter how much evidence there is stacked up against me, I'm always optimistic. It's a self-inflicted punishment. I'm like Sisyphus, only instead of a rock I've been sentenced to shove a square peg into a round hole for eternity, always certain it's about to fit. *"No" means nothing to me.* In another life I was probably a rapist.

But back to Africa.

The following morning, on a crowded bus that smelled of the worst BO I'd ever experienced, Alison, Pri, and I huddled underneath a BO shield that we created by draping a towel over our area and opening two bottles of deodorant.

"So, what happened?" Alison asked me. "Did you guys kiss?"

I told them the entire story. And you know, hearing it out loud, it sounded just as bad as it felt. But something about their eyes and the way that they listened made me forever grateful for female friends. At least they could empathize, and at least they were there, ready to laugh and tell me it was okay. *We all make asses of ourselves when we're with men.*

"Your ability to cockblock yourself is unprecedented," Pri said, "but it's too funny not to let it happen."

"Thanks," I said. "At least I'm good for something."

The bus ride was so long; we started to regret taking the trip. But the following day, when we got to Victoria Falls, it was all worth it. If you can only take one trip in your life, go to Victoria Falls. I've never seen anything like it. It was like ten Niagara Falls in a row, but taller. And there were no barricades, no walls, no safety precautions; it was just there, this huge opening in the earth that was gushing water and reflecting dozens of giant rainbows. I had no idea that the earth could look so majestic. Crossing a rickety rope bridge that took us to the other side of the falls, I was hit by so much spraying water, I started laughing like a kid. Because it was new, because I'd never experienced anything like it before, because it made me incredibly happy.

This high was short lived. After two days in Victoria Falls we went back to Lusaka and met Matt on safari. For four awkward nights we shared a tent, just he and I. I spent the rest of the trip fighting a downward spiral of self-doubt and self-loathing. Every night I'd crawl into my sleeping bag hoping he'd notice my carefully selected sleepwear and change his mind. On two occasions, I even laid in Matt's bed, hoping he'd want to cuddle. When he didn't make a move, I went back to my side and spent the rest of the night wondering what I could possibly do to make him love me. *What's wrong with me? Why won't anyone love me?* I tried spinning the ring on my finger and telling myself, *You don't need a man to make you happy*, over and over again. But I was too close to the scene of the crime for it to work.

On the last day of our safari, Pri, Alison, and I took an evening ride without Matt. We got to see elephants roaming in the wild, hippos, alligators, zebras, and lions. Toward the end of the tour, our guide got a call that someone had spotted a leopard, one of the rarest animals to see, as they're practically extinct. The driver stepped on the gas and we sailed through the brush trying to catch up with the cat. When we found it, fifteen bumpy minutes later, we slowed to a halt. There it was, a leopard, sitting underneath a tree, not ten feet away.

She carried herself differently than any animal I'd ever seen. Her neck was held high, her spots were lit up by the sun, and she was all at once powerful, wild, and unbroken.

And while I know this is going to sound incredibly cheesy, and I'd sooner admit to holding a penis than to being sentimental—seeing that leopard revived me. It was so unquestioningly *itself.* Sort of the exact opposite of me. I'd been seesawing between two completely different lives. A year earlier, I'd moved to Utah in hopes that Hayes would marry me and make me a Mormon—forever. Now I was in Africa hoping that Matt would sleep with me, and make me a non-Mormon until I ceased to exist.

Why couldn't I get either of them to go along with the plan? And more than that, why couldn't I get myself to go along with it? *I'm doing this to myself,* I realized. *I'm refusing to choose which kind of person I want to be. I'm saying yes to way too many things. I love that moment of unlimited possibilities so much that I've accidentally built my entire life there. I've extended this place ten years further than it was ever supposed to go. I'm a twenty-six-year-old virgin for God's sake!*

While I still haven't thought of a word for this liminal place, the transition from the many to the one, from possibility to actuality—there is a name for someone like me. An observer that floats in between two worlds is called a ghost.

It wasn't Matt's fault that things didn't work out. He didn't hate me or think I was repulsive. He'd simply asked me if I'd made up my mind. Which I hadn't. So we were back at square one. And the thing is, I think I'm courageous for staying true to myself but really I'm deathly afraid of making the wrong choice. For good reason. Either way I choose, my life will become so much smaller. If I stop being Mormon, I won't be allowed to attend my brother's and sisters' weddings in any Mormon temple. I'll break my mother's heart and I won't be with my family for eternity. But if I stay in the church, I can't wear the sleeveless dress I wore last night, I'll have to say fetch instead of fuck, and I won't get to live the rest of my life with any of the men I love most.

I've spent a decade saying yes to both sides, stalling and questioning, not ready to choose and watch my life become simpler and more ordinary. Only without definite or definable values I'm a genuine indeterminate. I am what I might be, not what I am.

I stared at that leopard for a long time until finally it ran off into the bush. Driving back to the lodge I was overcome with gratitude for the entire experience. The sun, which was just starting to set, was larger than any sun I'd ever seen. And not only that, the landscape was perfectly flat, so with an unobstructed view I got to see what it's like when the sun slides below the horizon—which was remarkable. I watched a circle being cut perfectly in half, more on fire than ever, followed by the moon, which came up to take its place—huge, white, iridescent.

"Hi, God—" I choked on the word.

AGE 27

What I believe:	What I used to believe:
- Life is funny. I am grateful for it.	
- This life is my chance to create my world.	- After I die, if I am righteous, I can become a God and create a world.
- I have to work to be happy. I also have to work to have peace.	- I can do anything I want to with my armpit.
- I learn from my mistakes.	- I should strive to live a life free of sin.
- I believe in the power of faith.	
- I believe in the power of uncertainty. Or do I?	
- I believe that there is more to each of us than we realize and that at every moment if I just close my eyes and listen to myself I know who I am, who I was, and who I will be.	- A chart can explain my complicated relationship to my faith.

I have no idea
how it's going to work out
for me though.
So maybe I just made that
last part up.

Acknowledgments

I am forever grateful for my mentor Elizabeth Swados, who taught me to "Just tell the story." Liz, without the countless hours you spent nurturing my voice, I could not have done any of this.

A special thank-you to all of my readers. This book was taken to an entirely different level thanks to thorough help from exceptional friends—Anaheed Alani, Ira Glass, and Kevin Townley, thank you for showing me how to be authentic, honest, and funny. Additional thanks to Andrew Sean Greer, Julie Orringer, David Dickerson, Kathryn Sheer, Alison Mayer, and Ayesha Rokadia for your support, wit, and wisdom.

This book was made possible in part due to The Moth. Thank you to George Green, Lea Thau, Jenifer Hixson, and Catherine Burns for their tireless efforts in creating a home for storytellers. A special thank-you to Catherine Burns for the original development of "My Grandmother's Dress" and "Yes Means Yes." I'd also like to thank Julie Snyder, Robyn Semien, and everyone at *This American Life* for their help on the essay "Babies Buying Babies." And a sincere thank-you to Lisa Chase and Roberta Myers at *Elle* magazine where "A Body of Work" originally appeared.

To David McCormick, my agent, I couldn't ask for a better person to have on my side. Thank you for believing in me from the beginning and making this book possible.

To my editor, Amy Hertz, thank you for taking a chance on me and trusting that I could do this even when I was certain we were lost in the dark. Through your faith, this became a lasting and authentic piece.

Additional thanks to Melissa Miller, Ava Kavyani, The Allen Room, the Cuba-Brown family, Michelle Cox, Peggy Huddleston, Jonathan Ames, Elaina Richardson, and everyone at Yaddo—a truly magical place where this book was conceived. Thanks also to Cheryl Young, David Macy, and everyone at the MacDowell Colony for providing me with the support and creative freedom to complete this book.

A quick shout-out to Heather Wright and Ayesha Rokadia for our *Ladies Vacation*. Special thanks to Nick Kahn-Fogel, Hazaa! To Heidi Bivens for graciously lending me her computer. To Dr. Harvey Levin for helping me change my life. A sincere thank-you to Hamid Naficy for his unique perspective and support. Last, a special thank-you to Kevin Townley for listening to every idea I've ever had and encouraging me to believe in myself.

I owe the biggest thank-you of all to my family. Mom, Dad, Tina, Julia, Britain, Jill, and my grandparents, you're more than just fodder, you're my source of happiness. Dad, I especially want to thank you for all of the sacrifices that you've made to help me achieve my dreams. I'm incredibly grateful for the patience and wisdom both Mom and you put into teaching me how to be a person. *Mi familia es para siempre. Familia Baker.*

And finally, God, thank you, this is way more than I expected.